Flying Saucer Esoteric

The Altered States of Ufology

Maxim W. Furek

BEYOND THE FRAY
Publishing

Published by Beyond The Fray Publishing

ISBN 13: 978-1-954528-77-2

Cover design: Disgruntled Dystopian Publications

Beyond The Fray Publishing, a division of Beyond The Fray, LLC, San Diego, CA
www.beyondthefraypublishing.com

BEYOND THE FRAY

Publishing

Contents

Introduction ix

Part One

1. Before Christ 3
2. Biblical Scripture 7
3. Saint Albert the Great: 1100s 15
4. Copernicus's Sun: 1500s 21
5. Galileo Galilei, Heretic: The 1600s 23
6. Sir Isaac Newton: 1700s 29
7. Verne & Wells: 1800s 35

Part Two

8. Prelude to Roswell: 1900s 57
9. Secrets Revealed: 1910s 63
10. The Book of the Damned: 1920s 71
11. Wormhole Theory: 1930s 79
12. The Shaver Mystery: 1940s 89

Part Three

13. Adamski's Wild Ride: 1950s 113
14. The Moon Landing: 1960s 159
15. Cattle Mutilations: 1970s 195
16. Majestic 12: 1980s 229

Part Four

17. The New Frontier: 1990s 247
18. Beyond the Cosmos: 2000s 267
19. Worlds Without End: 2010s 281
20. Conclusions 319

Acknowledgments 325
References 327
About the Author 351
Also by Maxim W. Furek 353

"If you want to know the secrets to the universe—think in terms of energy, frequency, and vibration."

Nikola Tesla

This is dedicated to the scientists, astrobiologists, and stargazers who honored science above pseudoscience, nurturing ufology closer to a more logical realm.

Introduction

I have seen the saucers!

As a radarman serving aboard the aircraft carrier USS *Constellation* (CVA-64) during the Vietnam conflict, I saw numerous unidentified flying objects we called "bogies." They were solid, tangible, and maneuverable contacts we documented in our ship's logbook as "UFOs" and included their range and bearing. And then—we were told, "Keep your mouths shut. You didn't see anything." The next day, those logbooks would disappear, replaced by new ones.

Since the beginning, flying saucers have been an important part of our cultural fabric, inspiring comic books, novels, motion pictures, and television series. UFOs have blurred the boundaries between science, science fiction, and religion, and despite the fog of confusion, a physical entity seems to exist beyond hoaxers, government denial, research hysteria, and myth.

In his 1956 book, *They Knew Too Much About Flying Saucers,* Gray Barker wrote, "But there is something about flying saucers and the prospect of space travel that almost takes over a person's entire life once he gets the 'bug.'"

I agree with Mr. Barker. It happened to me too.

I got the bug during the spring and summer of 2023, and I know exactly when it happened. My turning point was while I was attempting to read John le Carre's *The Mission Song*. Something shifted! The book wasn't tracking. I found it uninteresting and unreadable and couldn't finish it. It wasn't le Carre's fault—it was me.

UFOs seeped into my brain, whispered by some unknown apparition, and conjured through one of those unexplainable cosmic channels. I became obsessed and consumed with flying saucer literature. I stopped reading everything else, but voraciously read every UFO book I could, beginning with ones from the early 1950s. I read. I pondered. I took notes. I approached UFO literature as a student, as an academic. I wanted to learn the secret of the saucers.

Some of the books were interesting and thought-provoking, making me excited about turning the next pages. Others were boring with technical data and stiff archaic writing from earlier decades, as exciting as watching wallpaper dry. Still, I forged through, looking for possible gems, pieces of supplemental information I needed. I read on, looking for answers already discovered elsewhere. It became an abstract game of connecting the dots, from Jules Verne's lust for technological innovations to Alvin Toffler's warning of *Future Shock*. And, too, maybe it took a jolt of OCD to get the job done, as I worked on the project, like a madman, *every single day until it was completed!*

Flying Saucer Esoteric captures the incredible sequence flowing from contactees, abductees, space explorers, and hoaxers, into our collective unconsciousness. We have all formed our own immutable opinion based on what we have seen and heard and read. Many of us have reached the point where disbelief becomes belief and the whole becomes the sum of the parts. We have crossed the Rubicon. There is no going back.

We either believe—or we don't.

Part One

Chapter 1
Before Christ

1450 BC: One of the oldest known written records of UFOs was discovered during the reign of Pharaoh Thutmose III. An Egyptian papyrus recounted how the scribes of the House of Life were dumbfounded by the sight of a "circle of fire" in the sky and ran to tell the pharaoh the news. Thutmose and his army discovered a great number of fire circles in the sky, each "shining brighter than the sun." The Annals of Thutmose III described UFO-like circles of fire:

> *The scribes of the House of Life found a circle of fire that was coming in the sky ... it had no head, and the breath of its mouth had a foul odor. Its body was five yards long and five yards wide. It had no voice. Now after some days had passed, these things became more numerous in the sky than ever. They shone more in the sky than the brightness of the heavens and extended to the limits of the four supports of the heavens.*

610 BC: Pre-Socratic Greek philosopher Anaximander (610–546 BC), who lived in what is now modern-day Turkey, invented the idea of space, a place with no absolute up or down. He was the first to propose that Earth is a body floating

in an infinite void, held up by nothing. Philosopher Karl Popper called Anaximander's theory:

> *One of the boldest, most revolutionary, and most portentous ideas in the whole history of human thought.*

Anaximander was the first to leave open the theoretical possibility that there are or were other worlds like ours

May 28, 585 BC: During a battle between the Lydians and Medes, the Sun was suddenly obscured, and the astonished armies stopped fighting and made peace. After the ancient world learned that Thales of Miletus had predicted this eclipse, the study of the planets and stars assumed new significance.

500 BC: Greek philosopher Heraclitus offered these sage words:

> *If you do not expect it, you will not find the unexpected, for it is hard to find and difficult.*

500 BC: Greek philosopher Anaxagoras (500–428 BC) was born in the town of Clazomenae. He introduced the concept of the "Cosmic Mind" as an ordering force, and also "panspermia," that life began as "seeds" and existed throughout the universe. Anaxagoras incorrectly believed that the Earth was flat; he was the first to correctly explain the phenomenon of eclipses. Anaxagoras proposed the theory that extraterrestrial life existed on the Moon, most likely on its mountains.

460 BC: Philosopher Democritus (460–370 BC) proposed that the universe contained an infinite number of worlds, contradicting the later views of Plato and Aristotle, who argued that Earth was the only planet and the universe much smaller.

400 BC: Roman philosopher Metrodorus of Chios, in his book On Nature, contemplated the possibility of life in the universe:

> *Is it reasonable to suppose in a large field, that only one shaft of wheat should grow, and in an infinite Universe, to have only one living world*

428 BC: Ancient Greek philosopher Plato (428–348 BC) criticized Democritus's "plurality of worlds" on religious grounds. Plato, a monotheist, argued that because God is our only creator, there can be only one world, "if the created copy is to accord with the original." Plato is recognized as a prominent figure in the history of philosophy, along with his teacher Socrates and his student Aristotle.

380 BC: Greek philosopher Anaxarchus (c. 380–320 BC) thought infinite worlds existed.

341 BC: Greek philosopher Epicurus (c. 341–270 BC) founded Epicureanism, a highly influential school of philosophy. He studied the teachings of Democritus and absorbed his empiricist, atomist worldview, including the idea that there must be many worlds. Epicurus wrote, in a letter to the historian Herodotus:

> *There is an unlimited number of cosmoi* [worlds], *and some are similar to this one and some are dissimilar.*

50 BC: The Roman poet-philosopher Titus Lucretius Carus (99–55 BC), in his book *On the Nature of Things*, pondered:

> *Nothing in the Universe is unique and alone, and therefore in other regions there must be other earths inhabited by different tribes of men and breeds of beasts.*

Lucretius was recognized as the leading spokesman of the godless Epicurean philosophy and, because of his views, was castigated by those in authority. According to the *Stanford Encyclopedia of Philosophy*:

> *Because early Christianity branded Lucretius an enemy of religion, his life and death had to be depicted as appropriately wretched. Thus, according to St Jerome, he was driven mad by a love (potent), wrote poetry in his lucid intervals, and died by his own hand, leaving his poem to be edited posthumously by Cicero. This—apart from the last detail, which some have found credible—is a palpable fabrication.*

Chapter 2
Biblical Scripture

THE BIBLE CONSISTS of sixty-six books and older oral narratives written over a period of more than one thousand years. Proponents of the ancient alien theory offer biblical verses to support their premise that aliens visited Earth, interbred with humans to create hybrid creatures, and provided us with advanced technology far beyond man's primitive and unsophisticated reach. Included among these theorists are Josef F. Blumrich, Rev. Barry Downing, Graham Hancock, Dr. Morris K. Jessup, Meade Layne, James Moseley, Zecharia Sitchin, and, ultimately, Erich von Däniken, the movement's loudest voice. A selection of biblical references that are often cited include the following:

> Genesis 6:1–22: Genesis recounts that the Nephilim ("fallen ones") were the product of copulation between the divine beings (sons of god) and human women (daughters of Adam). The Nephilim are known as great warriors and biblical giants.
>
> > *The Nephilim were on the earth in*
> > *those days, and also afterward, when*

> *the sons of God came into the daughters of man and they bore children to them. These were the mighty men who were of old, the men of renown. The Lord saw that the wickedness of man was great in the Earth and that every intention of the thoughts of his heart was only evil continually ...*

Genesis 19:12–13: Sodom and Gomorrah were destroyed by angels from outer space.

> *And the men said unto Lot, Hast thou here any besides? Son in law, and thy sons, and thy daughters, and whatsoever thou hast in the city, bring them out of this place: for we will destroy this place, because the cry of them is waxen great before the face of the LORD, and the LORD hath sent us to destroy it.*

Genesis 19:24–28: The destruction of Sodom is detailed in both the Bible and the Koran. Some have speculated that a nuclear explosion destroyed the two "sinful" cities. Also, the Comet Research Group, in an essay published in *Nature*, proposed that a large meteor may have destroyed the ancient city of Tall el-Hammam, which formed the basis of the biblical story.

> *Then the Lord rained upon Sodom and*

upon Gomorrah brimstone and fire
from the Lord out of heaven;

And he overthrew those cities, and all
the plain, and all the inhabitants of
the cities, and that which grew upon
the ground.

But his wife looked back from behind
him, and she became a pillar of salt.

And Abraham got up early in the
morning to the place where he stood
before the Lord:

And he looked toward Sodom and
Gomorrah, and toward all the land
of the plain, and beheld, and, lo, the
smoke of the country went up as the
smoke of a furnace.

Exodus 3:2: The burning bush has often been interpreted by ufologists as authentic communication with extraterrestrials.

There the angel of the Lord appeared to
him in flames of fire from within a
bush. Moses saw that though the
bush was on fire it did not burn up.
So Moses thought, "I will go over
and see this strange sight—why the
bush does not burn up."

Exodus 13:21: Rev. Barry Downing in his controversial book The Bible and Flying Saucers: Did a UFO Part the Red Sea? claimed that the pillar of cloud and fire was a UFO that used its propulsion system to part the Red Sea:

> *And the Lord went before them by day*
> *in a pillar of a cloud, to lead them*
> *the way; and by night in a pillar of*
> *fire, to give them light; to go by day*
> *and night:*

Exodus 14:26: The parting of the Red Sea allowed Israelites safe passage before the waters swallowed the pursuing Egyptian soldiers. Many ancient astronaut theorists believe they were guided by alien advanced technology that parted the Red Sea:

> *Then the Lord said to Moses, "Stretch*
> *out your hand over the sea, that the*
> *water may come back upon the*
> *Egyptians, upon their chariots, and*
> *upon their horsemen." So Moses*
> *stretched out his hand over the sea,*
> *and the sea returned to its normal*
> *course when the morning appeared.*
> *And as the Egyptians fled into it,*
> *the Lord threw the Egyptians into*
> *the midst of the sea. The waters*
> *returned and covered the chariots*
> *and the horsemen; of all the host of*
> *Pharaoh that had followed them into*
> *the sea, not one of them remained.*
> *But the people of Israel walked on*

dry ground through the sea, the waters being a wall to them on their right hand and on their left.

Numbers 13:33:

We saw the Nephilim there (the descendants of Anak come from the Nephilim). We seemed like grasshoppers in our own eyes, and we looked the same to them.

Two Bible passages that could be interpreted as referring to UFOs are in 2 Kings:

2 Kings 2:11: Morris Jessup argued that the Bible demands a literal and physical interpretation. He concluded that Elijah's whirlwind was actually an extraterrestrial power blast.

As they were walking along and talking together, suddenly a chariot of fire and horses of fire appeared and separated the two of them, and Elijah went up to heaven in a whirlwind.

2 Kings 2:12: Some ufologists believe that this passage is a primitive description of a UFO abduction.

Elisha saw this and cried out, "My father! My father! The chariots and horsemen of Israel!" And Elijah saw

him no more. Then he took hold of
his own clothes and tore them apart.

Ezekiel 1:4–5: The prophet Ezekiel's vision of brightly lit creatures, wheels within wheels, and a vault may seem like a visitation from extraterrestrials and UFOs, but after experiencing this wondrous vision, Ezekiel concludes that it is a manifestation of God's glory, and said, "When I saw it, I fell facedown ..."

I looked, and I saw a windstorm coming
out of the north—an immense cloud
with flashing lightning and
surrounded by brilliant light. The
center of the fire looked like glowing
metal, and in the fire was what
looked like four living creatures ...

Zechariah 5:1–2: Zechariah sees what some have interpreted as a UFO:

Again I lifted my eyes and saw, and
behold, a flying scroll! And he said
to me, "What do you see?" I
answered, "I see a flying scroll. Its
length is twenty cubits, and its
width ten cubits."

Luke 17:29: Some ufologists asserted that Lot's wife was turned into a pillar of salt by a nuclear explosion from powerful aliens.

But the same day that Lot went out of

Sodom it rained fire and brimstone from heaven, and destroyed them all.

Luke 21:25:

And there shall be signs in the Sun, and in the Moon, and in the Stars.

Hebrews 11:

Faith is the substance of things hoped for, the evidence of things not seen.

Revelation 12:7:

Now war arose in heaven, Michael and his angels fighting against the dragon. And the dragon and his angels fought back.

Revelation 21:10–24: According to John, the Spirit showed him in a vision the holy city New Jerusalem coming down from God out of heaven.

He then carried me away in the Spirit to a great, high mountain and showed me the holy city, Jerusalem, coming down out of heaven from God.

Chapter 3
Saint Albert the Great: 1100s

1193: German Dominican friar and philosopher Albertus Magnus (1193–1280) is believed to have been born in Bavaria. Also known as Saint Albert the Great, he was among the first intellectuals to contemplate the existence of alien life:

> *Since one of Nature's most wonderful and noble questions is whether there is one world or many ... it seems desirable to ask questions about it.*

Albertus Magnus is recognized as the greatest German theologian of the Middle Ages. The Catholic Church distinguishes him as one of the thirty-seven Doctors of the Church. He was canonized as a Catholic Saint in 1931.

1200s

1207: Gervase of Tilbury, a wandering scholar and adventurer, writing in *Otio Imperialia,* described a UFO that caught its "anchor" in a pile of stones over a churchyard near the city of Bristol. A "sky sailor" attempted to dislodge the anchor but "died, stifled in our gross air, as a shipwrecked mariner would be in the sea." The craft flew away, leaving its anchor flukes hitched onto the church door.

1287: Medieval philosopher William of Ockham (1287–1347) considered the existence of other life and wrote of this possibility:

> *God could produce an infinite [number of] individuals of the same kind as those that now exist, but He is not limited to producing them in this world.*

1290: According to an ancient manuscript, while celebrating the Feast of Saints Simon and Jude, brothers from the Byland Abbey in Yorkshire, England, witnessed a UFO, causing "a great portent outside." The brothers documented:

> *A large round silver thing like a disc flew slowly over them and excited the greatest terror.*

1300s

1390: French philosopher and theologian William Vorilong (1390–1463) would articulate the possibility that Jesus could have visited extraterrestrial worlds to redeem their inhabitants. Vorilong wrote:

> *By what means are we able to have knowledge of [another world]? I answer by angelic revelation or by divine means. If it be inquired whether men exist on that world, and whether they have sinned as Adam sinned, I answer no, for they would not exist in sin and did not spring from Adam. But it is shown that they would exist from the virtue of God, transported unto that world as Enoch and Elias in this Earthly paradise. As to*

the question whether Christ by dying on this earth could redeem the inhabitants of another world, I answer that he is able to do this even if the worlds were infinite, but it would not be fitting for Him, to go into another world that He must die again.

1400s

June 24, 1400: Celebrated as one of the most influential men in history, Johannes Gensfleisch zur Laden zum Gutenberg (1400–1468) was born in Mainz, Germany. His invention of letterhead printing led to an information revolution and the unprecedented spread of literature throughout Europe, contributing to the Renaissance, Reformation, and Humanist Movements. Gutenberg's major work was the Gutenberg Bible, recognized for its superior aesthetic and technical quality.

August 11, 1401: Regarded as a "renegade thinker," German Catholic cardinal Nicholas of Cusa (1401–1464) was born in Kues, Germany. He became a leading theologian, noted for his deeply mystical writings about Christianity. He also contended that Earth was one of a multitude of worlds and theorized that all celestial planets could be inhabited by men, plants, and animals, including the Sun. In his famous treatise, *On Learned Ignorance* (1440), he wrote:

Life, as it exists on Earth in the form of men, animals and plants, is to be found, let us suppose, in a higher form in the solar and stellar regions. Rather than think that so many stars and parts of the heavens are uninhabited and that this Earth of ours alone is peopled—and that with beings, perhaps of an inferior type—we will suppose that in every region there are inhabitants, differing in nature by rank and all owing their

> *origin to God, who is the centre and circumference of all stellar regions.*

November 1, 1461: A hidden medieval document, discovered in the ancient town of Arras, in the Pas-de-Calais, France, recorded a strange UFO directly over the town—a day before All Souls' Day, dedicated to prayer for the souls of the dead. Jacques Duclerc, a chronicler, and counselor to King Philip the Good, wrote a detailed account of the event in his *Memoirs of a Freeman of Arras*:

> *... there appeared in the sky a brilliant object like an iron bar, long and wide as half the moon. For fifteen minutes it hovered motionless. Then, on a sudden, the strange object began to rise in spirals and twisted and writhed like an uncoiled mainspring of a watch, and after, it vanished in the sky.*

October 11, 1492: The first written record of a purported UFO sighting in the New World was made by Christopher Columbus, who reported green lights hovering above the Sargasso Sea, commonly referred to as the Bermuda Triangle. While patrolling the deck of the *Santa Maria* at about 10:00 p.m., Columbus thought he saw "a light glimmering at a great distance." He summoned Pedro Gutierrez, "a gentleman of the king's bed-chamber," who also saw the light. After a short time, it vanished, only to reappear several times during the night, each time dancing up and down "in sudden and passing gleams." The light was first seen four hours before land was sighted.

1493: One of the earliest European representations of a UFO was submitted by German humanist Hartmann Schedel, who described a strange cigar-shaped spherical object sailing against the sky, following a straight line from south to east, then turning toward the setting sun. The UFO was surrounded by flames. The actual date of the sighting is believed to have been 1034 and is contained in Schedel's book, now displayed in a museum in Verdun.

Chapter 4
Copernicus's Sun: 1500s

1520: German professor Conrad Wolffhart, writing under his assumed name of Greek philosopher Lycosthenes, recalled an unexplainable event he witnessed in Erfurt, Prussia:

> *A wonderful burning beam of light of great size. It suddenly appeared in the sky, fell on the ground, and destroyed many places. It then revolved, turned round and ascended in the sky, where it put on a circular form.*

1543: Polish mathematician and cleric Nicolaus Copernicus (1473–1543) published his radical theory that the Sun, not the Earth, sits in the center of our planetary system. Copernicus suggested that the six planets orbit around the Sun, as the Moon orbits around the Earth. Copernicus's "heliocentric theory" was in opposition to the "Ptolemaic geocentric theory," which espoused that the Earth was the center of the universe.

January 1548: Italian philosopher and cosmological theorist Giordano Bruno (1548–1600) was born in Nola, Italy. He proposed a position known as "cosmic pluralism," the philosophical belief that there are numerous planets, potentially inhabited, orbiting around numerous stars. He was among the first of critical thinkers to speculate that life existed on other planets. In his book *De I'Infinito, Universo e Mundi,* Bruno explained that other worlds similar to ours may exist:

> *There are innumerable suns and innumerable earths, which revolve around their suns, as our seven planets revolve around our sun ... These worlds are inhabited by living creatures.*

April 14, 1561: Numerous Germans witnessed an aerial battle over Nuremberg, the center of the German Renaissance in the fifteenth and sixteenth centuries. The event was described in a woodcut by Hans Glaser as a series of spheres and disks that appeared in the sky and engaged in an aerial ballet. These sightings happened a little after daybreak and featured what was appeared to have been hundreds of UFOs that appeared to be attacking each other.

January 8, 1564: Italian astronomer, physicist and engineer Galileo di Vincenzo Bonaiuti de' Galilei (1564–1642) was born in Pisa and recognized as the father of observational astronomy, the scientific method, and modern science. Because of his beliefs, he was tried as a heretic and spent the rest of his life under house arrest.

August 7, 1566: An infamous woodcut from a Swiss library described several strange aerial globes that were seen in the skies over Basil, Switzerland.

March 31, 1596: Descartes (1596–1650) wrote that there were no means to prove that the stars were not inhabited by "intelligent creatures," but their existence was a matter of speculation.

Chapter 5
Galileo Galilei, Heretic: The 1600s

The seventeenth century was marked by a limited understanding of celestial phenomena and the prevalence of primitive astrological beliefs. It was a volatile time when the church and state heard opposing voices.

1600: Dutch scientist Christiaan Huygens wrote in his *New Conjectures Concerning the Planetary Worlds, Their Inhabitants, and Productions*:

> *A man that is of Copernicus' opinion, that this Earth of ours is a planet ... like the rest of the planets, cannot but sometimes think that it's not improbable that the rest of the planets have ... their inhabitants too.*

February 17, 1600: Controversial Italian philosopher and monk Giordano Bruno was found guilty by the Roman Inquisition and burned alive at the stake in Rome's *Campo de' Fiori*. Bruno had been tried for heresy—charged with denying core Catholic doctrines, including eternal damnation, the Trinity, the divinity of Christ, the virginity of Mary, and transubstantiation. Some regarded him as a martyr for his scientific beliefs. Bruno had proposed the "heliocentric theory" of Copernicus and insisted that in the cosmos:

> *There must be an infinite number of suns with planets with life around them.*

1609–1619: German astronomer Johannes Kepler (1571–1630), a key figure in the seventeenth-century Scientific Revolution, discovered the mathematical properties of the orbits of the planets.

1610: Italian astronomer Galileo Galilei (1564–1642), looking through a telescope, discovered the phases of Venus, the moons of Jupiter, and the rings of Saturn.

1616: Rome declared the Copernican system dangerous to the faith, resulting in Galileo's trial before the Inquisition. Sixteen years earlier, Giordano Bruno had been burned at the stake for being a heretic and enemy of the Church.

1633: Italian astronomer Galileo Galilei went on trial in Rome for saying the Earth revolved around the Sun. Because of his beliefs, in opposition to the Catholic Church, he was tried as a heretic by the Roman Inquisition, found "vehemently suspect of heresy," forced to recant, and spent the rest of his life under house arrest.

December 20, 1642: English mathematician Sir Isaac Newton (1642–1727) born in Woolstorpe Manor, England, was celebrated as a natural philosopher and key figure in the seventeenth-century Scientific Revolution and Enlightenment. His pioneering book *Mathematical Principles of Natural Philosophy* (1687) formulated the laws of motion and universal gravitation that formed the dominant scientific viewpoint for centuries until it was superseded by Einstein's theory of relativity.

July 1, 1646: German philosopher and mathematician Gottfried Wilhelm Leibniz (1646–1716) suggested the possibility of extraterrestrials as a response to the problem of evil—Why does an omnipotent and omnibenevolent God allow evil? Leibniz argued that all the evil that exists in the universe happens on Earth and thus "is almost lost in nothingness" compared to the "good things which are in the universe."

1656: Dutch mathematician and astronomer Christiaan Huygens (1629–1695), considered a key figure in the seventeenth-century Scientific Revolution, discovered Saturn's largest moon, Titan, and identified that the changing appearance of Saturn was caused by its rings. In 1657, Huygens invented the pendulum clock—the most accurate timekeeper for almost three hundred years.

1659: Dutch astronomer Christiaan Huygens described the first surface feature of the planet Mars—a large triangular marking.

June 8, 1665: Italian-French astronomer Giovanni Cassini (1625–1712) was born in Imperia, Italy, and was responsible for a number of scientific discoveries and projects. He discovered Jupiter's Red Spot and the four moons of the planet Saturn. The *Cassini* spacecraft, which launched in 1997 and plunged into the planet in 2017, was named after him.

1666: Giovanni Cassini discovered bright polar caps on Mars. Cassini's innovations were widely recognized, and in 1650 the senate of Bologna designated him to occupy the principal chair of astronomy at the university.

1675: Giovanni Cassini discovered the internal structure of Saturn's rings.

1686: French scientist Bernard de Fontenelle (1657–1757) surveyed the prospects for life in the solar system in *Conversations on the Plurality of Worlds,* opening the discussion about possible life forms on other planets. The popular science book provided an early hypothesis of "cosmic pluralism," the idea that the stars are distant suns that might have their own planetary systems, including the possibility of extraterrestrial life. In *Conversations on the Plurality of Worlds*, an imaginary dialog between a philosopher and an uneducated but intelligent woman known as the Marquise read:

> *"It would be very strange that the Earth was as populated as it is, and the other planets weren't at all," the philosopher told the Marquise. Although he didn't think people could live on the sun (if there were any, they'd be blinded by its brightness), he sided with those who envisioned inhabitants on other planets and even the moon.*
>
> *Just as there have been and still are a prodigious number of men foolish enough to worship the Moon, there are people on the Moon who worship the Earth.*

1687: English mathematician Sir Isaac Newton published the pioneering book *Philosophiæ Naturalis Principia Mathematica* (*Mathematical Principles of Natural Philosophy*) formulating the laws of motion and universal gravitation. Newton's theory became the dominant scientific viewpoint for centuries until superseded by Albert Einstein's theory of special relativity (1905) and general relativity (1915).

1690: Dutch physicist Christian Huygens published *Cosmotheoros*, arguing that life can exist on many other planets. He also espoused the idea of the plurality of worlds by saying that:

> *Barren planets, deprived of living creatures which speak most eloquently of their Divine Architect are unreasonable, wasteful and uncharacteristic of God, who has a purpose for everything.*

Chapter 6

Sir Isaac Newton: 1700s

April 22, 1724: Immanuel Kant (1724–1804), born in Kaliningrad, Russia, was recognized as one of the greatest philosophers of all time and one of the foremost thinkers of the Enlightenment. Kant believed that life existed on other planets and issued what became known as Kant's Wager:

> *If it were possible to settle by any sort of experience whether there are inhabitants of at least some of the planets that we see, I might well bet everything that I have on it. Hence I say that it is not merely an opinion but a strong belief (on the correctness of which I would wager many advantages in life) that there are also inhabitants of other worlds.*

1726: Mathematical Isaac Newton, pondering the solar system, asserted that God controls the planets through the law of gravitation:

> *The wonderous disposition of the Sun, the planets, and the comets, can only be the work of an all-powerful and intelligent being.*

1726: Anglican priest, politician, and author Jonathan Swift, in his *Gulliver's Travels*, accurately described two "small stars" and their orbits revolving around Mars—Phobos and Deimos—one hundred and fifty years before contemporary astronomers even suspected they existed.

December 9, 1731: Numerous citizens of Florence, Italy, observed strange globes of light cavorting in the skies.

February 9, 1737: Thomas Paine (1737–1809), was born in Thetford, Norfolk, England, and emigrated to the British American Colonies. He was a Founding Father and political activist and participated in the American Revolution. His forty-seven-page pamphlet *Common Sense* called for independence from Great Britain. In *The Age of Reason,* he argued that the belief in the plurality of the worlds is fundamentally in conflict with Christianity:

> *From whence ... could arise the ... strange conceit that the Almighty ... should ... come to die in our world because they say, one man and one woman had eaten an apple! And on the other hand, are we to suppose that every world in the boundless creation had an Eve, an apple, a serpent, and a redeemer? In this case, the person who is irreverently called the Son of God, and sometimes God himself, would have nothing else to do than to travel from world to world, in an endless succession of death, with scarcely a momentary interval of life.*

In *The Age of Reason* and other writings, he advocated Deism, the belief in a God who does not intervene in the universe after creating it.

1745: French naturalist George-Louis Leclerc alleged that a comet, as large as a star, struck the Sun and ripped off clusters that eventually formed the planets. Since the strike was off-center, the Sun began spinning. As a consequence, the planets were thrust into orbits around the Sun while spinning on their own axes.

March 23, 1749: French physicist and scholar Pierre-Simon Laplace (1749–1827) was born in the Normandy region of France. He demonstrated mathematically, from Newtonian principles, that the solar system was stable and that planets orbited around the Sun and would continue to do so indefinitely. He developed the nebular hypothesis of the origin of the solar system and was one of the first scientists to suggest an idea similar to that of a black hole.

August 9, 1762: Two Swiss astronomers observed an enormous spindle-shaped UFO surrounded by a glowing outer ring. The sightings were reported separately from Basil and Sole.

April 21, 1774: French physicist, astronomer, and mathematician Jean-Baptiste Biot (1774–1862) was born in Paris. He co-discovered the Biot-Savart law of magnetostatics with Félix Savart and completed the first scientific hot-air balloon ride, reaching a height of 13,100 feet, measuring how the Earth's magnetic field varies with elevation. Biot was among a contingent promoting the extraterrestrial hypothesis that meteorites were rubble from outer space.

April 30, 1777: German astronomer and mathematician Carl Friedrich Gauss (1777–1855) was born in Brunswick, Principality of Brunswick-Wolfenbüttel, Holy Roman Empire. Gauss developed the first scientific proposal to communicate with extraterrestrials. His idea was to plant a colossal forest.

1777–1783: Sir William Herschel was the first to determine that Mars's rotation axis was tipped approximately thirty degrees from the perpendicular to its orbit, indicating that Mars experiences four seasons, similar to the Earth. Herschel also determined the planet's rotation period to be twenty hours thirty-nine minutes and 21.67 seconds. Herschel also observed a thin atmosphere around Mars, which is now known to be composed of ice particles.

March 13, 1781: English astronomer Sir William Herschel discovered Uranus, the seventh planet from the Sun. His was the first discovery of a new planet to be made in modern times by using a telescope. Uranus is the third-largest planet and orbits the Sun once every eighty-four Earth years.

September 19, 1783: The first "public" flight of a hot-air balloon was designed by brothers Joseph-Michel and Jacques-Étienne Montgolfier, in Annonay, France. The flight had a basket suspended below the balloon, containing a sheep, rooster, and duck. The experiment lasted eight minutes and was witnessed by the French king, Marie Antoinette, and a crowd of 130,000.

October 15, 1783: The first recorded manned hot-air balloon was launched by French brothers Joseph-Michel and Jacques-Étienne Montgolfier. Their balloon was launched on a tether with Jean-François Pilâtre de Rozier, a physics teacher, aboard. He stayed aloft for almost four minutes.

November 21, 1783: Pilâtre de Rozier and the Marquis d'Arlandes, a French military officer, made the first free ascent in a hot-air balloon. The pair flew from the center of Paris to the suburbs, about 5.5 miles, in twenty-five minutes. Benjamin Franklin wrote in his journal about witnessing the balloon take off:

> *We observed it lift off in the most majestic manner. When it reached around 250 in altitude, the intrepid voyagers lowered their hats to salute the spectators. We could not help feeling a certain mixture of awe and admiration.*

June 15, 1785: Pilâtre de Rozier, one of the first human passengers of balloon travel, died after his balloon, filled with a combination of hydrogen and hot air, exploded during an attempt to fly across the English Channel. He became the first victim of balloon travel, two years after his historic flight.

Chapter 7
Verne & Wells: 1800s

The new century was marked by the Industrial Revolution and enormous strides in industry, transportation, and manufacturing, but also the discovery of a dwarf planet and the introduction of an impressive cluster of individuals, who furthered the field of ufology—Charles Fort, Meade Layne, Jules Verne, Madame Blavatsky, H. G. Wells, Edgar Rice Burroughs, and George Adamski.

January 1, 1801: Giuseppe Piazzi (1746–1826), an Italian monk of the Theatine Order, discovered the first dwarf planet and named it "Ceres."

1803: Poet Ralph Waldo Emerson (1803–1882) said:

> *People only see what they are prepared to see.*

1803: The French astronomer and mathematician Jean-Baptiste Biot was sent by the French minister of the interior and the *Académie française* to investigate reports of a fireball and shower of debris over the Normandy town of L'Aigle. Biot reported back on three thousand meteorites, called "stones," and helped promote German physicist Ernst Chladni's 1794 theory that meteorites were remains from outer space.

October 3, 1815: The first Martian meteorite observed to have fallen to Earth landed near Chassigny, in the Burgundy region of France. Classified as type chassignite (dunite.)

August 25, 1865: The second Martian meteorite observed to have fallen to Earth landed near Shergotty in the state of Bihar, India. Classified as type basaltic shergottite.

1820: The American prophet Joseph Smith (1805–1844) wrote that at the age of fourteen he witnessed a bright aerial object near Manchester, New York. Known later as the First Vision, Smith was enveloped in a pillar of brilliant light that descended from above. He witnessed God the Father and His Son, Jesus Christ, standing above him.

1823: Church members believe that Smith was led to a hill near Palmyra, New York, where he received an ancient record from an angel known as Moroni. The ancient record, engraved on gold plates, gave the history of a people who lived on the American continent during the time of Christ. Smith translated the plates in about three months and then published the Book of Mormon.

September 22, 1827: Joseph Smith began translating an ancient record, inscribed on thin golden plates—its words by the "gift of God"—into the Book of Mormon.

February 8, 1828: Jules Verne (1828–1905) is born in Nantes, France. The prolific French author created much of the foundation of modern-day science fiction and is recognized as its patron saint. His works, which captured the innovations of the Industrial Revolution, include *From the Earth to the Moon*

(1865), *Journey to the Centre of the Earth* (1867), and *Twenty Thousand Leagues Under the Sea* (1870).

1830: German astronomer and mathematician Carl Friedrich Gauss suggested planting a colossal forest in the form of an orthogonal triangle to signal to extraterrestrials possibly observing the Earth with their powerful telescopes. Gauss wanted to communicate that Earth is populated by intelligent beings familiar with the Pythagorean theorem. This was the first scientific proposal to communicate with extraterrestrials.

April 6, 1830: After publishing the Book of Mormon in New York, Joseph Smith organized the Church of Jesus Christ of Latter-day Saints and became its first president.

1830: Alfred, Lord Tennyson (1809–1892) published the fifteen-line sonnet "The Kraken," about a sea monster sleeping for an eternity at the bottom of the ocean and destined to emerge from its slumber in an apocalyptic age. It is believed to have inspired science-fiction horror writer H. P. Lovecraft's Cthulhu Mythos, with its vivid images:

> *Below the thunders of the upper deep,*
>
> *Far, far beneath in the abysmal sea,*
>
> *His ancient, dreamless, uninvaded sleep*
>
> *The Kraken sleepeth: faintest sunlights flee About his shadowy sides; above him swell Huge sponges of millennial growth and height;*
>
> *And far away into the sickly light,*
>
> *From many a wondrous grot and secret cell Unnumbered and enormous polypi*

> *Winnow with giant arms the slumbering green. There hath he lain for ages, and will lie Battening upon huge sea worms in his sleep,*
>
> *Until the latter fire shall heat the deep;*
>
> *Then once by man and angels to be seen,*
>
> *In roaring he shall rise and on the surface die.*

August 12, 1831: Ukrainian mystic Helena Petrovna Blavatsky (1831–1891), often known as Madame Blavatsky, was born in Dniproin, Ukraine. She co-founded the Theosophical Society in 1875 and published *Isis Unveiled*, which described Theosophy as "the synthesis of science, religion, and philosophy," proclaiming that it was reviving an "Ancient Wisdom" that underlay all the world's religions. In *The Secret Doctrine,* Blavatsky asserted that ancient Greeks knew of the existence of extraterrestrial life and that aliens on the countless inhabited worlds, and the Moon in particular, may have "influence" or "control" over the Earth.

August 25, 1835: In what is now known as the "Great Moon Hoax," the *New York Sun* published a six-part science fiction series that was passed off as actual news. The articles described the findings of English astronomer Sir John Herschel, who allegedly built the world's largest telescope and discovered life on the Moon. The article offered:

> *We will state at once, that by means of a telescope of vast dimensions and an entirely new principle, the younger Herschel ... has already made the most extraordinary discoveries in every planet of our solar system; ... has obtained a distinct view of objects in the moon, fully equal to that which the naked eye commands of terrestrial objects at the distance*

> *of a hundred yards; ... [and] has affirmatively settled the question whether this satellite be inhabited, and by what order of beings.*

Years later, British writer Richard Adams Locke confessed that he wrote the articles as a satire reflecting on the skewed influence that religion was having on science. Also published in European newspapers, Locke's narrative became one of the greatest hoaxes of all time.

1836: Wilhelm Beer (1797–1850) and Johann von Mädler (1794–1874) created the most complete map of the Moon, *Mappa Selenographica*. It was the first lunar map to be divided into quadrants and provided micrometric measurements of the diameters of one hundred and forty-eight craters and the elevations of eight hundred and thirty mountains. It remained unsurpassed in its detail until J. F. Julius Schmidt's map of 1878.

1836: A large donut-shaped UFO is seen over the city of Cherbourg, France. Witnesses observed that the object was spinning on its own axis.

1840: Johan von Mädler and Wilhelm Beer published the first complete map of Mars. This was the first map to establish a latitude-longitude system for the planet, with the zero-longitude line defined through a small, very dark spot. They also refined the rotation period of Mars to twenty-four hours thirty-seven minutes 22.6 seconds (within 0.1 seconds of the currently accepted value).

February 26, 1842: The influential French astronomer Camille Flammarion (1842–1925) was born in Montigny-le-Roi, Haute-Marne, France. In his book *Astronomy for Amateurs*, Flammarion depicted a network of lines on the surface of Mars, interpreted as canals and indicating an intelligent civilization. Although his Mars theory was conclusively debunked, he has been best described as an:

> *"Astronomer, mystic and storyteller" who was "obsessed by life after death, and on other worlds, and [who] seemed to see no distinction between the two."*

A prolific and eclectic author, Flammarion influenced later writers with his belief in other planetary life forms, and with great commercial success, he blended:

> *Scientific speculation with science fiction to propagate modern myths such as the notion that "superior" extraterrestrial species reside on numerous planets, and that the human soul evolves through cosmic reincarnation.*

September 23, 1846: German astronomer Johann Gottfried Galle (1812–1910) and his assistant Heinrich D'Arrest discovered Neptune, named for the Roman god of the sea and the eighth planet from the Sun. Neptune is a blue gas giant, with a diameter four times that of Earth, that completes an orbit of the Sun once every one hundred and sixty-five years. In 1989, the US NASA *Voyager 2* became the first Earth spacecraft to visit Neptune.

November 26, 1846: The first recognized UFO episode in Brazilian history was documented by Imperial Navy vice-admiral Augusto João Manuel Leverger, baron of Melgaço, who, before words like UFO or UAP existed, called it an "extraordinary meteorological phenomenon." The significant event was published in the *Official Gazette of the Empire of Brazil* on November 26, 1846, as described by Leverger:

> *I observed phenomena this night like never before. At 5 hours and 57 minutes, the sky was perfectly clear, calm, 60° thermometer, a luminous globe made a rapidity curve of 30° in the NNO direction. The direction made with the horizon angles of approximately 75⁰ and 105⁰ by the Westside. It dropped a bright spot of 5 or 6 degrees of compliance and 30 to 35 degrees wide, in which three bodies were distinguished in the brightness, much brighter than that the spot of light, and even if it did not exceed in the intensity of the full moon in clear weather. They were superimposed and separated from each other. The one in the middle had the almost circular appearance; the lower one looked like a 120° circle segment with broken ends radiused; the one at the top was of an irregular quadrilateral shape; the largest dimension of the discs would be 20 to 25°.*

Experts believe that Leverger's sighting was not a meteorite because it lasted for twenty-five minutes and because of its trajectory. Leverger stated that it was not a balloon.

1846: In an ostensible Fortean event, a large, shiny disc flew over Lowell, Massachusetts, and dropped what was described as the:

> *Most fetid-smelling jelly which was found to weigh four-hundred and forty-two pounds and was four feet in diameter.*

September 24, 1852: During the height of the Industrial Revolution, the world's first powered, manned dirigible was flown. The steam-powered balloon was designed by Frenchman Henri Giffard and traveled about seventeen miles at five miles per hour.

1854: Sir David Brewster wrote in More Worlds Than One: The Creed of the Philosopher and the Hope of the Christian:

> *On a planet more magnificent than ours, could there not exist a type of intelligences the weakest of which would still be above that of Newton? Do they its inhabitants use telescopes more penetrating or microscopes more powerful than ours? Do they not have more subtle processes of induction, more fertile means of analyzing, and deeper combinations?*

February 27, 1861: Spiritualist Rudolf Steiner (1861–1925) was born in Kraljević, Austria. Steiner founded the Anthroposophical Society in 1912. His movement was based on the notion that a spiritual perception is independent of the senses, "knowledge produced by the higher self in man." Steiner believed that humans once participated more fully in spiritual processes through a dreamlike consciousness but had since become restricted by their attachment to material things.

1864: Jules Verne, an author and a visionary, published *Journey to the Center of the Earth,* combining the technology of the Industrial Revolution (roughly between 1760 and 1830) with fantasy and adventure—roughly eighty years before the appearance of the Shaver Mysteries.

1864: French astronomer Camille Flammarion, influenced by the writings of Jean Reynaud, published *In Real and Imaginary Worlds*, which described a range of exotic species and plants and a belief in extraterrestrial life.

1865: French astronomer Emmanual Liais (1826–1900) suggested that the dark albedo markings seen on Mars were patches of lush vegetation and not water—we know today that they are neither. A crater on Mars has been named after him.

1865: At age thirty-seven, Jules Verne published *From the Earth to the Moon: A Direct Route in 97 Hours, 20 Minutes,* the story of the fictitious Baltimore Gun Club and their attempts to build an enormous columbiad space gun, rather than a rocket ship, to launch three people to the Moon. Verne later wrote a sequel called *Around the Moon.* One hundred and three years later, Verne's affinity for technology was described by futurist Alvin Toffler in *Future Shock* as it offered a grim warning about:

> *The shattering stress and disorientation that we induce in individuals by subjecting them to too much change in too short a time.*

September 21, 1866: Prolific English writer Herbert George Wells (1866–1946) was born in Bromley, Kent, and would be called the "father of science fiction." Simon John James wrote in the *Independent*:

> *No writer is more renowned for his ability to foresee the future than HG Wells. His writing can be seen to have predicted the airplane, the tank, space travel, the atomic bomb, satellite television, and the worldwide web. His fantastic fiction imagined time travel, alien invasion, flights to the moon, and human beings with the powers of gods.*

His visionary science fiction includes *The Time Machine* (1895), *The Island of Doctor Moreau* (1896), *The Invisible Man* (1897), and *The War of the Worlds* (1898).

April 21, 1869: American history professor Paul August Kosok (1869–1959) was born in Long Island, New York. He is credited as the first serious researcher of Peru's Nazca

Lines and comprehended that some patterns represented living creatures, while other lines related to astronomical events.

1870: Jules Verne published *Twenty Thousand Leagues Under the Sea,* continuing to embrace his modern-day Industrial Revolution machines and technology. Verne's depiction of Captain Nemo's underwater vessel, the *Nautilus,* is regarded as prophetic and accurately describes many components of today's submarines, which in the 1870s were relatively primitive vessels.

April 24, 1874: Professor Schafarick, while in Prague, in the Austro-Hungarian Empire, observed:

> *An object of such a strange nature that I do not know what to say about it. It was of a blinding white and crossed slowly the face of the moon. It remained visible afterwards.*

August 6, 1874: Charles Fort (1874–1932) is born in Albany, New York. The writer and researcher specialized in anomalous phenomena. His terms "Fortean" and "Forteana" are often used to characterize such bizarre oddities. In *The Book of the Damned,* culled from the pages of the *Journal of the Royal Meteorological Society,* Fort documents an extract from the log of Capt. F. W. Banner aboard the *Lady of the Lake.* Sailors saw a remarkable object, light gray in color and much lower than the other clouds, which they reported to the ship's captain. Fort, who has been called the father of ufology, wrote:

> *According to Capt. Banner, was a cloud of circular form, with an included semicircle divided into four parts, the central dividing shaft beginning at the center of the circle and extending far outward, and then curving backward.*

> *It "traveled from a point at about 20 degrees above the horizon to a point about 80 degrees above," moving from the south, southeast, where it first appeared, to the northeast, traveling against the wind.*
>
> *For half an hour this form was visible. When it did finally disappear [it] was not because it disintegrated like a cloud, but because it was lost to sight in the evening darkness.*

September 1, 1875: Edgar Rice Burroughs (1875–1950) is born in Chicago, Illinois. He has inspired other writers and scientists and is recognized for his prolific output in the adventure, science fiction, and fantasy genres. He was the creator of the characters Tarzan and John Carter. He also wrote the Pellucidar series, the Amtor series, and the Caspak trilogy.

1875: The term *occultism* was introduced into the English language by the Ukrainian mystic Madame Blavatsky (1831–1891), an esotericist who co-founded the Theosophical Society and, in 1877, published *Isis Unveiled, a* book outlining her Theosophical worldview.

August 16, 1877: The two small moons of Mars, Phobos and Deimos (Fear and Dread), were discovered by American astronomer Asaph Hall at the US Naval Observatory in Washington, DC.

1877: Giovanni Schiaparelli, using an eight-and-three-quarter-inch refracting telescope, discovered *canali* (channels) on the planet Mars. He theorized that the canals were possibly built to link melting polar icecaps with water-starved areas.

January 24, 1878: One of the first mentions of the word "saucer" came after Texas farmer John Martin observed a dark flying UFO high in the sky, cruising "at a wonderful speed."

The story appeared the next day in the Dennison *Daily News*, titled "A Strange Phenomenon." The article read:

> *When directly over him, it was about the size of a large saucer and was evidently at a great height.*

March 14, 1879: Albert Einstein (1879–1955) was born, now widely acknowledged as one of the greatest and most influential physicists ever. Best known for developing the theory of relativity, he also made important contributions to the development of the theory of quantum mechanics. His mass-energy equivalence formula, $E = mc^2$, which arises from relativity theory, has been dubbed "the world's most famous equation." He received the 1921 Nobel Prize in Physics "for his services to Theoretical Physics, and especially for his discovery of the law of the photoelectric effect."

May 15, 1879: The crew of the brig *Victoria,* sailing just off the coast of Malta, observed three luminous UFOs rise out of the sea about a half mile from their ship, as reported in the *Malta Times*.

September 8, 1882: UFO researcher Meade Layne (1882–1961) was born in Viroqua, Virginia, and founded the Borderland Sciences Research Associates (BRSA). Layne is recognized for proposing an early version of the interdimensional hypothesis to explain flying saucer sightings. Layne believed that UFOs were sent from "Etheria," a parallel dimension. These interdimensional UFOs were invisible but could be viewed when their atomic motion became slow enough. As a pioneer of the ancient astronaut hypothesis, Layne postulated that Etherians inspired much of Earth's religious beliefs and mythology. His books included *The Ether Ship Mystery and Its Solution* (1950) and *The Coming of the Guardians* (1954).

August 12, 1883: While observing the Sun, the first known photos of a UFO were taken by Jose Bonilla, a Mexican astronomer at the Zacatecas Observatory. Bonilla witnessed almost one hundred and fifty strange passing objects. The photographs he took showed a series of cigar- and spindle-shaped objects, which were solid and non-celestial.

August 20, 1890: Howard Phillips Lovecraft (1980–1937) was born at his family home in Providence, Rhode Island. The precocious youth was reciting poetry at age two, reading at age three, and writing at age six or seven. His earliest enthusiasm was for the *Arabian Nights*, Greek mythology, and weird fiction, his interest fostered by his grandfather, who entertained Lovecraft with off-the-cuff weird Gothic tales.

Lovecraft wrote extensively about what we now call "cosmic horror," a mix of elder beings, forgotten gods, and alien beings. All these beings have one thing in common: their chaotic nature.

April 17, 1891: UFO "contactee" George Adamski (1891–1965) was born in Poland, emigrating to the USA when he was around four years old. In the 1940s and 1950s, he claimed to have taken numerous photographs of flying saucers and said that he met with friendly Nordic aliens, claiming to have taken flights with them to the Moon and other planets. Adamski billed himself a "philosopher, teacher, student and saucer researcher," although skeptics concluded his claims were an elaborate hoax, and that Adamski himself was a charlatan and a con artist.

January 1, 1892: Robert Potter, an Australian clergyman, published *The Germ Growers*, which described a covert invasion by aliens who take on the appearance of human beings and develop a virulent disease to assist in their plans for global conquest. Potter's alien invasion novel was not widely read, and consequently, H. G. Wells's more successful *War of the Worlds* (1898) is credited as the seminal and much-imitated alien invasion story.

February 15, 1892: James Vincent Forrestal (1892–1949) was born in Matteawan, New York, and would become the first United States Secretary of Defense. According to ufologists, Forrestal received an executive order authorizing him to establish a board of experts, answerable only to President Truman, to be called Majestic 12 (MJ-12). Their job was to investigate the Roswell crash. While being treated for depression at Bethesda Naval Hospital, Forrestal died by suicide from fatal injuries sustained after falling out a sixteenth-floor window.

April 28, 1892: Francis Joseph Xavier Scully (1892–1964) was born. He was a noted columnist for the entertainment trade magazine *Variety*. Scully publicized the Aztec, New Mexico, UFO hoax when, in 1949, he authored two columns in *Variety* claiming that dead extraterrestrial beings were recovered from a flying saucer crash. His book *Behind the Flying Saucers* (1950) expanded on the themes of flying saucer crashes and dead extraterrestrials, with Scully describing one of his sources as having "more degrees than a thermometer."

1894: Percival Lowell founded the Lowell Observatory in Flagstaff, Arizona—the same year that H. G. Wells wrote his classic science fiction novel *The War of the Worlds*. Lowell developed the idea that canals on the surface of Mars were artificial, indicating that the planet had intelligent life. According to author Ronald Story:

The accounts of Martian life given by Wells and Lowell were strikingly similar in certain respects, even though one was writing fiction and the other expounding a serious hypothesis.

June 10, 1895: Psychoanalyst and catastrophist Immanuel Velikovsky (1895–1979) was born in Vitebsk, Russia. He wrote several books offering pseudoscientific interpretations of ancient history, and his 1950 book, *Worlds in Collision*, became a bestseller. The book espoused the idea that Earth suffered catastrophic close encounters with other planets in ancient history.

January 1, 1896: *The Book of the Secrets of Enoch* was translated from the Slavonic language by W. R. Morfill. This document is an important work for scholars and patrons of Christianity and specifically of apocalyptic works, as it delves into the early origins of Christianity. The text, also called the *Slavonic Enoch*, was known only in Russia for over 1,200 years. The work is recognized academically as an example of *pseudepigrapha*, which were purportedly written by biblical figures, but is not accepted as such.

November 17, 1896: In one of the earliest records of UFOs, numerous airships, with underslung gondolas, appeared up and down the California coast. The low-flying and illuminated UFOs were witnessed by numerous individuals and prominent citizens, who described the "wandering apparitions" as being one hundred feet long and gray-colored, "like a Jules Verne illustration." Additional West Coast reports of whirring machinery and aerial searchlights sweeping the ground became commonplace well int The German-manufactured Zeppelin airship did not take to the air until July 1900.

April 16, 1896: Peruvian archaeologist Manuel Toribio Mejía Xesspe (1896–1983) was born. In 1926 he became the first to systematically study the mysterious Nazca Lines, south of Lima, Peru. Because the lines are virtually impossible to identify from ground level, they only gained widespread recognition after pilots flew over them in the 1930s. Experts have debated the purpose of the lines, and ancient astronaut theorists claim that they were designed by extraterrestrials. The lines consist of:

> *More than 800 straight lines on the coastal plain, some of which are thirty miles (48 km) long. Additionally, there are over three hundred geometric designs, which include basic shapes such as triangles, rectangles, and trapezoids, as well as spirals, arrows, zig-zags and wavy lines.*

1887: Frenchman Jules Verne's *Robur the Conqueror* was published in the United States. Verne's science-fiction novel described the globe-circling airship the *Albatross*. The sequel, *Master of the World*, was published in 1904 and adapted into a 1961 film, *Master of the World*, with Vincent Price, who, as Robur, planned to conquer the world to put an end to tyranny and war.

April 6, 1897: According to an article in the *Chicago Tribune*, several hundred residents witnessed a mobile, steel-bodied airship estimated to be about fifteen feet in length, hovering over Omaha, Nebraska.

1897: The *Washington Times* speculated that the mysterious and widely seen airships were "a reconnoitering party from Mars," while the *Saint Louis Post-Dispatch* suggested "these may be visitors from Mars, fearful, at the last, of invading the planet they have been seeking."

April 17, 1897: The Houston, Texas, *Daily Post* reported on what was later called "The Great Airship Flap of 1897," noting that:

> *The much talked of airship was seen here last night at about 1:16 o'clock. The Reverend J. W. Smith was the first to discover the curious aerial monster. He thought at first that it was a star shooting but, after watching it a moment or two, saw that it was not ... It soon disappeared, traveling in a westerly direction.*

April 19, 1897: Yates Center, Kansas, farmer Alexander Hamilton was awakened by his cattle to witness "an airship slowly descending upon my cow lot about forty rods from the house." Hamilton, a much-respected former member of the House of Representatives, saw a craft that rose and hoisted away a two-year-old heifer, discovered the next day—four miles away. Hamilton also stated that the craft was manned by "six of the strangest beings I ever saw, all jabbering in an unknown tongue." The traumatized farmer told the local newspaper:

> *I don't know whether they were angels or devils, but I don't want any more to do with them.*

June 20, 1897: Major Donald Edward Keyhoe (1897–1988) was born in Ottumwa, Iowa. He became a Marine Corps naval aviator and served as the tour manager of aviation pioneer Charles Lindbergh. Keyhoe wrote for pulp magazines such as *Weird Tales* and *Dr. Yen Sin*, but, in the 1950s, became a UFO researcher, publishing *Flying Saucers from Outer Space* (Henry Holt & Company, 1953.) Kehoe encouraged the government to research UFOs and release this information to the public.

1887: French astronomer Camille Flammarion published *Lumen,* describing a fictional human character who meets the soul of an alien able to cross the universe faster than light. Flammarion wrote that the alien had been reincarnated on other worlds, each with its own gallery of organisms and unique evolutionary history.

1897: H. G. Wells's *The War of the Worlds* was serialized in *Pearson's Magazine* in the United Kingdom and by *Cosmopolitan* magazine in the United States. Based on an original novel by Robert Potter, Wells's vision of alien invasion was published in book form the following year.

1898: H. G. Wells's *The War of the Worlds* is published. The novel details a catastrophic conflict between humans and extraterrestrial "Martians." It is considered a landmark work of science fiction. Dr. Oliver Tearle of Loughborough University has recognized the continued relevance of *The War of the Worlds*, which has inspired numerous reworkings and imitations, constantly being adapted for radio, film, and television. He points out that in 2019 alone there were two television revisions by Fox and the BBC:

> *Curiously, the most famous adaptation of all, Orson Welles's 1938 radio broadcast in the United States, is also the most misunderstood, and contrary to popular belief there was no widespread panic among Americans who thought Welles's adaptation was a news broadcast.*

August 21, 1898: Truck driver Truman Bethurum (1898–1969) was born in Gavilan, California. He claimed he was contacted on eleven separate occasions by an extraterrestrial group near Nevada's Mojave Desert. He conversed in English with its beautiful and voluptuous female captain, Aura Rhanes, from the planet Clarion. Bethurum claimed to possess physical evidence of extraterrestrial existence but was widely dismissed by UFO researchers as a con artist and charlatan. In 1954 he published *Aboard a Flying Saucer*.

1898: Garrett P. Serviss published the science fiction novel *Edison's Conquest of Mars*, which featured inventor Thomas Edison leading a group of scientists to develop ships and a disintegration ray to defend Earth from hostile aliens.

Part Two

Chapter 8
Prelude to Roswell: 1900s

THIS DECADE GAVE us Enrico Fermi, Robert Oppenheimer, Morris K. Jessup, Donald Howard Menzel, Richard Sharpe Shaver, Ray A. Palmer, "panspermia" and the Tunguska Object.

March 20, 1900: Morris K. Jessup (1900–1959) was born in Rockville, Indiana. Jessup became a well-known figure in the UFO community and an important participant in the Philadelphia Experiment narrative. He published several books on a range of topics, including UFOs, the paranormal, and unexplained phenomena, including his controversial *The Case for the UFO* (1955). Jessup has been referred to in ufological circles as:

> *Probably the most original extraterrestrial hypothesiser of the 1950s.*

December 1900: The Flannan Isles Lighthouse was the site of a mystery surrounding the disappearance of lighthouse keepers James Ducat, Thomas Marshall, and Donald MacArthur. Their disappearance remains one of the most perplexing and enduring mysteries of the twentieth century. Relief lighthouse keeper Joseph Moore climbed the one hundred and sixty steps to the lighthouse, and according to *SkyHistory:*

> *Reaching the lighthouse compound and entering the living quarters, Moore noticed that the clock on the kitchen wall had stopped, the table was set for a meal that had never been eaten and a chair had been toppled over. A canary in a cage was the only sign of life.*

The lighthouse incident has been intertwined with conspiracy circles, the supernatural, and even the visitation of extraterrestrials, and remains one of the most baffling episodes in Scottish maritime history.

1901: Despite his reputation as a child genius, engineer, inventor, and physicist, Nikola Tesla lost the race to invent the radio to Italian inventor Guglielmo Marconi—even though he gave short-range demonstrations of radio communication two years before Marconi. In 1943 the US Supreme Court voided four of Marconi's key patents, belatedly acknowledging Tesla's innovations in radio.

April 11, 1901: Theoretical astrophysicist and UFO debunker Donald Howard Menzel (1901–1976) was born in Florence, Colorado. During World War II, Menzel was commissioned as a lieutenant commander in the United States Navy and asked to head a division of intelligence. He was appointed acting director of the Harvard Observatory in 1952 and was the full director from 1954 to 1966. He discovered the chemistry of stars, the atmosphere of Mars, and the nature of gaseous nebulae. His published books include *The World of Flying Saucers: A Scientific Examination of a Major Myth of the Space Age* (1963) and *The UFO*

Enigma: The Definitive Explanation of the UFO Phenomenon (1977).

September 29, 1901: Italian and later naturalized American physicist and creator of the world's first nuclear reactor, Enrico Fermi (1901–1954), was among the few scientists who excelled in both theoretical physics and experimental physics. He was recognized as the "architect of the nuclear age" and the "architect of the atomic bomb." In 1938 he was awarded the Nobel Prize in Physics. The synthetic element fermium was named after him, making him one of only sixteen scientists who have elements named after them.

July 5, 1902: Army Lt. Gen. Arthur Gilbert Trudeau (1902–1991) was born in Vermont and is known for his command of the 7th Infantry Division during the Battle of Pork Chop Hill in the Korean War. He was named chief of Army Intelligence in October 1953, and in 1958, returned to Washington as director of Army Research and Development.

In Colonel Philip J. Corso's book, *The Day After Roswell*, Trudeau, his immediate supervisor, was instrumental in resurrecting the long-hidden Roswell wreckage, hidden within a Pentagon basement, and encouraged Corso:

> *To introduce components of the Roswell debris to defense contractors for technical analysis that would yield breakthroughs in fiber optics, lasers, silicon chips, electromagnetic propulsion, and wireless pilot-to-aircraft control systems in years to come.*

Without going public on his UFO views, Trudeau advanced state-of-the-art military and civilian applications through his secretive direction of Roswell technology, according to Corso.

1903: Swedish chemist Svante August Arrhenius (1859–1927) was awarded the Nobel Prize for Chemistry. His theory of "panspermia" proposed that life on Earth was created from bacterial spores transported through space by light pressure. The panspermia hypothesis argues that life did not begin on Earth but that the seeds of life were extraterrestrial in origin, carried here by meteorites or other space bodies.

April 22, 1904: American theoretical physicist Julius Robert Oppenheimer (1904–1967) was born in New York City. He became the director of the Manhattan Project's Los Alamos Laboratory "Project Y." Regarded as the "father of the atomic bomb," he helped create the first nuclear weapons during World War II.

March 18, 1905: Thomas Townsend Brown (1905–1985) was born in Zanesville, Ohio. The researcher spent his life attempting to develop an antigravity device, connecting electric fields and gravity. *The Philadelphia Experiment: Project Invisibility* (1979) implied that Townsend's "electrogravitics" was the propulsion used by advanced extraterrestrial technology. Chapter 10 of the aforementioned book was titled "The Force Fields of Townsend Brown."

July 7, 1907: Robert A. Heinlein (1907–1988) was born in Butler, Missouri. Heinlein was a prolific writer and is considered to be one of the most literary and sophisticated science-fiction writers. He helped develop the genre and is recognized for his Hugo Award-winning novel, *Stranger in a Strange Land* (1961).

1907: French astronomer Camille Flammarion wrote that he believed that dwellers on Mars had tried to communicate with Earth in the past. He also warned that a seven-tailed comet was heading toward Earth.

October 7, 1907: Richard Sharpe Shaver (1907–1975) was born in Berwick, Pennsylvania. He claimed to have been a prisoner of subterranean evil robots. Along with publisher Ray A. Palmer, they co-created the controversial Shaver Mystery and possibly the UFO hysteria investigated by the FBI.

June 30, 1908: The Tunguska Object entered Earth's atmosphere over Siberia and exploded with the devastating force of a ten-megaton thermonuclear bomb. The massive explosion flattened seventy thousand square miles of forests in a remote region of Eastern Siberia along the Tunguska River. The explosion left no crater, creating a mystery that has puzzled scientists ever since. Scientists at the Siberian Federal University in Russia theorized the explosion was caused by an asteroid that grazed the Earth, entering the atmosphere at a shallow angle and then passing out again into space. *Astronomy*, reviewing the near miss, concluded:

> *A direct impact with a 656-foot-wide (200-meter-wide) asteroid would have devastated Siberia, leaving a crater two miles (three kilometers) wide. It would also have had catastrophic effects on the biosphere, perhaps ending modern civilization.*

But author Erich A. Aggen Jr., writing in *Flying Saucers* (September 1970) asserted that, because the object altered its course twice, it was extraterrestrial:

> *Only a piloted or intelligently guided object could have executed such a maneuver.*

1908: The US Army received its first tender for a dirigible from Captain Thomas Scott Baldwin.

March 23, 1909: Police constable Kettle of Peterborough witnessed a UFO some 1,200 feet above the ground. The craft was described as a "dark, oblong body" having the "steady buzz of a high-powered engine" and a "powerful light."

1909: Turkish-born French astronomer Eugenios Antoniadi concluded that the "canals" on Mars were psychological interpretations of faint, blotchy structures seen through the wobbly terrestrial atmosphere and were not real. He made his observations through a large telescope in Meudon, France.

Chapter 9

Secrets Revealed: 1910s

1910: Astronomer Josef Allen Hynek (1910–1986) is born. Hynek is recognized as one of the twentieth century's leading UFO experts.

February 27, 1910: American aeronautical and systems engineer Clarence Leonard "Kelly" Johnson (1910–1990) was born in the remote mining town of Ishpeming, Michigan. He is recognized as one of the most talented and prolific aircraft design engineers in the history of aviation, contributing to over forty advanced aircraft designs, most notably the Lockheed U-2 and SR-71 Blackbird. Kelly also produced the first fighter capable of Mach 2, and the first fighter to exceed 400 mph. Known as an "organizing genius," he was the first team leader of the Lockheed Skunk Works.

August 1, 1910: Raymond A. Palmer (1910–1977) is born in Milwaukee, Wisconsin. Although he was known to his friends as "RAP," his biographer Fred Nadis called him "the Man from Mars." Palmer became editor of *Amazing Stories* in 1938 and began to publish the Shaver Mysteries, "true" accounts of underground civilizations visited by controversial writer Richard Sharpe Shaver.

January 24, 1911: Catherine Lucille Moore (1911–1987) was born in Indianapolis, Indiana, and, writing as C. L. Moore, was among the first female science fiction writers. Her rogue antihero "Northwest Smith" was featured in "Shambleau," published in *Weird Tales,* as he wandered the solar system with a raygun and his sidekick, the Venusian, Yarol.

June 11, 1911: Long John Nebel was born (1911–1978) in Chicago. He became an influential New York City talk radio host from the mid-1950s until he died in 1978. His syndicated program dealt mainly with anomalous phenomena, UFOs, and other offbeat topics.

June 28, 1911: The third Martian meteorite observed to have fallen to Earth landed at Nakhla near Alexandria, Egypt. A much-repeated story is that one of the meteorites struck and killed a dog, making it the only recorded instance of an earthling being killed by a Martian. Classified as type clinopyroxenite (nakhlite.)

July 9, 1911: American theoretical physicist John Archibald Wheeler (1911–2008) was born in Jacksonville, Florida. He was largely responsible for reviving interest in general relativity after World War II. He helped design and build the hydrogen bomb in the early 1950s and, along with Edward Teller, was the main civilian proponent of thermonuclear weapons. Stephen Hawking referred to him as the "hero of the black hole story."

1911: Edgar Rice Burroughs started writing his twelve-book Martian Adventures, which included *Swords of Mars, A Fighting Man of Mars,* and *The Warlord of Mars,* inspiring writers like Ray Bradbury and scientists like Carl Sagan. According to Burrough's website:

> *With his opening trilogy, considered one of the landmarks of science fiction, Burroughs created a vast and sweeping epic. Captain John Carter of the Confederate Army is whisked to Mars (Barsoom) and discovers a dying world of dry ocean beds where giant four-armed barbarians rule, of crumbling cities home to an advanced but decaying civilization, a world of strange beasts and savage combat, a world where love, honor, and loyalty become the stuff of adventure.*

September 18, 1911: Ufologist Brinsley Le Poer Trench (1911–1995) was a leading British ufologist and, as a member of the House of Lords, introduced a serious debate on UFOs. This historic occasion was the first in which the subject was discussed by the British Parliament. Trench later became the editor of *Flying Saucer Review*.

April 2, 1912: American occultist and saucerian Riley Hansard Crabb (1912–1994) was born in Minneapolis, Minnesota. He succeeded Meade Layne as director of the Borderland Sciences Research Associates (BSRA) from 1959 until 1985, writing and lecturing extensively on flying saucers, mediumship (particularly the Mark Probert seances), and occult matters, such as Kabbalah. He was an enthused member of the Theosophical Society and a prolific writer who theorized about everything from flying saucers and Forteana to radionics and subtle energy.

1912: Rudolf Steiner founded the Anthroposophical Society based on the notion that there is a spiritual perception independent of the senses, "knowledge produced by the higher self in man." The renewed perception of spiritual things required training the human consciousness to rise above attention to the matter. The ability to achieve this goal by an exercise of intellect is theoretically innate in everyone.

1912: Although the Nobel Committee announced that Nikola Tesla and Thomas Edison were the recipients of the Physics Prize, it went to Gustav Dalen. Tesla had refused the prize and the $20,000 that came with it, saying he wouldn't have accepted the prize because he wouldn't share it with Edison. He differentiated himself as a pure scientist and Edison as an applied scientist, arguing they should not be in combination. In a letter to a friend, Tesla demonstrated his arrogance:

> *In a thousand years, there will be many recipients of the Nobel Prize, but I have not less than four dozen of my creations identified with my name in the technical literature. These are honors real and permanent, which are bestowed, not by a few who are apt to err, but by the whole world which seldom makes a mistake and for any of those I could give all the Nobel prizes which will be distributed during the next thousand years.*

March 17, 1913: Josef F. Blumrich (1913–2002) is born in Steyr, Austria. He published *The Spaceships of Ezekiel,* about a spaceship that was supposedly observed by the prophet Ezekiel, and another of numerous ancient alien hypotheses. Blumrich created detailed drawings of Ezekiel's "alien craft," concluding that the technology of the builders was more advanced than mankind's.

1913: Ancient alien theorist W. Raymond Drake (1913–1989) was born. The British disciple of Charles Fort published nine books about ancient astronauts, many predating Erich von Däniken. Drake spent his career researching obscure archives of material, searching for anomalies to support his theory of space aliens impacting human history. As Drake himself said:

I aspired to collect as many facts as possible from ancient literature to chronicle for the past what Charles Fort has so brilliantly done for the present century.

1913: Rudolf Steiner built his first Goetheanum, which he characterized as a "school of spiritual science," in Dornach, near Basel, Switzerland. The Waldorf School movement, derived from his experiments with the Goetheanum, in the early twenty-first century, had more than one thousand schools around the world.

October 6, 1914: Thor Heyerdahl (1914–2002) is born and would become one of history's most famous explorers. In 1947 he crossed the Pacific Ocean on the balsawood raft *Kon-Tiki*. This was his first expedition to be captured on film and was later awarded the Academy Award for best documentary in 1951. He later completed similar achievements with the reed boats *Ra*, *Ra II*, and *Tigris*.

March 29, 1915: American aviator Kenneth Albert Arnold (1915–1984) is born in Sebeka, Minnesota. He is known as "the man who started it all" after witnessing the first widely reported modern UFO sighting in the United States. Arnold claimed that he saw nine discs, called "flying saucers" by a reporter, flying in tandem near Mount Rainier, Washington, on June 24, 1947.

May 6, 1915: American actor and director George Orson Welles (1915–1985) was born in Kenosha, Wisconsin, and is remembered as one of the most influential filmmakers of all time. Wells co-wrote, produced, and directed *Citizen Kane* (1941), ranked as one of the greatest films ever made, and starred as the title character, Charles Foster Kane. Welles's radio adaption of H. G. Wells's *War of the Worlds*, at the age of twenty-three, gave him international notoriety, as it caused some listeners to believe that there was an actual Martian invasion.

1915: Paranormal researcher Charles Fort began organizing a book project called *X*, theorizing that we were being controlled by a race of Martian aliens, retaining Earth as a type of intergalactic petting zoo. One of Fort's best-known sayings is "I think we're property." But science-fiction author H. G. Wells, after examining *The Book of the Damned,* called Fort:

> *One of the most damnable bores who ever cut scraps from out-of-the-way newspapers, who writes like a drunkard.*

May 22, 1915: Philip James Corso (1915–1998) was born in California, Pennsylvania. He served in the US Army and earned the rank of lieutenant colonel. In 1997 Corso published *The Day After Roswell* about his alleged involvement in reverse engineering the extraterrestrial technology recovered from the Roswell Incident.

November 17, 1915: MIT physics professor Philip Morrison (1915–2005) was born in Somerville, New Jersey. He is recognized for his work on the Manhattan Project and the development of the world's first atomic bomb. Morrison published papers on cosmic rays, and his 1958 paper marked the birth of gamma ray astronomy. Morrison transported the core of the Trinity test device, detonated on July 16, 1945, to the test site in the back seat of a Dodge sedan.

1917: The American Institute of Electrical Engineers persuaded a reluctant and arrogant Nikola Tesla to accept the Edison Medal.

October 13, 1917: During a fierce rainstorm in Fatima, Portugal, a crowd of fifty thousand people witnessed a huge silver disk spinning, windmill-like, about the sky. This UFO sighting fulfilled the prophecy of three young peasant girls who claimed that the Virgin Mary told them she would reveal herself on October 13. While many viewed the event as a spectacular UFO sighting, the Catholic Church declared the Fatima event a miracle.

December 16, 1917: Sir Arthur Charles Clarke (1917–2008) was born in Minehead, United Kingdom, and became one of the most important and influential figures in twentieth-century science fiction. He wrote over fifty books but is best known for the novel and movie *2001: A Space Odyssey*, which he co-created with the assistance of Stanley Kubrick.

1919: Albert Einstein published Relativity: The Special and General Theory, "written for those not acquainted with the underlying math," and listed by Discovery as one of the 25 Greatest Science Books of All Time:

> *To explain the special theory of relativity, Einstein invites us on board a train filled with rulers and clocks; for the more complex general theory, we career in a cosmic elevator through empty space. As Einstein warns in his preface, however, the book does demand a fair amount of patience and force of will on the part of the reader.*

1919: Charles Fort publishes *The Book of the Damned: The Original Classic of Paranormal Exploration.* Fort's collection of the damned (data that science has excluded) brought together a bizarre compilation of visitors from space, monsters, poltergeists, and floating islands, and a world where frogs fall from the sky, mysterious airships take flight in an age before the airplane, and people disappear, reappear, and spontaneously combust.

December 10, 1919: Fred Lee Crisman (1919–1975) was born in Oregon. Crisman, connected to several conspiracy theories, was involved in the Maury Island incident, convincing two flying saucer witnesses that debris had been dropped from a flying saucer. He was subpoenaed in 1968 by a New Orleans grand jury in the prosecution of a man for the assassination of President John F. Kennedy.

Chapter 10

The Book of the Damned: 1920s

THE WORLD of ufology celebrated the collective birthdays of individuals destined to play key roles in the field—Carl M. Allen, James Edward McDonald, Albert K. Bender, Gray Barker, John Mack, Zecharia Sitchin, Leonard H. Stringfield, as well as the Scopes Monkey Trial, and "The Colour Out of Space."

May 7, 1920: James Edward McDonald (1920–1971) was an American physicist and ufologist born in Duluth, Minnesota. McDonald campaigned in support of expanding UFO studies, arguing that UFOs represented an important unsolved mystery and argued in favor of the extraterrestrial hypothesis. McDonald testified before Congress during the 1968 UFO hearings. McDonald was the senior physicist at the Institute for Atmospheric Physics and a professor in the Department of Meteorology, University of Arizona, Tucson.

July 11, 1920: Ancient astronaut theorist Zecharia Sitchin (1920–2010) was born in Baku, the capital of the then Soviet Union. Sitchin was among the first to suggest that extraterrestrials played a significant role in ancient human history. His books, such as *The 12th Planet* (Ishi Press, 1976), have sold millions of copies and have been translated into over twenty-five languages. Sitchin's ideas easily pre-dated those of Erich von Däniken. Critic Michael S. Heiser has called Sitchin:

> *Arguably the most important proponent of the ancient astronaut hypothesis over the last several decades.*

July 17, 1920: American ufologist, author, and researcher Leonard H. Stringfield (1920–1994) was born in Cincinnati, Ohio. During World War II, he served as a military intelligence officer and pilot in the US Army Air Forces, which provided him with insights into the inner workings of the US military. He was an early member of the National Investigations Committee on Aerial Phenomena (NICAP) and served as the organization's public relations director. His first book, *Situation Red: The UFO Siege* (1970), detailed numerous UFO sightings and encounters, propelling him to the forefront of ufology.

June 16, 1921: Ufologist and writer Albert K. Bender (1921–2016) was born in Duryea, Pennsylvania. Obsessed with the UFO phenomenon, he founded the International Flying Saucer Bureau and wrote *Flying Saucers and the Three Men* (1962). Bender claimed that in March 1953 he had been approached by three Men in Black (MIB), which became a staple for ufologists.

February 17, 1922: The charismatic contactee Howard Menger (1922–2009) was born in High Bridge, New Jersey. He claimed that in the late 1950s, he met extraterrestrials, documented in his books *From Outer Space to You* and *The High Bridge Incident.* Explaining where the aliens actually came from, Menger stated:

> *Years ago, on a T.V. program, when I first voiced my opinion that the people I met and talked with from the craft might not be extraterrestrial, it was thought that I had recanted. However, they (the aliens) said they had just come from the planet we call Venus (or Mars). It is my opinion that these space travelers may have bypassed or visited other planets (as we are planning) but were not native to those planets any more than our astronauts are native to the moon.*

June 3, 1922: One of the foremost figures in ufology, 1st Lt. Walter Haut (1922–2005) was born in Chicago, Illinois. He stepped into the role of public information officer at the 509th Bomb Group based in Roswell, New Mexico. Haut was directed by the base commander, Colonel William Blanchard, to draft an announcement that the United States Army Air Forces had recovered a crashed "flying disc" from a nearby ranch. The US Army Air Forces retracted the claim later the same day, explaining that the UFO was actually a weather balloon.

1922: Albert Einstein received the 1921 Nobel Prize in Physics "for his services to Theoretical Physics, and especially for his discovery of the law of the photoelectric effect," referring to his 1905 paper, "On a Heuristic Viewpoint Concerning the Production and Transformation of Light." Einstein took a pivotal step in the development of quantum theory. His mass-energy formula, $E = mc^2$, has been dubbed "the world's most famous equation."

November 11, 1924: Ufologist hoaxer Gabriel Green (1924–2001) was born in Whittier, California. He claimed to have contacted flying saucer extraterrestrials from the planet Korendor, orbiting the triple star Alpha Centauri. Green was a write-in candidate for US president, representing the Universal

Flying Saucer Party. He published *Let's Face Facts about Flying Saucers* in 1972.

May 2, 1925: Paranormal author Gray Barker (1925–1984) was born in Riffle, Virginia. His 1956 book *They Knew Too Much About Flying Saucers* introduced Albert K. Bender's Men in Black mythology. Barker's critics claim that he was an opportunist who participated in hoaxing the UFO community.

May 31, 1925: Carl Allen (or Carlos Miguel Allende) was born on a farm outside of New Kensington, Pennsylvania. The ex-merchant mariner claimed to have witnessed a strange experiment at the Philadelphia Naval Shipyard, sometime around October 28, 1943, and began warning Dr. Morris Jessup not to investigate the levitation of UFOs. Allende believed that, based on Albert Einstein's unified field theory, Jessup's work was too dangerous.

July 10, 1925: The Scopes Monkey Trial, with an obvious comparison to similar trials in the 1500s, saw high school teacher John Thomas Scopes accused of violating Tennessee's Butler Act, deeming it illegal for teachers to teach human evolution. The trial exposed two extreme viewpoints—Modernists, who said evolution could be consistent with religion, and Fundamentalists, who said the word of God as revealed in the Bible took priority over all human knowledge. Scopes was found guilty, but the verdict was overturned on a technicality.

1925: Morris Jessup earned a bachelor of science degree in astronomy from the University of Michigan while working at the Lamont-Hussey Observatory. He received a master of science the following year. In UFO circles, he has been referred to as "probably the most original extraterrestrial hypothesiser of the 1950s" with an educational background in both astronomy and archeology.

1926: The American Museum of Natural History's Roerich Expedition described one of the first accounts of a UFO—a shiny, disc-shaped object spotted high in the skies over Altai-Himalaya.

1927: The Nazca Lines were first discovered by the Peruvian archaeologist Toribio Mejia Xesspe but were later popularized as evidence of the ancient astronaut theory. James Moseley, in a 1955 *Fate* magazine article, was the first to suggest that they represented intriguing Fortean phenomena, suggesting a mysterious origin long before alternative writers such as Erich von Däniken (1968), Henri Stierlin (1983) and Gerald Hawkins (1990) took notice.

March 1927: H. P. Lovecraft published his science fiction/horror story "The Colour Out of Space." The short piece depicted an area known by the locals as "the blasted heath," west of the fictional town of Arkham, Massachusetts, where a meteorite had crashed, poisoning or killing every living thing. The story first appeared in the September 1927 edition of Hugo Gernsback's science fiction magazine *Amazing Stories*. It has been adapted to film several times, such as *Die, Monster, Die!* (1965), *The Curse* (1987), *Colour from the Dark* (2008), *The Colour Out of Space* (*Die Farbe*) (2010), and *Color Out of Space* (2019). Stephen King's 1987 novel, *The Tommyknockers*, was also inspired by Lovecraft's story.

September 29, 1927: UFO investigator Paul Frederic Bennewitz Jr. (1927–2003) was born in Kansas and is believed to have been a part of a government disinformation campaign. He was an active member of Arizona's Aerial Phenomena Research Organization (APRO), a civilian UFO investigation group. Bennewitz claimed that an extensive network of secret UFO bases, called Dulce Base, was located outside of Albuquerque, New Mexico, with intentions to control mankind.

1927: German theoretical physicist and Nobel laureate Weiner Heisenberg (1901–1976) proposed his revolutionary "uncertainty principle." Heisenberg stated that any realistic description of the universe must describe it in all possible states at the same instant in time. For example, a man could be alive, dead, and unborn at the same time. Heisenberg's principle also states that we cannot know both the position and speed of a particle, such as a photon or an electron, with perfect accuracy, because the more we determine the particle's position, the less we know about its speed and vice versa. In summary, the uncertainty principle described a balance between two complementary properties, such as speed and position.

February 1928: H. P. Lovecraft published his short story "The Call of Cthulhu," in *Weird Tales,* delving into inhuman statues, ancient relics, and hieroglyphs left behind by aliens who had been visiting Earth for millennia. Lovecraft's themes were later appropriated by both author Erich von Däniken and the History Channel's *Ancient Aliens,* while author Jason Colavito believed that the 1964 cult classic *The Morning of the Magicians,* written by French journalists Louis Pauwels and Jacques Bergier, had been influenced by "The Call of Cthulhu."

May 19, 1928. West Virginia's two-thousand-and-two-hundred-foot Silver Bridge opened to traffic and was the first bridge in the nation to use an innovative eyebar-link suspension system rather than a traditional wire-cable suspension. Thirty-nine years later, the bridge collapsed, killing forty-six people, as documented in John A. Keel's *The Mothman Prophecies* and celebrated during the annual Mothman Festival.

1928: Controversial ufologist and contactee G. George Adamski founded the Royal Order of Tibet. In 1934, he moved to Laguna Beach, teaching a philosophy of life course he called "Universal Law."

January 7, 1929: The *Buck Rogers in the 25th Century A.D.* comic strip debuted and was initially syndicated in forty-seven newspapers. The space hero, created by Philip Francis Nowlan, was inspired by literary giants Jules Verne and H. G. Wells but also inspired copycats like Flash Gordon, Brick Bradford, and Speed Spaulding.

1929: The regarded observer of Mars, French astronomer Eugene Antoniadi (1870–1944), after using the Meudon Observatory's eighty-three-centimeter telescope, suggested that the Martian "canali" were simply optical illusions created by attempting to see immense distances through the Earth's dense atmosphere. In 1934, Antoniadi created the first map of Mercury.

October 4, 1929: John Edward Mack (1929–2004) was born in New York City. As the head of psychiatry at Harvard Medical School, he later researched the psychology of alien abduction experiences. In 1977, Mack won the Pulitzer Prize for Biography for his book *A Prince of Our Disorder* on T. E. Lawrence.

Chapter 11
Wormhole Theory: 1930s

January 22, 1930: Comic hero Buck Rogers first ventured into outer space aboard a rocket ship in "Tiger Men from Mars," his fifth newspaper comic story. Buck Rogers paralleled the development of space technology in the twentieth century and introduced Americans to outer space, combining Western with science fiction.

March 25, 1930: John Alva Keel (1930–2009) was born in Hornell, New York, the son of a small-time bandleader. After serving in the US Army during the Korean War, he worked as a foreign radio correspondent in Paris, Berlin, Rome, and Egypt. Keel became a leading ufologist, best known as the author of *The Mothman Prophecies* and for popularizing the Men in Black concept.

1930: American astronomer Clyde William Tombaugh (1906–1997) discovered Planet X, which some scientists initially thought might be as massive as Earth. The planet was later renamed Pluto but was then reclassified in 2006 as a dwarf planet or a "trans-Neptunian object." Tombaugh also discovered numerous asteroids and called for serious scientific research on flying saucers.

May 1930: Ray A. Palmer, "the Man from Mars," is credited, along with Walter Dennis, with creating the Science Correspondence Club and editing what some consider the first fanzine, *The Comet*. Palmer went on to promote UFOs and Richard Sharp Shaver's Shaver Mysteries in *Amazing Stories*. In 1952, Palmer collaborated with Kenneth Arnold, "the Man Who Started It All," on *The Coming of the Saucers: A Documentary Report on Sky Objects that Have Mystified the World*.

May 28, 1930: American astrophysicist and astrobiologist Frank Donald Drake (1930–2022) was born in Chicago, Illinois. Drake was a pioneer in the search for extraterrestrial intelligence (SETI), beginning with Project Ozma in 1960. He developed the Drake equation, which attempted to quantify the number of intelligent lifeforms that could potentially be discovered, and, working with Carl Sagan, helped design the Pioneer plaque, the first physical message flown beyond the solar system. Drake played an important role in developing the Voyager record.

August 4, 1931: James Willett Moseley (1931–2012) is born. He published the UFO newsletters *Saucer News* and its successor *Saucer Smear*—the longest continuously published UFO journal in the world. Over his nearly sixty-year career, he cleverly exposed UFO hoaxes but also contrived hoaxes of his own. Someone had called Moseley the "Voltaire of ufology," and, according to Antonio Huneeus:

> *Like the famous 18th-century wit, who used his pen to ridicule the Catholic Church, the French monarchy, and everything else in the society of his time, Moseley was critical and sarcastic regarding just about everything and everybody in UFOlogy. Yet Jim did believe a core of the UFO*

phenomenon was real and truly unexplained after filtering out all the hoaxes, *conspiracy theories, misidentifications, and just plain nonsense that pervades much of the field.*

1930: Considered to be the first UFO religion, the "I AM" Activity Movement was founded by Guy Ballard (1878–1939) and his wife, Edna Anne Wheeler Ballard (1886–1971), in Chicago, Illinois. Ballard claimed that, while hiking on Mount Shasta, he met "Saint Germain," an ascended master, one of the supernatural beings that included the original theosophical masters such as Jesus Christ, El Morya Khan, and Maitreya, as described by Helena Petrovna Blavatsky. The movement had up to a million followers in 1938.

June 15, 1931: Elliott Budd Hopkins (1931–2011) was born in Wheeling, West Virginia. Hopkins is widely credited for initiating the alien-abduction movement, a subgenre of UFO studies. High-profile writers on the subject, including Whitley Strieber and the Harvard psychiatrist John Mack, credited him with having ignited their interest in the field.

December 15, 1931: Saint Albertus Magnus was canonized by Pope Pius XI in Vatican City, Rome, and made a "Doctor of the Church." He was among the first intellectuals to contemplate the existence of extraterrestrial life.

1932: German theoretical physicist and Nobel laureate Weiner Heisenberg, one of the main pioneers of the theory of quantum mechanics, was awarded the 1932 Nobel Prize in Physics "for the creation of quantum mechanics." He is recognized for his 1927 "uncertainty principle," which states that the position and velocity of an object cannot both be measured exactly at the same time, even in theory.

1932: Charles Fort published *Lo!*, considered by some as his best work, combining detailed research with a comprehensive writing style. Fort viewed unexplainable phenomena as signs of possible extraterrestrial lifeforms:

> *Unknown, luminous things, or beings, have often been seen, sometimes close to this earth, and sometimes high in the sky. It may be that some of them were living things that occasionally came from somewhere in our existence, but that others were lights on the vessels of explorers, or voyagers, from somewhere else.*

1933: Film director Robert Bresson (1933–1983) suggested what could be interpreted as an unexpected key to understanding the paranormal:

> *Make visible what, without you, might perhaps never have been seen.*

November 1933: Catherine Lucille Moore's character Northwest Smith, "a rogue and adventurer who wandered through the solar system," was the first space Western hero. Smith, an outlaw, appeared in "Shambleau," the first in a series of stories in *Weird Tales*. "Shambleau" is a retelling of the Medusa myth combined with Moore's additional themes of sexuality and addiction.

1933–1938: Dozens of mysterious "Ghost Flyers," pre-dating World War II "foo fighters," were seen over Norway, Sweden, and Finland. The phantom "Ghost Flyers" were described as large airplanes with ordinary wings and tail—flying during impossible weather conditions at extremely low altitudes, over treacherous mountain terrain, and never landing for fuel or repairs.

July 29, 1934: Nuclear physicist Stanton Terry Friedman (1934–2019) was born in New Brunswick, Canada. Friedman was an early civilian investigator of the Roswell UFO incident, co-authoring with Don Berliner the 1992 book *Crash at Corona: The U.S. Military Retrieval and Cover-Up of a U.F.O.* He believed that alien spaceships and extraterrestrials had walked the Earth, and that the United States government had engaged in a "cosmic Watergate" to cover up evidence of alien visitations, most notably Roswell. Along with Kathleen Marden, he co-authored *Captured! The Betty and Barney Hill U.F.O. Experience* (2007).

November 9, 1934: Carl Sagan (1934–1996) is born in New York City. He later described himself as a childhood science fiction addict. He was fascinated by astronomy after learning that every star in the night sky was a distant Sun. His scientific curiosity led him to earn four degrees in physics, astronomy, and astrophysics from the University of Chicago. He said:

> *The nature of life on Earth and the search for life elsewhere are two sides of the same question—the search for who we are.*

March 10, 1935: The comic strip *Smokey Stover,* written and drawn by cartoonist Bill Holman, began a thirty-seven-year run, describing the misadventures of a zany fireman. Distributed by the Chicago Tribune Syndicate, the strip ran from 1935 to 1972. In Holman's strip, Smokey calls himself a "foo fighter" and is often seen riding in his two-wheeled "Foomobile." The term "foo fighter" came to be used to describe unidentified or mysterious aerial phenomena seen in the skies over both the European and Pacific Theaters of Operations during World War II.

April 14, 1935: Erich von Däniken is born in Zofingen, Switzerland. The "ancient astronauts" and "paleo contact" would sell over seventy million copies of his books, including *Chariots of the Gods* (1968), *Gods from Outer Space* (1968), and *The Gold of the Gods* (1973).

1935: Albert Einstein collaborated with physicist Nathan Rosen to produce a model of a wormhole, often called Einstein-Rosen bridges. His motivation was to use his theory of general relativity to expand on the idea of the existence of "bridges" connecting two different points in space-time, theoretically creating a shortcut that could reduce travel time and distance. The wormholes described theoretical black holes as portals to parallel universes—currently an essential theory researchers use to explain both UFOs and Bigfoot encounters.

1938: Renowned physicist Enrico Fermi was awarded the Nobel Prize in Physics for his work on induced radioactivity by neutron bombardment and for the discovery of transuranium elements. Later addressing the possibility of actual extraterrestrial contact, Fermi theorized that intelligent species have a determined window of time needed to develop technology allowing them to leave their home base. But, he added, if that window closed due to wars, societal collapse, or the cessation of scientific progress, that opportunity would disappear.

1935: J. Allen Hynek completed his PhD in astrophysics at Yerkes Observatory of the Department of Astronomy and Astrophysics at the University of Chicago.

February 19, 1936: Brad Steiger (1936–2018) was born at the Fort Dodge Lutheran Hospital during a blizzard. At the age of eleven, a near-death experience altered his life and his religious beliefs. He wrote almost one hundred and seventy books, which have sold seventeen million copies, including fiction and non-fiction works on the paranormal, spirituality, UFOs, true crime, and biographies. He was a proponent of the ancient astronauts theory, stating that many humans descend from alien "star people." His popular books were widely criticized by academics for making far-fetched claims without scientific evidence.

1936: J. Allen Hynek joined the Department of Physics and Astronomy at Ohio State University.

1938: Ray A. Palmer became the editor of *Amazing Stories* after Ziff Davis purchased it and fired then-editor T. O'Conor Sloane. Palmer took over from 1938 through 1949, driving up circulation with the Shaver Mystery, written by Richard Sharpe Shaver, and loathed by loyal science fiction fans. Freelance writer Andrew Liptak noted:

> *In the 1940s, Palmer was able to tap into the growing idea that there was much that was unexplainable about the world and turn it into a cottage industry that has endured in the decades since. While widely ridiculed by the government and public at large, the notion of UFOs is a romantic one, something Palmer certainly recognized as a storyteller and editor.*

April 18, 1938: Superman, the American comic book hero, created by Jerry Siegel and Joe Shuster, debuted in *Action Comics #1*, which sold for ten cents. It is considered to be both the beginning of the superhero genre and the most valuable comic book in the world, selling on eBay for $3,207,852 in 2014.

October 30, 1938: On Halloween eve, the Columbia Broadcasting System aired Orson Welles's radio adaption of H. G. Wells's *The War of the Worlds*, heard by approximately one million people. Welles and his *Mercury Theatre on the Air* used fake news bulletins describing a Martian invasion of New Jersey. Writing for *Smithsonian*, A. Brad Schwartz observed:

> *Some listeners mistook those bulletins for the real thing, and their anxious phone calls to police, newspaper offices, and radio stations convinced many journalists that the show had caused nationwide hysteria. By the next morning, the 23-year-old Welles's face and name were on the front pages of newspapers coast-to-coast, along with headlines about the mass panic his CBS broadcast had allegedly inspired.*

Although much was written about the resulting panic and suicides, Robert E. Bartholomew, an American medical sociologist, journalist, and author, a purported authority on mass hysteria and social delusions, said that there was:

> *a growing consensus among sociologists that the extent of the panic ... was greatly exaggerated.*

1939: Statesman Winston Churchill penned an eleven-page essay on alien life that revealed his curiosity about the universe and outlined his definition of life:

> *I, for one, am not so immensely impressed by the success we are making of our civilization here that I am prepared to think we are the only spot in this immense universe that contains living, thinking creatures, or that we are the highest type of mental and physical development which has ever appeared in the vast compass of space and time.*

September 24, 1939: Jacques Fabrice Vallée was born (1939–) emerging as an important figure in the study of UFOs. He is an internet pioneer, computer scientist, venture capitalist, and author. His scientific career began as a professional astronomer at the Paris Observatory. Vallée is recognized for defending the scientific legitimacy of the extraterrestrial hypothesis and later for promoting the interdimensional hypothesis.

Chapter 12
The Shaver Mystery: 1940s

During the World War II era, we witnessed mysterious "foo fighters," Kenneth Arnold's Mount Rainier sightings, the Roswell Incident, and the UFO pandemic of the '40s, when thousands reported sightings of unknown aerial objects.

May 1940: A suspected flying saucer landing occurred near Montana's Boulder Mountain, seven years before the Roswell crash. Udo Wartena witnessed a large disc-shaped object, over one hundred feet across, hovering above a meadow. Wartena watched as a staircase unfolded from the UFO and a man emerged, asking if the ship could take some water. Wartena was invited inside the object, where he met another man who told him they had come from a distant planet and were 609 years old. Wartena refused to acknowledge the incident, but just before his death in 1989, he confided what he had seen to two close friends.

1941: The Rev. William Huffman, pastor of the Cape Girardeau, Missouri, Baptist Church, was asked to accompany local police to the site of a suspected plane crash. But when Huffman and the rescue team arrived, they saw a disc-shaped object and "non-human people" lying on the ground. The bodies were hairless with large heads, big eyes, small mouths and very small ears. They were about four feet tall and had very long arms and fingers. According to the *Columbia Daily Tribune,* Rev. Huffman was asked to pray over the bodies:

> *Upon doing so, he was escorted by military officials to a nearby location where he was sworn to secrecy and strongly warned to never discuss the crash with anyone. Huffman did not know what was told to others at the scene, but he was told, "This didn't happen, you didn't see this. This is national security and is to never to be talked about again."*

Of note is that this obscure UFO sighting occurred several years before the 1947 Roswell Incident.

December 7, 1941: The comic strip *John Carter of Mars* first appeared. It was based on Edgar Rice Burroughs's 1912 character but also inspired by the success of *Buck Rogers*, which debuted in 1929. *John Carter of Mars* ran from 1941 to 1943. The strip debuted on the same day as the infamous Pearl Harbor attack and lasted only one year and four months, ending on April 18, 1943.

January 20, 1942: Investigative journalist Linda Moulton Howe is born in Boise, Idaho. Howe is recognized as a ufologist and advocate of a variety of conspiracy theories. She investigated cattle mutilations, concluding that they are performed by extraterrestrials. She also believes that the US government is working with aliens.

1942: Wandering the woods outside the Swiss town of Bülach, five-year-old Eduard Albert Meier (later known as "Billy" Meier), encountered an elderly-looking gentleman named Sfath, wearing what resembled a deep-sea diving suit. Meier claimed that the two communicated telepathically on Sfath's spacecraft and would maintain contact throughout his life.

February 25, 1942: The "Battle of Los Angeles" took place in the aftermath of the 1941 Pearl Harbor attacks and after US Secretary of War Henry Stimson warned that American cities should be prepared to accept "occasional blows" from enemy forces. After military radar picked up what appeared to be an enemy Japanese contact, air-raid sirens announced a citywide blackout, and troops began manning anti-aircraft guns and sweeping the skies with searchlights. As the *Los Angeles Times* wrote:

> *Powerful searchlights from countless stations stabbed the sky with brilliant probing fingers, while anti-aircraft batteries dotted the heavens with beautiful, if sinister, orange bursts of shrapnel.*

The anti-aircraft barrage continued for over an hour, pumping over 1,400 rounds of ammunition into the sky. This war hysteria later translated into the Cold War and UFO hysteria that would soon grip the nation.

February 26, 1942: Sailing in the Timor Sea, the Royal Netherlands Navy cruiser *Tromp* witnessed a large aluminum-shaped UFO flying towards them at an estimated speed of 3,500 mph. The officer on duty was unable to identify it as any known aircraft.

December 2, 1942: The first human-created, self-sustaining nuclear chain reaction went critical, developed by Enrico Fermi, who led the University of Chicago's team that constructed Chicago Pile-1. The experiment used 771,000 pounds of graphite to build fifty-seven layers. The pile also used 80,590 pounds of uranium oxide and 12,400 pounds of uranium metal, approximately $1 million worth of materials. Fermi, the "architect of the atomic age," was present at the Trinity test on July 16, 1945, where he used his Fermi method to estimate the bomb's yield.

December 3, 1942: John Olsen Lear (1942–2022), son of Learjet magnate Bill Lear, was born in Ohio. Lear became an accomplished aviator who set multiple Lear Jet records with flights around the world. In the 1980s, Lear began espousing reports of alien collusion with secret governmental groups and became one of the most influential voices of UFO conspiracy theories. Lear referenced three saucer crashes—one near Roswell; another near Aztec, New Mexico; and a third near Laredo, Texas.

January 7, 1943: Nikola Tesla died alone and in debt, in room 3327 of the Hotel New Yorker. He had been living in small hotel rooms for decades. His cause of death, at age eighty-six, was coronary thrombosis. The FBI immediately searched his hotel room and retrieved all his notes and drawings, including his "death ray" documents. *New York Times* best-selling author Sam Kean observed Tesla's new device:

> *Instead of lightning, Tesla said his new weapon would harness a beam of metal ions hurtling along at 270,000 miles per hour. As for how this beam was possible, Tesla was always coy, citing new laws of physics that "no one has ever dreamed about"—the "all-penetrating" beam would pack one-hundred billion watts into just one one-hundred-millionth of a square centimeter.*

Tesla claimed that his "teleforce" weapon could shoot down airplanes from two hundred and fifty miles away, but never provided proof that the mysterious death ray worked.

1943: Ufologist and author William Leonard Moore (1943–) co-authored two books with Charles Berlitz, including *The Roswell Incident*. Moore became the Arizona state section director of the Mutual UFO Network and left teaching to pursue a career as a researcher and freelance writer.

Moore wrote *The Philadelphia Experiment: Project Invisibility* with Charles Berlitz (Fawcett Crest, 1979), about the USS *Eldridge* and a secret 1943 military experiment. In 1980, Moore collaborated again with Berlitz, on *The Roswell Incident*, investigating the legendary UFO crash and extraterrestrials.

1943: Robert Oppenheimer, the "father of the atomic bomb," was appointed director of the Manhattan Project's Los Alamos Laboratory in New Mexico. His task was to develop the first nuclear bomb. Oppenheimer was present at the first test of the atomic bomb, Trinity, on July 16, 1945.

August 27, 1943: The USS *Eldridge* (DE-173) was commissioned and designated to escort men and materials to North Africa and South Europe. The ship allegedly became part of a secret government degaussing project called the Philadelphia Experiment.

October 28, 1943: According to the Philadelphia Experiment, the USS *Eldridge*, a destroyer escort, was transported through a hole in space-time from Philadelphia to Norfolk, Virginia, more than two hundred miles away. The ship's crew suffered various side effects, including insanity, intangibility, and being "frozen" in place. Several died in the experiment.

Scientist Dr. Franklin Reno, believed to have masterminded the Philadelphia Experiment, claimed that his experiment was based on Albert Einstein's unified field theory. The USS Eldridge crew was told that it would be just a simple weapons test. Tesla coils were attached to the front, back, and each side of the ship and would generate the "cloak." When the equipment was turned on, a greenish fog appeared around the vessel.

Replete with time travel, teleportation, possible homicide, and government cover-up, the Philadelphia Experiment has been celebrated in books and at least three motion pictures, sharing a direct connection to Dr. Morris K. Jessup's 1955 book, *The Case for the UFO: Unidentified Flying Objects*.

1943: The US Supreme Court voided four of Guglielmo Marconi's key patents, belatedly acknowledging Nikola Tesla's innovations in radio. The AC system he championed and improved remains the global standard for power transmission. Tesla died in his room, earlier that year, on January 7, 1943.

December 5, 1943: Newspaper journalist and academic James Farrell Marrs Jr. (1943–2017) was a *New York Times* best-selling author of books and articles on a wide range of cultish topics. His book *Crossfire* was a source for Oliver Stone's film *JFK*. Marrs authored books about aliens, government conspiracies, and secret societies. He was a member of the Scholars for 9/11 Truth.

November 1944: "Foo fighters," mysterious flying objects, harassed and mystified World War II Allied aircraft pilots, who described what they believed to be UFOs or any other unexplained aerial phenomena. These sightings were seen in the skies over both the European and Pacific theaters. Witnesses assumed that the "foo fighters" were secret weapons employed by the Axis powers.

March 1945: Ray A. Palmer published "I Remember Lemuria," a rewriting of Richard Sharp Shaver's ten-thousand-word manuscript titled "Warning to Man." Palmer skillfully presented the Shaver Mysteries as "factual" and included footnotes and annotations that gave the piece an air of authenticity. Together, Palmer and Shaver created an amazing narrative that involved UFOs and hollow-Earth conspiracies and was one of the most important contributions to the pulp era.

June 17, 1945: Arthur William Bell III (1945–2018) was born in North Carolina. Art Bell became the founder and original host of the paranormal-themed radio program *Coast to Coast AM* and also created and hosted its companion show *Dreamland.*

1945: Fred Tracy, serving aboard the USS *Antietam* (CV-36), an Essex-class aircraft carrier, claimed that he was personally involved in a degaussing operation conducted in a top-secret Annapolis, Maryland, installation. Wrapped with three-inch-diameter cables spaced fifteen feet apart, the *Antietam* was bombarded with vast amounts of electricity for three days, time enough to penetrate the eight-inch-thick steel hull.

May 8, 1945: Citing an official document from Secretary of the Navy Admiral Forrestal, Fred Tracy offered proof that the Philadelphia Experiment occurred. This official memo was read to them during the final days of World War II, sometime between May 8, 1945, and May 19, 1945.

July 16, 1945: Known as the Trinity Test, Los Alamos scientists detonated a plutonium bomb at a test site located at Alamogordo, New Mexico, some 120 miles south of Albuquerque. The Trinity Test's mushroom cloud, stretching some forty thousand feet across, represented a power equivalent to around twenty-one thousand tons of TNT, or 18.6 kilotons of power, announcing the arrival of the nuclear age.

August 6, 1945: An American B-29 bomber dropped the world's first deployed atomic bomb, called Little Boy, over the Japanese city of Hiroshima. Little Boy, which used uranium-235, immediately killed an estimated eighty thousand people. Tens of thousands more would later die of radiation exposure.

August 9, 1945: After Hiroshima, a second B-29 dropped the Fat Man plutonium bomb on Nagasaki, killing an estimated forty thousand people. Japan's emperor, Hirohito, announced his country's unconditional surrender in World War II in a radio address on August 15, citing the devastating power of "a new and most cruel bomb."

June 1946: *Amazing Stories* published a pseudonymous letter by Fred Lee Crisman claiming to have battled "mysterious and evil" underground creatures with submachine guns—while in Burma, during World War II. Crisman was involved in the Maury Island incident and later, in 1968, was subpoenaed by a New Orleans grand jury in the prosecution of a man for the assassination of President John F. Kennedy.

1946: The UFO frenzy continued during the summer and fall, as thousands of "ghost rockets," cigar-shaped craft with orange flames shooting from the tails, were reported over Europe. Pilots described them differently from "foo fighters."

August 1, 1946: Captain Jack E. Puckett, while flying a twin-engine C-47 from Langley Field to Florida's MacDill Air Force Base, avoided a collision with a bright horizontal UFO with a fiery tail and reported:

It continued toward us on a collision course at our exact altitude. At about 1,000 yards, it veered to cross our path. We observed it to be a long, cylindrical shape, approximately twice the size of a B-29 bomber, with luminous portholes ...

September 3, 1946: President Harry S. Truman approved Project Paperclip, which allowed US military departments to sponsor the immigration of "chosen, rare minds." The secret program sent reconnaissance teams into Germany to secure scientists and military technology before other powers could capture them. Project Paperclip secured V-2 missiles and the infamous aerospace engineer Wernher von Braun, who invented the V-2 and later designed the Saturn V rocket for NASA's Apollo program. According to legend, Die Glocke, an antigravity and time travel device, was reportedly one such German *wunderwaffe* (wonder weapon), that some alleged crashed in Kecksburg, Pennsylvania, in 1965.

June 24, 1947: Boise businessman Kenneth Arnold, "the man who started it all," while flying from Chehalis to Yakima, Washington, saw a formation of nine unidentified shiny crescent-shaped objects flying at high speed in front of his plane. He estimated their speed at about 1,200 miles an hour—a speed unattainable by any known aircraft at that time. He described them as crescent-shaped, silvery and shiny, and flying in a V formation. They had no tails. Another individual, a prospector named Fred Johnson, witnessed the same ariel formation and verified Arnold's account sighted near Mount Rainier.

According to *Mysterious Universe*:

Whether Arnold encountered a number of extraterrestrial craft, advanced creations of the Soviet Union, or the then-

> *latest developments of the US military remains unknown. The theories are many. The hard answers are scant.*

June 25, 1947: Kenneth Arnold told Associated Press reporter Bill Bequette that the UFOs behaved like a rock or saucer skipping across water. *East Oregonian* reporter Bill Bequette filed the UFO sighting, referring to "flying saucers," even though the objects Arnold reported were crescent, not saucer, shaped. The headline at the bottom of the front page of the newspaper read:

> *Impossible! Maybe, But Seein' Is Believin', Says Flyer.*

In the legendary seven sentences that followed, Bequette reported Arnold's claims that he saw "nine saucer-like aircraft flying in formation" at an altitude between 9,500 and 10,000 feet between Mount Rainer and Mount Adams, moving at "the amazing speed of about 1,200 miles an hour." Bacquette's report remains one of the most momentous accounts in ufology's history.

June 27, 1947: The Men in Black mythology is believed to have started with Navy Seaman Harold Dahl, who saw six donut-shaped obstacles hovering about half a mile above his boat near Maury Island in Washington State's Puget Sound. Metallic debris, which fell on Dahl and his son, killed the family dog. Dahl was able to take several photographs of the UFO, but the following morning, he was visited by a man in a black suit, who warned him not to speak of the incident—or bad things would happen. Dahl's supervisor, Fred Crisman, became a significant player in this bizarre scenario.

June 28, 1947: A group of pilots and intelligence officers observed a brightly lit UFO performing "impossible maneuvers" over Maxwell Air Force Base in Montgomery, Alabama.

July 1, 1947: Radar stations at Roswell Air Base and nearby White Sands missile testing base picked up a UFO that did not maneuver like known aircraft. It was not viewed visually.

July 4, 1947: Both radar and visual sightings of a UFO took place over Roswell, New Mexico, during an intense thunderstorm. Rancher W. W. "Mac" Brazel did not see the object but heard what he thought was a loud explosion over his ranch.

July 5, 1947: After a violent storm, rancher W. W. "Mac" Brazel and his two children discovered an area seven hundred yards wide littered with strange mechanical debris, on their sheep ranch outside of Roswell, New Mexico. The debris consisted of thin, silver-colored materials and lightweight struts with odd markings.

July 6, 1947: Rancher W. W. "Mac" Brazel gathered up some of the debris and took them over to the Roswell sheriff, George Wilcox, who reported the discovery to the Roswell Air Base. Maj. Jesse Marcel, the base intelligence officer, returned to the site with Brazel and decades later recalled:

> *One thing I was certain of, being familiar with all our activities, was that it was not a weather balloon, nor an aircraft nor a missile. It was something else which did not know what it was. There were just fragments strewn over an area about three-quarters of a mile long and several hundred feet wide.*

July 7, 1947: Two photographs, sometimes called the shoeheel UFO photos, taken by amateur astronomer William Albert Rhodes, are believed to show a disc-like object flying above Phoenix, Arizona. The photos were published in Kenneth Arnold's 1952 book *The Coming of the Saucers* and reprinted multiple times by editor Raymond A. Palmer. Air

Force files categorized the Rhodes photos as a "possible hoax."

July 10, 1947: The FBI's E. G. Fitch circulated a memo, from Army/Air Force intelligence officer Brigadier General George Schulgen, titled "Flying Disks." Schulgen requested that every effort should be made to determine whether flying disks are real and, if so, to learn all about them. Schulgen thought the disks might be foreign bodies mechanically devised and controlled.

July 13, 1947: Ufologist and paranormal pioneer Timothy Green Beckley (1947–2021) was born in New Brunswick, New Jersey. Although *UFO Magazine* called him "the Hunter Thompson of UFOlogy," he was widely known as "Mr. UFO." He was an author, editor, and producer, publishing over two hundred books. He authored over thirty books, including *The Truth About Crashed UFOs, MJ 12 and the Riddle of Hangar 18,* and *Our Alien Planet: This Eerie Earth.* He was invited to speak before closed-door meetings on UFOs presided over by the Earl of Clancarty at the House of Lords in England. He was a podcast host on KCOR Radio's *Exploring the Bizarre* with Tim Swartz. Beckley was eclectic, prolific, and bizarre, and a personal friend and mentor.

June 1947: *Amazing Stories* published "The Shaver Mystery, the Most Sensational True Story Ever Told." The ninety-thousand words and four stories were attributed to writer Richard Sharpe Shaver, who wrote about ancient civilizations who dwelled in subterranean cities. The final Shaver story was published in the summer of 1948.

July 7, 1947: A meeting was held at the Pentagon in the office of General Schulgen, chief of the Air Forces' Air Intelligence Requirements Division. It was decided that reports from "more qualified" observers of flying discs should be selected for follow-up investigation, and Project Sign was born.

July 8, 1947: Roswell Air Base public information officer Walter Haut issued a press release that a flying disc had crashed near the base and was recovered by the 509th Bomb Group near the small town of Roswell:

> *The many rumors regarding the flying disc became a reality yesterday when the intelligence office of the 509th Bomb group of the Eighth Air Force, Roswell Army Air Field, was fortunate enough to gain possession of a disc through the cooperation of one of the local ranchers and the sheriff's office of Chaves County.*
>
> *The flying object landed on a ranch near Roswell sometime last week. Not having phone facilities, the rancher stored the disc until such time as he was able to contact the sheriff's office, who in turn notified Maj. Jesse A. Marcel of the 509th Bomb Group Intelligence Office.*
>
> *Action was immediately taken and the disc was picked up at the rancher's home. It was inspected at the Roswell Army Air Field and subsequently loaned by Major Marcel to higher headquarters.*

The government claimed it was simply a weather balloon, but in 1978, the issue was revisited when ufologist Stanton T. Friedman interviewed Major Jesse Marcel, involved in the original incident. He believed the military had covered up the recovery of an alien spacecraft.

1947: According to the children of WWII ace Marion "Black Mac" Magruder, their father claimed to have seen alien bodies at Wright Field, and one of them was alive. He dubbed it "Squiggly." Magruder told his family:

> *It was alive but we killed it. It was a shameful thing that the military destroyed this creature by conducting tests on it.*

He explained that it was not on purpose, because there was no way to know how to treat the injuries of the alien, and their attempts could not save "Squiggly's" life.

1947: In an FBI Office memorandum, "Flying discs, Richard Shaver," the FBI concluded that publisher Ray A. Palmer and sci-fi writer Richard Sharpe Shaver conspired to create the "flying disc" hysteria through articles in *Amazing Stories*.

October 14, 1947: US Air Force officer, World War II flying ace, and test pilot Chuck Yaeger made the first supersonic flight. Yeager broke the sound barrier when he tested the X-1, although the feat was not announced to the public until 1948.

The X-1 (which Yeager named the *Glamorous Glennis*) reached Mach 1.06 or 700 mph, making Yeager the first man to travel faster than the speed of sound and earning him the title of "Fastest Man Alive," flying over Southern California's Rogers Dry Lake.

August 1, 1947: After being summoned by Kenneth Arnold, two Army A-2 Intelligence officers, Captain William L. Davidson and Lt. Frank Brown, investigated flying saucer claims from Harold Dahl and Fred Crisman. Both men claimed they witnessed falling debris and received threats from Men in Black—after viewing flying saucers over Puget Sound's Maury Island. But, after leaving in their B-25 Mitchell aircraft, the plane caught fire and crashed outside of Kelso, Washington, killing Davidson and Brown. Flying saucer conspiracists concluded that Davidson and Brown met their untimely demise due to knowledge of undisclosed secrets.

Crisman and Dahl, in subsequent confessions to Air Force investigators, admitted that they had fabricated the original story.

December 30, 1947: Project Sign (1947–1949) was created by the Army Air Forces to examine sightings of UFOs, in response to numerous reports of "flying saucers." But, in discussing nearby star systems, Project Sign's report concluded:

> *Outside the solar system other stars—twenty-two in number —have satellite planets. Our star has nine. One of these, the Earth, is ideal for existence of intelligent life. On two others there is a possibility of life. Therefore, astronomers believe reasonably the thesis that there could be at least one ideally habitable planet for each of the twenty-two other eligible stars.*

1948: In his new consulting role for Project Sign, J. Allen Hynek studied UFO reports and decided whether the described phenomena suggested known astronomical objects. He was among the first people to conduct scientific analysis of reports and especially of trace evidence purportedly left by UFOs.

1948: Two airline pilots saw something that they described as a cigar-shaped UFO with square windows, while others argued that it could have been very bright meteors called "bolides."

July 24, 1948: A UFO encounter occurred in the skies near Montgomery, Alabama, when chief pilot Clarence S. Chiles and co-pilot John B. Whitted, flying an Eastern Airlines DC-3 at about five thousand feet altitude, claimed to have observed a "glowing object" almost strike their plane before it appeared to pull up into a cloud and travel out of sight. They described the UFO as being:

> *A torpedo-shaped UFO about one hundred feet long, with two rows of brightly lit windows along the side.*

The Chiles-Whitted sighting, the Mantell UFO incident, and the Gorman Dogfight were listed as "classic" 1948 UFO incidents, ostensibly convincing Project Sign "that UFOs were real."

Spring 1948: Kenneth Arnold is featured as the cover story in the premier issue of *Fate*, Ray A. Palmer's new magazine. Arnold, "the man who started it all," described the nine infamous flying disks he observed near Mount Rainier:

> *I had not flown more than two or three minutes on my course when a bright flash reflected on my airplane. It startled me as I thought I was too close to some other aircraft. I looked every place in the sky and couldn't find where the reflection had come from until I looked to the left and the north of Mt. Rainier where I observed a chain of nine peculiar-looking aircraft flying from north to south at approximately 9,500 feet elevation and going, seemingly, in a definite direction of about one hundred and seventy degrees north to south.*

January 7, 1948: Kentucky Air National Guard pilot Captain Thomas Mandell, flying from Marietta, Georgia, to Standiford Field, Kentucky, blacked out and crashed his P-51 Mustang into a Kentucky farm. His final moments and last words were recorded:

> *I see something above and ahead of me., and I'm still climbing. It looks metallic and is tremendous in size ... it's above me and I'm gaining on it. I'm going to 20,000 feet.*

A MUFON article cites historian David Michael Jacobs, who argues the Mantell case marked a sharp shift in both public and governmental perceptions of UFOs.

> *Previously, mass media often treated UFO reports with a whimsical or glib attitude reserved for silly season news. Following Mantell's death, however, Jacobs notes "the fact that a person had died in an encounter with an alleged flying saucer dramatically increased public concern about the phenomenon. Now a dramatic new prospect entered thought about UFOs: they might be not only extraterrestrial but potentially hostile as well."*

Mantell was an experienced pilot. His flight history consisted of 2,167 hours in the air, and he had been honored for his part in the Battle of Normandy during World War II. Although many ufologists believe that a UFO was involved in Mantell's death, the most frequently cited "scientific" explanation was reflected in Jenny Randles and Peter Hough's *The Complete Book of UFOs:*

> *In reality, we now know that Mantell was almost certainly chasing a "Skyhook"—a huge silvery device that was floating far too high in the atmosphere for his F-51 ever to have reached it. The Navy were testing these monster aerial devices secretly and had not told the Army/Air Force about their exercise.*

January 22, 1948: The Air Force officially entered the "flying saucer arena" in response to an exchange of letters between the commanding general of the Army Air Forces and the chief of the Air Materiel Command, Air Technical Intelligence Center at Wright-Patterson Air Force Base. The concerned parties were alarmed at the rash of UFO sightings during the summer of 1947.

October 1, 1948: The Gorman Dogfight was a widely publicized UFO incident that took place over Fargo, North Dakota. George F. Gorman, twenty-five, a veteran World War II fighter pilot, was participating in a cross-country flight with other National Guard pilots. Flying a P-51 Mustang, Gorman saw a UFO that was also viewed by a Piper Cub flying in the area. After a near collision, Gorman attempted to pursue the craft, but the UFO accelerated faster than him. He described the object as a simple blinking "ball of light" about six to eight inches in diameter.

October 23, 1948: Pilot George F. Gorman, involved in the Gorman Dogfight, gave a sworn account of the incident to investigators that read:

> *I am convinced that there was definite thought behind its maneuvers. I am further convinced that the object was governed by the laws of inertia because its acceleration was rapid but not immediate and although it was able to turn fairly tight at considerable speed, it still followed a natural curve. When I attempted to turn with the object I blacked out temporarily due to excessive speed. I am in fairly good physical condition and I do not believe that there are many if any pilots who could withstand the turn and speed effected by the object, and remain conscious. The object was not only able to out turn and out speed my aircraft ... but was able to attain a*

> *far steeper climb and was able to maintain a constant rate of climb far in excess of my aircraft.*

December 12, 1948: Dr. Lincoln La Paz, a world authority on meteorites and a professor at the University of Albuquerque, New Mexico, observed a green fireball moving horizontally, atypical of a meteorite. Copper dust was later recovered under the fireball's flight path, a substance rarely found in meteorites. La Paz is believed to have been one of the advisors consulted by the US government regarding the Roswell Incident.

December 1948: James Lipp, a member of the US Air Force's Project Sign, wrote in a report:

> *The Martians have kept a long-term watch on Earth, and have been alarmed by the sight of our A-bomb shots as evidence that we are warlike and on the threshold of space travel.*

January 13, 1949: Leading up to Project Twinkle, and concerned about the frequent sightings of green fireballs, especially in the southwest, the director of Army Intelligence from Fourth Army Headquarters in Texas proposed that the green fireballs may be:

> *The result of radiological warfare experiments by a foreign power and that they are of such great importance, especially as they are occurring in the vicinity of sensitive installations, that a scientific board [should] ... study the situation.*

Lincoln La Paz, from the University of New Mexico, believed that the objects, observed by military and civilian pilots, were atypical of meteors.

June 27, 1949: *Captain Video and His Video Rangers* was considered the first science-fiction television program and ran on the Dumont Network from Monday through Saturday at 7:00 p.m. and starred Richard Coogan, Al Hodge, Don Hastings, and Ben Lackland. The final episode was aired on April 1, 1955.

Captain Video was performed live, with obvious flubbed lines and amateurish special effect gimmicks, and developed on a shoestring budget. At least ten minutes of each episode was inserted with stock footage from an old Western movie, which had nothing to do with the rest of the show. Premiums sold via the show included a flying saucer ring, a "secret seal" ring, cast photos, electronic goggles, a "secret ray gun," a rocket ship key chain, decoders, membership cards, and a set of twelve plastic spacemen.

May 22, 1949: Secretary of the Navy, Admiral James Vincent Forrestal (1982–1949) jumped to his death in an apparent suicide. Forrestal was being treated for depression on the sixteenth floor of the Bethesda Naval Hospital. Writer James Rink believed that Forrestal was silenced for objecting to government secrecy and talking about extraterrestrials:

> *When he began to talk to leaders of the opposition party and leaders of Congress about the alien problem he was asked to resign by Truman ... In fact, it was feared that Forrestal would begin to talk again and he had to be isolated and discredited. Sometime in the early morning of May 22, 1949, he became one of the first victims of the cover-up.*

August 1949: The Air Force's Air Technical Intelligence Center (ATIC) concluded that UFOs constituted "no direct threat to the national security."

August 20, 1949: Professor Clyde W. Tombaugh, during an evening outside his home in Las Cruces, New Mexico, witnessed a craft with six or eight green lights and what he thought may have been windows. Tombaugh is recognized for having discovered what was known as the "planet" Pluto.

December 9, 1949: Japanese astronomer Tsuneo Saheki detected a mysterious explosion on the planet Mars. The explosion caused a brilliant glow for several minutes, followed by a luminous yellowish-gray cloud forty miles high and seven hundred miles in diameter. Saheki concluded that it was either a volcanic eruption or an artificial atomic explosion.

February 11, 1949: Project Sign was changed to Project Grudge because, according to author Ed Ruppelt, the code name had been compromised. Widely referred to as "the Grudge Report," Project Grudge's (1949–1951) final six-hundred-page report, released in December of 1949, was officially titled *Unidentified Flying Objects—Project Grudge, Technical Report No. 102-AC-49/15-100.*

December 1949: After Project "Saucer" was changed from a "special-type project to a standard intelligence function," the Air Force invited all citizens to report their sightings to the nearest Air Force installation:

> *All reports will be given expert consideration and those of special interest will be thoroughly investigated. The identity of those making such reports will be kept in confidence; no one will be ridiculed for making one.*

February 1949: Project Twinkle, a grouping of the military, intelligence officers, and astronomers, was organized to investigate the rampant sightings of unexplained Kelly-green fireballs seen by thousands over New Mexico and Colorado. Dr. Joseph Kaplan, a leading geophysicist and specialist in phenomena within the atmosphere, was placed in charge of the organization. After two months of discussion and investigation, Project Twinkle was abandoned "as a waste of time." The unknown objects were believed to be unusual meteorites or other natural phenomena.

December 26, 1949: *True* magazine published former US Marine major Donald E. Keyhoe's article "The Flying Saucers Are Real," a widely read and controversial article. Keyhoe, who had privileged information from the Air Force Press Desk, claimed that elements within the Air Force knew that saucers existed and had concluded they were likely "'interplanetary machines." When Keyhoe expanded the article into a book, *The Flying Saucers Are Real* (Henry Holt & Company, 1950), it sold over half a million copies in paperback, a testament to the topic's appeal.

December 27, 1949: In an obvious pushback, the US Air Force issued this public statement:

> *The saucers are misinterpretations of various conventional objects, mild hysteria, meteorological phenomena, aberrations, or hoaxes.*

Part Three

Chapter 13
Adamski's Wild Ride: 1950s

IN THE '50s we continued to look up into the skies, as we also witnessed Hollywood's commercialization of the UFO, the Washington Flap, Project Twinkle, Project Blue Book, and the popular pseudoscience of "contactee" G. George Adamski.

January 1, 1950: Frank Scully, a reporter for Variety, wrote Behind the Flying Saucers, describing alien encounters from the Pacific Northwest to the towns of Aztec and Farmington, New Mexico. Scully claimed that UFOs, occupied by extraterrestrials, were landing in people's backyards. His focus on the 1948 Aztec, New Mexico, crash was proved later to be a hoax.

January 1950: *True Magazine* celebrated a sold-out issue after Donald E. Keyhoe alluded that extraterrestrials could be piloting flying saucers. The December 1949 article was later reworked by Keyhoe into a best-selling paperback book, *The Flying Saucers Are Real.*

1950–1960: Project Orion was a study conducted by the US Air Force, DARPA, and NASA to calculate the efficacy of a rocket ship driven by nuclear pulse propulsions, a series of explosions of atomic bombs behind the craft. The project was eventually abandoned after the Partial Test Ban Treaty banned nuclear explosions in space, and widespread concerns over nuclear fallout. Another technical consideration was that some believed that Project Orion would have required a rocket the size of the Empire State Building.

April 3, 1950: Immanuel Velikovsky published his controversial book *Worlds in Collision*, proposing that around the fifteenth century BC, the planet Venus passed near Earth and changed Earth's orbit and axis, causing untold cataclysms—documented in early mythologies and religions. Although the book was criticized by the scientific community as "pseudoscience," it became a *New York Times* bestseller and placed in the Top Ten for twenty-seven straight weeks.

1950: The Fermi paradox is believed to have originated over a lunch conversation between Nobel Prize-winning nuclear physicist Enrico Fermi, sometimes known as "the architect of the atomic bomb," and his colleagues. While discussing the existence of alien life, at the Los Alamos National Lab, Fermi's response became infamous in its simplicity: "Where is everybody?" Writing about Fermi's paradox in *Britannica*, Kate Lohnes said:

> *The Milky Way is about ten billion years old and 100,000 light-years across. If aliens had spaceships that could travel at one percent of the speed of light, the galaxy could have already been colonized 1,000 times. Why haven't we heard from any other life?*

Fermi's question remains unanswered—if there are civilizations scattered across the stars by the billions, why haven't we made contact with them?

April 24, 1950: Italian farmer Bruno Facchini witnessed a UFO and four humanoids, about five feet tall, who blasted him with a laser-like device. Afterward, Facchini discovered physical markings on the ground.

1950: Meade Layne published *The Ether Ship Mystery and Its Solution* (a BSRA Publication, 1950). In the book's preface, Director Layne wrote:

> *No attempt is made in the following pages to prove the objective and factual existence of the Flying Discs and other strange sky craft, since on this point there is no longer any doubt. On account of the great variety in shape, color and behavior of these flying objects, a generic name is needed. The term Ether Ships or Ether Craft has been adopted since it indicates the true nature and origin of all these diversified phenomena.*

As director of the Borderland Sciences Research Associates (BSRA), Layne proposed the interdimensional hypothesis as an explanation for flying saucer sightings. Layne produced four booklets on the flying saucer problem—*The Mystery of the Flying Discs* (1948, out of print), *The ESM and Its Solution* (1950), *The Ether of Space* (1953), and *The Coming of the Guardians* (1953.)

March 18, 1950: About five thousand residents of the small town of Farmington, New Mexico, witnessed countless UFOs flying at speeds estimated at over one thousand miles per hour and performing "impossible" aerial acrobatics.

April 1, 1950: The Air Force established "Project Twinkle" to investigate sightings by hundreds of pilots, weather observers, and atomic scientists of kelly-green fireballs larger than the moon and blazing several times more brightly. Project Twinkle established a triple phototheodolite post (a precision optical instrument used to measure meteorological events or rocket launches) at Vaughn, New Mexico, to obtain scientific data on the fireballs. The project was later transferred to the Holloman Air Force Base at Alamogordo, New Mexico.

May 11, 1950: An alleged flying saucer, photographed in black and white with a simple Kodak camera by farmer Paul Trent, was shown flying over his farm in McMinnville, Oregon. According to historian John Killen:

> *The McMinnville photos weren't the first reports of UFOs, but they are considered by many who study the topic to be among the best photographic evidence of flying saucers. And even skeptics see them as the best fake photos of flying saucers ever found.*

Optics expert Dr. Bruce S. Maccabee, commissioned by the Condon Committee to examine the photos, concluded:

> *This is one of the few UFO reports in which all factors investigated—geometric, psychological, and physical—appear to be consistent with the assertion that an* extraordinary flying *object, silvery, metallic, disc-shaped, tens of meters in diameter and evidently artificial, flew within sight of two witnesses.*

1950: Arthur C. Clarke published his short article "The Sentinel," where Earth astronauts discover a four-million-year-old artifact on the moon. Clarke's story provided the plot for his award-winning *2001: A Space Odyssey.* According to author Ronald Story:

> *It was, in effect, a space-age Genesis; a creation story featuring mankind as the product of a cosmic experiment being carried out, not by the traditional Judeo-Christian God, but by extraterrestrial intelligences who, because of attributes acquitted during their own long evolution, might themselves be defined as gods.*

Story points out that the motion picture and novel "contained the essential elements of the ancient astronaut theory before the fame and plagiarism of von Däniken."

June 23, 1950: A DC-4 airliner, with fifty-eight aboard, crashed over Benton Harbor, Michigan. A prolonged flash in the sky, described by witnesses as a ball of fire, might have brought the plane down. Some alleged that a UFO crashed into the aircraft.

1950: Donald E. Keyhoe published the best-selling paperback book *The Flying Saucers Are Real* (Fawcett Gold Medal, 1950)—a reworking of his *True Magazine* article about extraterrestrials and UFOs. The one-hundred-and-seventy-five-page book cost twenty-five cents and sold over half a million copies in paperback while popularizing many themes in ufology that are still widely believed today. According to the former director of Project Blue Book Edward J. Ruppelt:

> *The article was one of the most widely read and widely discussed magazine articles in history.*

July 4, 1950: Contactee Daniel W. Fry claimed that he rode in a flying saucer from White Sands, New Mexico, to New York in thirty minutes and at eight thousand miles per hour. He claimed that he communicated telepathically with unseen extraterrestrials who lectured him about Earth's prehistory, including Atlantis and Lemuria.

1950: Astronomer and paranormal researcher Dr. Morris Jessup published four books during the 1950s—*The Case for the UFO* (1955), *The UFO Annual* (1956), *UFOs and the Bible* (1956), and *The Expanding Case for the UFO* (1957). Still, his impact on ufology was undeniable, and according to Nick Redfern, *The Case for the UFO* was of special interest:

> *His book was a detailed study of theoretical power sources for UFOs: what was it that made them fly? How could they perform incredible aerial feats, such as coming to a complete stop in the skies, hovering at incredible heights? Jessup believed that the vitally important answers lay in the domain of gravity. Or, as he saw it: anti-gravity.*

1950: Pilot Kenneth Arnold, the man who introduced the world to flying saucers, initially emphasized that he believed the objects were experimental military craft. However, interviewed by TV's Edward R. Murrow on the *CBS Evening News*, Arnold made a complete reversal of his original statement:

> *I more or less have reserved an opinion as to what I think. Naturally, being a natural-born American, if it's not made by our science or our Army Air Forces, I am inclined to believe it's of an extra-terrestrial origin.*

August 15, 1950: An Air Force investigation team concluded, after reviewing a film taken of a UFO sighting near Great Falls, Montana, the film showed sunlight reflecting off the surface of two Air Force interceptor jets.

September 27, 1950: The *Philadelphia Inquirer* carried the story of a flying saucer that dissolved, titled "*Pfft—It's Gone: Flying 'Saucer' Just Dissolves.*" The odd purple *gelatinous mass*, about six feet in diameter and a foot thick in the middle, was investigated by two patrolmen, Collins and Keenan, cruising in their patrol car. They said, "it *quivered as though it were alive.*" The incident became the genesis of the 1958 science fiction film *The Blob* and was documented fourteen years later by Frank Edwards in his 1964 book, *Strange World.*

1950: Dr. Urner Liddel of the Office of Naval Research publicly revealed facts about the secret Skyhook Balloon program. Liddell believed that many flying saucer reports were actually caused by Skyhook balloons.

December 15, 1950: Hollywood Variety writer Frank Scully published his bestseller, Behind the Flying Saucers, while assuming a defensive posture:

> *Though I have not the slightest interest in what the military may or may not say about this book, I want my readers to understand my position. I have never seen a flying saucer. I have never had a hallucination that I have seen a flying saucer. I have never joined in any mass hysteria on the subject, and to the best of my knowledge and belief, I have never participated in the perpetration of any hoax on flying saucers.*

Scully revealed that he had spoken to "men of science" who had not only seen UFOs but had secretly worked on them. Still, the Aztec, New Mexico, saucer is believed to have been a not-so-elaborate hoax.

January 27, 1951: An era of atomic testing in the Nevada desert began as an Air Force plane dropped a one-kiloton bomb on Frenchman Flat. Over one thousand nuclear explosions were detonated at the site over the following four decades. The mushroom clouds could be seen from almost one hundred miles away.

1951: The USS *Eldridge* (DE-173), believed to have been part of the secret Philadelphia Experiment, is transferred to the Royal Hellenic Navy and then to Greece, where it was redesignated the HS *Leon* (D-54). Forty-two years later the ship was sold for scrap.

February 1951: In an article published in *Look* magazine, Dr. Urner Liddel, Office of Naval Research, wrote:

> *There is not a single reliable report of a flying saucer sighting which cannot be attributed to an ordinary cosmic (Skyhook) balloon.*

1951: *The Thing from Another World* is among the sci-fi classics. Scientists at an Arctic research station discover a spacecraft buried in the ice with a frozen humanoid creature. When they take him back to their station, he is accidentally thawed out. Directed by Howard Hawks.

1951: *The Day the Earth Stood Still* is one of the best science fiction movies of all time. Better crafted than other 1950s offerings, it is considered a classic of the genre, reflecting the fears and anxiety of the Cold War era. Critic Nick Riganas noticed:

> *Encircled by large yet feeble military forces, the peaceful intergalactic ambassador, Klaatu, emerges from the mysterious vessel accompanied by the silently dangerous robot of*

> *incomprehensible power, Gort, only to witness firsthand the earthlings' hospitality. The sophisticated humanoid declares that he comes in peace; however, he needs to assemble the world's greatest minds to hear his merciful warning and a definitive ultimatum.*

Klaatu was sent to Earth to warn humankind about their experiments with atomic weapons. He warns that unless humankind gives up violence, other planets will destroy Earth in their defense. Directed by Robert Wise. *Klaatu barada nikto.*

August 25, 1951: On a summer night in Lubbock, Texas, a handful of scientists from Texas Technical College were gathered in the backyard of geology professor Dr. W. I. Robinson, chemical engineering professor Dr. A. G. Oberg, physics professor Dr. George, and Dr. W. L. Ducker, head of the petroleum-engineering department. Around 9:20 p.m., the university colleagues saw a V-shaped formation of fifteen to thirty blueish-green lights passing overhead. The lights reappeared about an hour later, in a more haphazard formation. The scientists were all in agreement that they had witnessed something fantastic. US Air Force Captain Edward J. Ruppelt, in his definitive 1956 casebook, *The Report on Unidentified Flying Objects,* observed:

> *If a group had been hand-picked to observe a UFO, we couldn't have picked a more technically qualified group of people.*

In the early 1950s, Ruppelt served as lead investigator for Project Blue Book, the official Air Force investigation into UFO sightings, after working on its precursor effort, Project Grudge.

August 30, 1951: Eighteen-year-old Carl Hart Jr. used a Kodak 35 mm camera at f3.5, 1/10 of a second, and shot five exposures of the Lubbock Lights. As reported in *Life*:

> *His photographs show eighteen to twenty luminous objects, more intense than the planet Venus, arranged in one or a pair of crescents. In several photographs, off to one side of the main flight, a larger luminosity is visible—like a mothercraft hovering near its aerial brood.*

November 2, 1951: At least one hundred and sixty-five people saw a kelly-green fireball that flashed eastward across the skies of Arizona. It raced, straight as a bullet, parallel to the ground, and then exploded in a silent burst of light.

1952: Dr. J. Allen Hynek, at a meeting of the American Optical Society, became the first American scientist to publicly state that UFOs, which he called "persistent," demanded serious study.

March–June 1952: The number of UFO sightings officially reported to the US Air Force jumped from twenty-three to one hundred and forty-eight.

1952: Albert K. Bender founded the International Flying Saucer Bureau (IFSB), acknowledged as the first major civilian UFO club in the world). Although the organization was initially successful, he suddenly shut it down in 1953, revealing to Gray Barker that he was being threatened by mysterious agents known as the Men in Black.

April 4, 1952: *Life* magazine published a story called "Have We Visitors from Space?" The article, written by H. B. Darrach Jr. and Robert Ginna, said:

> *These objects cannot be explained by present science as natural phenomena—but solely as artificial devices created and operated by a high intelligence.*

Life's article provided a detailed listing of ten previously unpublished UFO reports, arguing that these events could not be explained as balloons, mirages, or mental aberrations.

April 5, 1952: One day after the *Life* magazine article, the Air Force announced a new directive, ordering the commanding officers of all Air Force installations to make immediate, high-priority reports of all UFO sightings in their areas.

1952: Kenneth Arnold and Raymond A. Palmer published *The Coming of the Saucers: A Documentary Report on Sky Objects that have Mystified the World*. The book, believed to be the first account of UFOs, was published five years after Arnold's legendary Mount Rainier sighting. The book contained reprints and expanded articles the two had published in Palmer's *Fate* magazine. Air Force UFO investigator Edward J. Ruppelt was critical of Arnold's account:

> *As Arnold's story of what he saw that day has been handed down by the bards of saucerism, the true facts have been warped, twisted, and changed. Even some points in Arnold's own account of his sighting as published in his book,* The Coming of the Saucers, *do not jibe with what the official files say he told the Air Force in 1947.*

1952: John Keel produced the popular radio program *Things in The Sky* about unidentified flying objects and heard by millions. Keel later wrote scores of ufology's most celebrated titles, including *Operation Trojan Horse, Our Haunted Planet,* and *The Mothman Prophecies*. His "Beyond the Known" was published in a monthly column for *Fate* magazine.

April 1952: In keeping with the intense public interest in the subject, *Life* magazine published a story titled "Have We Visitors from Space?" that promised to offer "scientific evidence that there is a real case for interplanetary saucers."

1952: UFO debunker Donald Howard Menzel was appointed acting director of the Harvard Observatory and became the full director from 1954 to 1966. In 1963, he published the blistering, anti-UFO book *The World of Flying Saucers: A Scientific Examination of a Major Myth of the Space Age*.

May 7, 1952: Ed Keffel took a series of five photographs of a UFO seen above Barra da Tijuca, Brazil, and later published in the Brazilian magazine *O Cruzeiro*. The craft was also observed by multiple witnesses.

June 1952: An article about a crashed UFO titled "Auf Spitzbergen landete Fliegende Untertasse" appeared in the German newspaper *Saarbrücker Zeitung*. According to the account, the Norwegian Air Force spotted a crashed disc-shaped UFO with a series of jets around the rim of the disc while flying over Spitsbergen on maneuvers. The event was documented by popular American columnist Dorothy Kilgallen.

June 4, 1952: US Air Force Secretary Thomas K. Finletter issued a public statement about flying saucers:

> *No concrete evidence has yet reached us either to prove or disprove the existence of the so-called flying saucers. There remain, however, several sightings that the Air Force investi-*

> *gators have been unable to explain. As long as this is true, the Air Force will continue to study "flying saucer" reports.*

July 19, 1952: A series of UFO sightings were reported in Washington, DC, and tracked on radar scopes at Washington National Airport and Andrews Air Force Base. Air Force jets were sent to investigate the objects but found nothing. Edward Nugent, an air traffic controller at Washington National Airport (today Ronald Reagan Washington National Airport), spotted seven mysterious objects on his radar. The objects were located fifteen miles (24 km) south-southwest of the city, no known aircraft were in the area, and the objects were not following any established flight paths. Nugent's superior, Harry Barnes, a senior air-traffic controller, watched the objects on Nugent's radarscope and later wrote:

> *We knew immediately that a very strange situation existed ... their movements were completely radical compared to those of ordinary Aircraft.*

The objects, known as the "Washington Flap" and the "Washington Airport sightings," returned the following day, and again on July 26, viewed by numerous military and civilian personnel. Air Force investigators concluded the sightings were due to "mirage effects created by a double-temperature inversion," and dismissed the incidents.

June 24, 1952: Prompted by *Life* magazine's well-received April 4, 1952, article, *Look* magazine published an article titled "Hunt For the Flying Saucers!"

July 27, 1952: Construction worker Truman Bethurum encountered a UFO from the planet "Clarion," with a crew and female captain, Aura Rhanes, who wore "a black and red beret tilted on the side of her head." He later created an alien-inspired philosophical group called the Sanctuary of Thought.

July 27, 1952: Another continuation of the "Washington Flap" was experienced as a rash of UFO sightings was reported over Washington, DC. The incidents made headlines across the country. The Pentagon later said the unknown radar blips were false images caused by temperature inversion.

August 13, 1952: Sixty-eight UFOs, which were tracked by radar and reported by airline pilots, flew over Washington, DC.

1952: Author and paranormal researcher Gray Barker began collecting stories about an alleged West Virginia extraterrestrial called the Flatwoods monster. After submitting an article to *Fate* magazine, he later began writing regular pieces about UFOs for *Space Review*, a magazine published by Albert K. Bender's International Flying Saucer Bureau.

1952: Project Blue Book launched, the latest iteration of the Air Force's UFO investigative teams. After interviewing project members Captain Edward J. Ruppelt and astronomer J. Allen Hynek, the panel concluded that many sightings Blue Book had tracked were, in fact, explainable.

August 19, 1952: D. S. "Sonny" DesVergers, a scoutmaster of West Palm Beach, Florida's Troop 33, observed a UFO while driving three scouts home. Upon investigating, DesVergers experienced a hot sensation, "just like walking into an oven," and realized that the heat was coming from a large oval object hovering about thirty feet overhead:

> *I shined the light up and saw a flat surface of a round object about ten m in diameter, about three m above me. I guess I was absolutely paralyzed; I could not move a*

> *muscle; I was scared to death. It must have been a good minute that I was under this thing. I wanted to run but my feet just wouldn't work. I realized there was something abnormal about this.*

Not everyone believed the scoutmaster, who described being burned by a ball of red fire, causing him to be momentarily blinded and blacking out for about twenty-five minutes. According to *NexusNewsfeed*:

> *Captain Edward J. Ruppelt, chief UFO investigator for the US Air Force, would later call the entire event a hoax. DesVergers was painted as an opportunist and media-hungry conman who sold his story to* The American Weekly *newspaper the following year.*

Still, the case remains unexplained. Physical evidence of the grass samples taken at the site was charred black, and the lower leaves deteriorated as if by heat. The only way a laboratory could duplicate the effect was to place live clumps of grass in a pan of sandy soil and heat it to about three hundred degrees Fahrenheit.

August 24, 1952: Bill Squyres, radio announcer at Pittsburg, Kansas's KOAM, saw a UFO with a "dull, aluminum appearance," hovering ten feet off the ground. He described the craft as having "propellors all around the middle." Gray Barker said that this was designated Case No. 12 in the "Twelve Good Sightings" listed in the three-hundred-and-sixteen-page Project Blue Book Special Report No. 14.

August 30, 1952: At the tenth annual World Science Fiction Convention, held at Chicago's Morrison Hotel, Ray A. Palmer was awarded a bronze plaque honoring him as a "Son of

Science Fiction." The convention was held over the Labor Day weekend and was chaired by Julian May.

September 12, 1952: After a pulsing red light was seen crossing the skies, a group of witnesses, including a member of the National Guard, saw a tall "man-like figure with a round, red face surrounded by a pointed, hood-like shape," in the town of Flatwoods in Braxton County, West Virginia. The humanoid creature, which emitted a hissing sound, became known as the Flatwoods monster. UFO writer Gray Barker described the figure as approximately ten feet tall with a round blood-red face, a large pointed "hood-like shape" around the face, eyelike shapes that emitted greenish-orange light, and a dark black or green body. The following day, two parallel skid marks and a large circular area of flattened grass were discovered.

1952–1969: Project Blue Book replaced Project Grudge, headed by director Capt. Edward J. Ruppelt.

1952: Photos taken by George Adamski, who claimed they were Venusian spacecraft, were dismissed by Donald Menzel as being a simple chicken brooder, a heating and incubation device used to hatch chicks. A similar UFO drawing was featured on the 1977 cover of Ray Palmer's *Search Magazine*.

1952: *True Magazine* published articles by *San Francisco Chronicle* reporter John Philip Cahn that exposed Frank Scully's sources as con artists who had hoaxed the author. The Aztec, New Mexico, "crashed saucer" story was deceptively provided by Silas Newton and Leo Gebauer.

November 20, 1952: G. George Adamski (1891–1965) reported that he had met and conversed with a visitor from Venus in a California desert, using a combination of hand gestures and telepathy. Adamski became one of the most controversial characters in ufology, his flying saucer photographs dismissed by experts such as J. Allen Hynek as crude fakes.

January 1953: The CIA's Office of Scientific Intelligence, in collaboration with Howard Percy Robertson, a professor of mathematical physics at the California Institute of Technology, organized a panel of nonmilitary scientists to review Air Force UFO accounts going back to 1947.

After only four days of study, the Robertson Panel declared that UFOs, including "foo fighters," were not a threat and unworthy of further investigation. The panel offered other probable explanations such as electrostatic phenomena similar to St. Elmo's fire, electromagnetic phenomena, or simply reflections of light from ice crystals. The group had been convened after a cluster of UFOs flew over the skies of Washington, DC, in 1952.

January 26, 1953: Albert M. Chop, Air Force Press Desk, wrote to publishers Henry Holt & Company:

> *The Air Force and its investigating agency "Project Bluebook," are aware of Major (Donald) Keyhoe's conclusion that the "Flying Saucers" are from another planet. The Air Force has never denied that this possibility exists. Some of the personnel believe that there may be some strange natural phenomena completely unknown to us, but that if the apparently controlled maneuvers reported by many competent observers are correct, then the only remaining explanation is the interplanetary one.*

February 1953: Titanium miners John Van Black and John Allen, near Brush Creek, California, watched an alien emerge from a "metallic saucer" and scoop up water from a creek with a strange cone-shaped bucket and hand it to someone inside the craft. The saucer returned four times over the next four weeks. Black observed what he thought was a small child with a bucket. According to *Anomalien.com*:

> *Looking closer, he saw it was a small man wearing green pants, unusual shoes, a jacket, and a green cap. He was very pale and had black hair. Says Black, "He looked like someone who had never been out in the sun much."*

1953: Ufologist James Moseley requested an interview with former president Harry Truman, about flying saucers. Truman took Moseley into his private office in Independence, Missouri, where the former president confessed he'd never seen a flying saucer and didn't know anything about them. The interview happened just over a year after the 1952 "flying saucer invasion" of Washington, DC, while Truman was still president. But in what became one of Moseley's favorite anecdotes, Truman responded jokingly, "I've never seen a purple cow. I never hope to see one."

April 1953: J. Allen Hynek wrote a report for the *Journal of the Optical Society of America* titled "Unusual Aerial Phenomena," arguing that "ridicule is not a part of the scientific method." His report contained one of his best-known statements:

> *The steady flow of reports, often made in concert by reliable observers, raises questions of scientific obligation and responsibility. Is there ... any residue that is worthy of scientific attention? Or, if there isn't, does not an obligation exist to say so to the public—not in words of open ridicule but seri-*

ously, to keep faith with the trust the public places in science and scientists?

1953: *Flying Saucers from Outer Space,* written by retired US Marine Corps Maj. Donald E. Keyhoe, reflected his belief that certain aerial phenomena were interplanetary in origin. Keyhoe, who had several credible government contacts, aptly documented the Air Force's back-and-forth public explanations of flying saucers.

August 13, 1953: H. G. Wells's classic novel of alien invasion, *War of the Worlds,* was brought to the screen. The residents of a small California town watch as a flaming meteor, landing in the hills, contains dangerous Martians armed with death rays. The film won an Academy Award for Best Visual Effects and went on to influence other science fiction films. Directed by Byron Haskin, it starred Gene Barry, Ann Robinson, and Les Tremayne.

August 1953: After years of vacillating between openness and secrecy, all UFO reports became classified and suppressed—whenever possible. The Joint Chiefs of Staff, in December, made the unauthorized release of information a crime under the Espionage Act, punishable by a $10,000 fine or up to ten years in prison.

September 1953: Albert K. Bender abruptly discontinued his organization, the International Flying Saucer Bureau. Bender claimed that he could not continue writing about UFOs because of "orders from a higher source," claiming he was threatened by three men dressed in black—the beginnings of the Men-in-Black syndrome, as recounted in Gray Barkers' *They Knew Too Much About Flying Saucers* (University Press, 1956). Bender told close associates that he had found the solution to the flying saucer mystery but had been frightened into silence by three "men" in dark suits who warned him not to divulge his fantastic discovery.

1953: Twenty-two-year-old James Moseley, a large trust fund beneficiary, drove across the country "tracking the elusive flying saucer" in preparation for a planned book. He interviewed almost one hundred UFO experts and eyewitnesses and visited the Pentagon, where he examined their UFO files and the Project Blue Book facilities at Wright-Patterson Air Force Base in Dayton, Ohio.

1953: G. George Adamski published *Flying Saucers Have Landed*, co-written with Desmond Leslie. It became a cult classic, including his alleged contact with a beardless, suntanned Venusian who communicated by telepathy. Adamski wrote:

> *The beauty of his form surpassed anything I had ever seen. And the pleasantness of his face freed me of all thought of my personal self. I felt like a child in the presence of one with* great *wisdom and much love, and I became very humble within myself.*

December 7, 1953: During the tense days of the Cold War, Radio Moscow offered their assessment of the flying saucer hysteria:

> *Flying saucers are figments of the imaginations of Western War Mongers designed to make taxpayers swallow heavier military budgets.*

December 31, 1953: Marines at Virginia's Quantico Marine Base witnessed a UFO landing nearby and then flying away.

The craft was described as being rounded with pulsating red lights.

January 21, 1954: The first atomic submarine, the USS *Nautilus*, was launched at Groton, Connecticut; however, the submarine did not make its first nuclear-powered run until nearly a year later.

January 25, 1954: The British Air Ministry warned all personnel not to talk about flying saucers.

February 23, 1954: *Rocky Jones, Space Ranger* began a thirty-three-episode run that ended on November 16, 1954, after two seasons. The black-and-white television serial was recorded on film rather than broadcast live, as were most other space operas of the day, which allowed more elaborate special effects, such as the animated Orbit Jet XV-2 taking off and landing. One variable that set *Rocky Jones* apart from its space opera competitors—*Captain Video, Flash Gordon, Buck Rogers,* and *Commander Cody*—was his clear role as a pacifist:

> *Although (the Space Rangers) might destroy a rocketship full of unseen villains, their space pistols were never fired at people, and conflicts were always resolved with only fistfights.*
>
> The half-hour program starred Richard Crane, Sally Mansfield, and Scotty Beckett, and was directed by Hollingsworth Morse.

1954: Jack Finney published *The Body Snatchers,* which, in 1956, was turned into the classic science-fiction horror film *Invasion of the Body Snatchers*. Reviewing the novel in *The Science Fiction Encyclopedia,* John Clute remarked:

Horrifyingly depicts the invasion of a small town by interstellar spores that duplicate human beings, reducing them to dust in the process; the menacing spore-people who remain symbolize, it has been argued, the loss of freedom in contemporary society.

June 5, 1954: Russian astronomer Nikolai Barabashov said that large areas of Venus are covered with water, similar to the Earth three hundred million years ago, when organisms began to evolve and life first appeared. He contended:

Life may develop on Venus, any time now.

June 2, 1954: Lord Dowding, British air chief marshal and former head of the British Fighter Command, tells a conference of spiritualists at Herne Bay, Kent, England:

I believe people on other planets are operating through flying saucers to help our world in its present crisis.

June 1954: Dr. Hermann Oberth, famed German rocket and space travel authority, addressed an Innsbruck press conference:

These objects (the UFOs) are conceived and directed by intelligent beings of a very high order. They probably do not originate in our solar system, perhaps not even in our galaxy.

1954: Princeton University mathematician doctoral candidate Hugh Everett III developed the radical theory that parallel universes, exactly like our universe, exist. His "many-worlds" interpretation of quantum mechanics hypothesized that these universes are all interrelated—they branch off from ours, as our universe has branched off from others. Within these parallel universes, our wars have had different outcomes, and species that are extinct in our universe have evolved and adapted in others. In other universes, we humans may have become extinct. To the fans of science fiction, Everett is viewed as a pioneering folk hero and the man who invented a quantum theory of multiple universes—a theory that remains popular today.

June 30, 1954: Captain James Howard, on a BOAC airliner bound from New York to London, watched as seven black metallic flying objects trailed his plane for eighty miles near Goose Bay, Labrador. The objects and Howard's aircraft were at approximately the same altitude of nineteen thousand feet. The captain described the largest object as "a flying jellyfish," while co-pilot Len Boyd recalled:

> *I am willing to swear that what we saw was something solid, something maneuverable, and something that was being controlled intelligently.*

The objects, viewed by the crew, passengers, and two radar scopes, continued to change shape and appeared like a swarm of bees in flight. In an article written for *Everybody's Weekly*, Captain Howard recalled:

> *It was a solid thing. I'm sure of that, maneuverable and controlled intelligently—a sort of base ship linked somehow with those smaller attendant satellites ... It must have been some weird form of spaceship from another world.*

July 1954: The Australian Flying-Saucer Investigation Committee issued a report on fifty-five UFO sightings, concluding:

> *We are still far from deciding what these things are. It would be only guesswork to say they are actual spaceships from another planet. But we are fully agreed that these things are material objects—not optical illusions or hallucinations.*

1954: Contactee Truman Bethurum published the book Aboard a Flying Saucer: A Nonfiction Story of True Personal Experience, writing about the purported Captain Aura Rhanes and planet Clarion. It was reprinted in 2017 by New Saucerian Press. Bethurum later published The Voice of the Planet Clarion (1957), Facing Reality (1958), and The People of the Planet Clarion (1970).

September 14, 1954: Metalworker Marius Dewilde, along with his dog "Kiki," claimed to have seen two four-foot-tall extraterrestrials emerge from a cylindrical cigar-like UFO in Northern France's wine region. Dewilde described the humanlike visitors as being of small stature, clad in something resembling a deep-sea diver's costume. Dewilde said that he was paralyzed by a green beam of light from the "flying cigar." The local mayor, Lucien Jeune, and the village council sprang into action and quickly passed a municipal decree to keep aliens out of the local skies and protect the Châteauneuf-du-Pape vineyards.

> *Article 1. The overflight, the landing, and the takeoff of aircraft known as flying saucers or flying cigars, whatever their nationality is, are prohibited on the territory of the community.*

> *Article 2. Any aircraft, known as a flying saucer or flying cigar, which should land on the territory of the community will be immediately held in custody.*
>
> *Article 3. The forest officer and the city policeman are in charge, each one in what relates to him, of the execution of this decree.*

1954: An inquiry into theoretical physicist and Los Alamos Laboratory director J. Robert Oppenheimer's leftist politics, by a McCarthy-era Atomic Energy Commission, stripped him of his security clearance. Oppenheimer was a brilliant physicist and was recognized as the "father of the atomic bomb."

November 1954: The CIA began testing the secret and experimental U-2. The high-altitude "overhead reconnaissance project" could fly at sixty thousand feet, dramatically higher than most mid-1950s commercial airliners, which flew between ten thousand feet and twenty thousand feet. The high-technology U-2 was a CIA-funded venture between the Skunk Works, Lockheed's Advanced Development facility in Burbank, California, and aeronautical engineer Kelly Johnson. Some researchers believe that after the agency began U-2 test flights in August 1955, commercial pilots and air traffic controllers began reporting a large increase in UFO sightings.

1955: The US government purchased Area 51, a highly classified US Air Force air base in the remote Nevada desert. Although it was officially known as Homey Airport or Groom Lake, CIA documents referred to it by the codename "Area 51." The original rectangular base measures twenty-three by twenty-five miles of restricted airspace. The air base borders the Yucca Flat region of the Nevada Test Site, where 739 nuclear tests were conducted by the US Department of Energy.

Conspiracy theorists allege the area is holding retrieved spacecraft and extraterrestrial aliens, sparked by the 1947 Roswell Incident.

Area 51 is believed to be used as a secret testing area for experimental stealth aircraft and weapons. The area is heavily restricted, and foolhardy trespassers can face huge fines and lengthy prison sentences for trespassing.

March 1955: *The Case for the UFO* was published by New Saucerian Books (Point Pleasant, WV) and written by Dr. Morris Jessup, astronomer and paranormal researcher, who published four books during the 1950s. He argued that UFOs represented a mysterious subject worthy of study, speculating that they were "exploratory craft of 'solid' and 'nebulous' character." Jessup also "linked ancient monuments with prehistoric superscience" years before similar claims were made by von Däniken in *Chariots of the Gods* and other books. According to Nick Redfern, *The Case for the UFO* was of special interest:

> *His book was a detailed study of theoretical power sources for UFOs: what was it that made them fly? How could they perform incredible aerial feats, such as coming to a complete stop in the skies, hovering at incredible heights? Jessup believed that the vitally important answers lay in the domain of gravity. Or, as he saw it: anti-gravity.*

July 10, 1955: *This Island Earth*, directed by Joseph M. Newman and Jack Arnold, was released, based on the 1952 novel by Raymond F. Jones. It starred Jeff Morrow, Faith

Domergue, and Rex Reason and was praised for the well-written script and flying saucer special effects in Technicolor.

1955: Carl M. Allen (Carlos Miguel Allende) sent a package marked "Happy Easter" to the US Office of Naval Research. Inside was a copy of Dr. Morris K. Jessup's book *The Case for the UFO: Unidentified Flying Objects,* with bizarre annotations in the margins.

1955: Derek Dempster, a former Royal Air Force pilot, founded the quarterly British magazine *Flying Saucer Review.* It was the first international saucer journal to be published on a regular basis, with editorial direction from Brinsley le Poer Trench, Charles Bowen, and Gordon Creighton.

August 21, 1955: Three children and eight adults witnessed a UFO landing behind their farmhouse in Kelly, Kentucky. The group saw a "little man" about three feet tall with huge eyes and ears, wearing a metallic garment. The alien held its hands over its head, in a possible gesture of peace, but was shot at point-blank and knocked off its feet. Other creatures who appeared were also shot at; .22-caliber bullets just ricocheted off their bodies. More than a dozen police officers, including Kentucky State Police, were "unable to fault the story."

1955: The remote Area 51 site, in southern Nevada, was created during the Cold War between the US and the Soviet Union as a secret testing and development facility for aircraft, including the U-2 and SR-71 Blackbird reconnaissance planes. Because the U-2 could reach altitudes much higher than any other planes at the time, it accounted for many of the UFO sightings in the area. The facility is next to two other restricted military areas: the Nevada Test Site, where US nuclear weapons were tested from the 1950s to the 1990s, and the

Nevada Test and Training Range. The entire range covers more than 2.9 million acres of land.

October 9, 1955: In a *New York Times* interview, General Douglas MacArthur, when asked about the possibility of World War III, has been widely misquoted about preparation for the next major war:

> *The nations of the world will have to unite, for the next war will be an interplanetary war. The nations of the Earth must someday make a common front against attack by people from other planets.*

McArthur's quote has been distorted and taken out of context by hardline ufologists. MacArthur did suggest the notion of an eventual interplanetary war on several occasions; one of them was in 1955, and one of them was during a speech at West Point. He never stated it would be the "next war" fought by Earth, but that it would happen in the very distant future. The only comments MacArthur made about the next war were that he had no idea what form it would take.

1955: G. George Adamski's sequel, *Inside the Space Ships*, described further meetings with his Venusian contact and emissaries from Mars and Saturn. Adamski preached that every planet in our solar system was populated with humanlike inhabitants, including the dark side of the Earth's moon. *History.com*'s Greg Daugherty observed that:

> *Adamski claimed that his new friends took him aboard one of their scout ships, flew him to an immense mother ship hovering over the earth, gave him a ride around the moon, and treated him to a colorful travelogue about life on Venus.*

Inside the Space Ships and his previous *Flying Saucers Have Landed* (1953) became bestsellers, and by 1960 they had sold a combined two hundred thousand copies. Adamski was widely read at the time, gaining a new generation of fans during the psychedelic 1960s.

1955: The Skunk Works, Lockheed's Advanced Development facility in Burbank, California, received a contract from the CIA to build a spy plane known as the U-2. The high-altitude "overhead reconnaissance project" was designed to fly over the Soviet Union at sixty thousand feet, photographing sites of strategic interest. After pilot Gary Powers was shot down over Russia, the overflights were discontinued. The "official" contract for the U-2 followed the Skunk Work's traditional gentleman's agreement and handshake.

October 1955: Ufologist James Willett Moseley, in a *Fate* magazine article, suggested that the Nazca Lines were intriguing Fortean phenomena. Moseley proposed a mysterious origin long before they involved alternative writers such as Erich von Däniken (1968), Henri Stierlin (1983), and Gerald Hawkins (1990). The Nazca Lines were first discovered in 1927 by Peruvian archaeologist Toribio Mejia Xesspe.

1956: Long John Nebel began his twenty-year career working on New York's WOR all-night radio. After getting involved in the occult, the slender six-foot-three-inch on-air personality soon attracted insomniacs, the paranormal community, and "night people." He frequently invited people who claimed to have been from outer space as guests. He later co-hosted a show with his wife, model Candy Jones, on WMCA from midnight to 5:30 a.m. Dennis Israel, vice president and general manager of the station, said:

> *He was the first to do an all-night talk show on the radio and the first to have a network talk show.*

1956–1963: Bill Kaysing was in charge of the technical presentations unit at the Rocketdyne Propulsion Field Laboratory during the seven years when the major planning for the engine and components of the Apollo project was completed.

Kaysing held security clearances with the US Air Force and the Atomic Energy Commission, but, in 1976, published *We Never Went to the Moon: America's Thirty Billion Dollar Swindle*, which kicked off the conspiracy theory that the six Apollo moon landings, which took place between 1969 and 1972, were hoaxes, and that the photographs released by NASA documenting them were faked.

1956: Carl M. Allen (Carlos Miguel Allende) began sending over fifty handwritten letters to Dr. Morris K. Jessup. He also sent Jessup's book *The Case for the UFO: Unidentified Flying Object,* with bizarre annotations in the margins, indicating some knowledge about propulsion systems.

1956: Gray Barker published *They Knew Too Much About Flying Saucers* (University Books, 1956), the first book to document the mysterious Men in Black, who, according to conspiracy theorists, intimidate individuals into keeping silent about UFOs. Barker recounted Albert K. Bender's alleged encounters with the Men in Black, believed to travel in groups of three, wear black suits, and drive large black automobiles, usually Cadillacs. Barker also acknowledged that:

> *(Richard Sharpe) Shaver wrote about flying saucers before Kenneth Arnold saw "a chain of saucer-like things" skipping along above Mt. Rainier in 1947, and told the press about the*

experience, thus coining a word that will forever plague saucer research, and attaching a humorous and therefore necessarily suspicious connotation to the mystery.

1956: Townsend Brown helped found the National Investigations Committee On Aerial Phenomena, although, the following year, he was forced out as director after allegations he was using funds to further his antigravity research. Brown alleged that he had discovered a connection between electric fields and gravity, producing an antigravity effect. A chapter in Charles Berlitz and William L. Moore's book *The Philadelphia Experiment: Project Invisibility* (Fawcett, 1979) was titled "The Force Fields of Townsend Brown," implying Brown's electrogravitics was the secret behind UFO propulsion.

February 5, 1956: The black-and-white American science-fiction horror film *Invasion of the Body Snatchers* was released. Directed by Don Siegel, it was shot in the film noir style and starred Kevin McCarthy and Dana Wynter in a story about an extraterrestrial invasion. The film was based on Jack Finney's 1954 novel, *The Body Snatchers*.

1956: *True Magazine* published articles by *San Francisco Chronicle* reporter John Philip Cahn that exposed Silas Newton and Leo Gebauer as con artists. These two hoaxers convinced best-selling author Frank Scully that a UFO crashed in Aztec, New Mexico.

June 4, 1956: Leonor Zalles Freeland, of New York, received a patent from the United States Patent Office for a circular flying saucer. Listed as Serial Number 41,763, the patent was granted a fourteen-year term.

1956: Dr. Morris Jessup publishes *UFO and the Bible*, one of the first postulations that ancient astronauts may have visited

Earth during biblical times. He developed themes that were later referenced by author Erich von Däniken in *Chariots of the Gods*. Jessup has been referred to as "the most original extraterrestrial hypothesiser of the 1950s," and became a key player in the Philadelphia Experiment.

June 13, 1956: *Earth vs the Flying Saucers* was released as a double feature with *The Werewolf*. The storyline was suggested by the best-selling 1953 book *Flying Saucers from Outer Space* by Maj. Donald Keyhoe. Special effects legend Ray Harryhausen created the flying saucers and supervised the animations. Hugh Marlow and Joan Taylor starred in this film directed by Fred F. Sears.

1956: Former director of Project Blue Book, Capt. Edward J. Ruppelt's *Report on Unidentified Flying Objects*, (Doubleday, 1956) claims that "UFO is the official term that I created to replace the words 'flying saucers.'" Ruppelt took over Project Grudge, later renamed Blue Book, and left the agency and the Air Force in September 1953.

1956: American military spy technology continued after the U-2 spy plane was put into service. Area 51 was used to develop additional top-secret aircraft, including the A-12 reconnaissance plane (also known as OXCART) and the stealth fighter F-117 Nighthawk.

September 1956: Dozens of witnesses witnessed a domed, disk-shaped UFO land near US Highway 70, twelve miles west of Holloman Air Force Base (currently the White Sands Proving Grounds). The craft was viewed for more than ten minutes and then ascended "with a whirring sound." A wire sent to the Pentagon by the official evaluation team stated that the craft "was definitely not any type of aircraft under development by the US or any foreign terrestrial power."

April 4, 1957: An impressive series of radar observations were viewed at Scotland's RAF West Freugh by military and civilian operators at three separate military bases; however, an official press release stated that the UFO may have been a balloon. Wing Commander Walter Whitworth, when approached for a comment, stated:

> *I have been ordered by the Air Ministry to say nothing about the subject.*

April 30, 1957: A secret Air Ministry report revealed that the Scotland UFOs exceeded known aircraft capabilities. The objects were observed at seventy thousand feet and accelerated to 240 mph. The AM report concluded:

> *There were not known to be any aircraft in the vicinity nor were there any meteorological balloons. Even if balloons had been in the area these would not account for the sudden change of direction and the movement at high speed against the prevailing wind.*

1957: Gray Barker and James Moseley mailed a fake letter, written on State Department stationery, to "contactee" George Adamski, telling Adamski that the United States Department of State was pleased with Adamski's flying saucer research. The letter, signed by the fictitious "R. E. Straith," was described by Barker as "one of the great unsolved mysteries of the UFO field" in his 1967 *Book of Adamski*.

1957: C. G. Jung published the "slender text," *Flying Saucers: A Modern Myth of Things Seen in the Skies*, offering his perspective on the then-raging UFO phenomenon. He asked, "Why are so many people thinking and envisioning UFOs at this particular moment?" Jung was "puzzled to death" by flying saucers. He likened UFOs to a "technological angel" or a "physicists' miracle," writing that they were shaped like mandalas and seemed to have a similar effect on our psyche—a "symbol of wholeness" that appears in "situations of psychic confusion and perplexity." Jung believed that because people are struggling and unable to become fully integrated and actualized individuals, their acute social anxieties are projected as mandala-like UFOs, itself a symbol of the collective unconscious, and:

> *Forced to manifest itself indirectly in the form of spontaneous projections. The projected image then appears as an ostensibly physical fact independent of the individual psyche and its nature. In other words, the rounded wholeness of the mandala becomes a spaceship controlled by an intelligent being.*

Jung described the mandala as an archetypal symbol and an image of wholeness and integration, that may appear in all cultures.

September 4, 1957: A flight of four Portuguese Air Force fighter-bombers, under the command of Captain Jose Lemos Ferreira, witnessed an expanding and contracting UFO and three other emerging multicolored craft, near the Spanish town of Granada. The incredulous crew had no explanation for the sighting, while Captain Ferreira remarked:

> *After this please do not give us the old routine of Venus, balloons, aircraft, and the like which has been given as a general panacea for almost every case of UFOs.*

October 4, 1957: The Soviet satellite Sputnik was launched into space and became the first spacecraft to orbit Earth. Sputnik opened the new frontier of outer space.

October 15, 1957: In one of the first reported abduction cases, Antonio Villas Boas, a young Brazilian farmer, claimed he was abducted aboard a UFO, stripped naked, probed with needles and other implements, and forced to have intercourse with a "beautiful" naked female entity. Villas Boas described the female as having blonde hair, a wide face, which came to a point at her chin. She had elongated blue eyes and thin lips. Her breasts were high and well separated. The female grunted while they copulated.

1957: Princeton physicists John A. Wheeler and Hugh Everett developed the Everett-Wheeler interpretation, suggesting a universe where every point in space connected with every other point in space, but was also interconnected with every point of time as well—past, present, and future. They argued that in order to realistically describe the universe, we must accept the reality of other universes and worlds besides our own. The Everett-Wheeler interpretation appeared to confirm "non-scientific" occult, science fiction, and contactee theories of space and time.

November 6, 1957: Research engineer James Stokes observed a five-hundred-foot-long elliptical-shaped UFO flying between Alamogordo, New Mexico's US Air Force Missile Development Center, and the White Sands. The unidentified craft killed his car's ignition, and Stokes suffered from sunburn caused by the UFO's tremendous heat.

November 6, 1957: On the same day as the James Stokes event, Richard Kehoe, an employee of the General Telephone Company, witnessed an egg-shaped, tan UFO alighted on two metal rings. It was wrapped in "a blue haze" that killed his car's ignition. Kehoe saw two men, with yellow-green skin and about five and a half feet tall, who questioned him about the time of day. The contact occurred in Playa del Rey, California.

1957: Ufologist and Fortean researcher John A. Keel published *Jadoo*, a book describing his time in Egypt and India, where he investigated the rope trick and the legendary creature called "yeti." He later explored reported UFO sightings called "windows," "waves" or "flaps," offering his well-crafted literary skills and humor to the paranormal field.

December 12, 1957: Writing to New *Republic* editor Gilbert A. Harrison, psychotherapist Carl Jung wrote:

> *The problem of the UFOs is, as you rightly say, a very fascinating one, but it is as puzzling as it is fascinating; since, in spite of all* observations *I know of, there is no certainty about their very nature.*

Jung observed that there was "an overwhelming material pointing to their legendary or mythological aspect," and that "the psychological aspect is so impressive, that one almost must regret that the UFOs seem to be real after all," adding:

> *I have followed up the literature as much as possible and it looks to me as if something were seen and even confirmed by radar, but nobody knows exactly what is seen.*

1957: Major Donald E. Keyhoe, director of NICAP, lodged a formal complaint with a member of the US Senate, charging that the US Air Force made continuous false statements about flying saucers to the press, public, and members of Congress.

Keyhoe provided summaries of more than two hundred UFO cases to support his claims.

December 17, 1957: The United States successfully test-fired the Atlas intercontinental ballistic missile for the first time.

January 6, 1958: *Life* magazine issued a curious political statement when an article read:

During the ensuing year there will be authenticated sightings of roughly two hundred Unidentified Flying Objects, of which the Pentagon will be able to disprove two hundred and ten.

January 16, 1958: Brazilian photographer Almiro Baraúna claimed to have shot a photographic sequence of a flying disc on the coast of Trindade Island, while on board the Brazilian Navy ship *Almirante Saldanha*. Ufologist Antonio Huneeus remarked:

> *These UFO photos are among the best known ever in the history of ufology, not just because of their quality but also due to their background, such as the fact that were taken in a navy ship; that the object was seen by many of the crewmen; that the case was officially investigated by the Brazilian Navy; and last but not least, that the case became known when Brazil's President, Juscelino Kubitschek, gave copies of the photos to a reporter from the Rio de Janeiro newspaper* Correio da Manha, *where they were published on the front page on February 21, 1958.*

January 23, 1958: Captain G. H. Oldenburgh, information service officer at Langley Air Force Base, wrote:

> *The public dissemination of data on Unidentified Flying objects ... is contrary to Air Force policy and regulations.*

Jan. 31, 1958: The US military launched the country's first satellite, the Explorer 1, into space via the Jupiter-C rocket. NASA was established later that year after President Dwight Eisenhower signed the National Aeronautics and Space Act.

June 9, 1958: The novelty song "The Purple People Eater," written and performed by Sheb Wooley, reached No. 1 on the Billboard pop charts and became an international hit. Wooley, capitalizing on the UFO frenzy of the times, wrote the song in less than an hour.

September 10, 1958: The science-fiction horror film *The Blob* featured an alien red slime that consumes everything in its path as it grows larger and larger. It starred Steven McQueen and Aneta Corseaut, and was directed by Irvin Yeaworth, Russell Doughten, and Irvin S. Yeaworth Jr.

Conor Feehly, writing for *Nautilus*, described the amorphous alien that hitchhiked a ride to Earth on a meteorite:

> *Upon landing, the translucent extraterrestrial began to devour humans, growing larger and redder with each meal. While the amoeba-like alien in the cult classic was famous for its insatiable hunger,* The Blob managed *to articulate something that previous science fiction movies hadn't: There's no guarantee aliens will look anything like the lifeforms that we are familiar with.*

October 1958: Paramount Pictures released the horror-science fiction film *I Married a Monster from Outer Space,* produced and directed by Gene Fowler Jr., and starring Thomas Tryon and Gloria Talbott. The film was released as a double feature with *The Blob.* The storyline is about a young wife who discovered that her husband is actually an alien humanoid.

January 1, 1959: Riley Crabb published the staple-bound *Flying Saucers and America's Destiny: An Illustrated Analysis of the World Crisis with Reference to the Role of the Space Visitors, the Prophecy of Washington, Projection for Disaster, Trance of* [*etc.*]. His other books included *The Reality of the Underground Cavern World*, (1960) and the forty-page *Flying Saucers on the Moon* (1960). All of his books were published by the Borderland Sciences Research Foundation.

January 26, 1959: Robert Lazar was born in Coral Gables, Florida. Lazar claimed he was hired in the 1980s to reverse engineer alien technology while working at a secret site called "S-4", a subsidiary installation allegedly located south of the US Air Force's Area 51. He purports to have examined an alien craft and read US government briefing documents that described alien involvement in human affairs over the past ten thousand years. Lazar's assertions have been analyzed and rejected by skeptics, such as journalist Ken Layne, who charged:

> *A lot of credible people have looked at Lazar's story and rationally concluded that he made it up.*

March 1959: During the heat of the "Space Race," Army Lt. Gen. Arthur G. Trudeau tasked the Army's chief of ordnance to develop a secret study for a manned lunar outpost. Called Project Horizon, the goal was to construct an Army base on the moon by 1966 and "protect potential United States interests." Having already launched the Sputnik satellite, the Soviet Union was threatening to claim the moon for the Red Army by 1967. In his tell-all book, *The Day After Roswell* (Gallery Books, 1997), Major Philip J. Corso included fifty-nine pages of official documents and schematics pertaining to Project Horizon.

April 19, 1959: Dr. Morris Jessup contacted his friend, oceanographer Dr. J. Manson Valentine. Claiming to have made a breakthrough regarding the Philadelphia Experiment, Jessup arranged to meet with him the next day. According to Valentine:

> *He was convinced that the Navy, in seeking to create a magnetic cloud for camouflage purposes in October 1943, had uncovered a potential that could temporarily, and if strong enough, perhaps permanently, rearrange the molecular structure of people and materials so that they would pass into another dimension with further implications of predictable and as yet uncontrolled teleportation.*

April 20, 1959: A Florida park attendant discovered Dr. Morris Jessup's still body inside a 1958 Chevy Station Wagon, located in Miami's Matheson Hammock Park. The car's engine was still running, and a hosepipe attached to the exhaust had been fed through the driver's side window. His death appeared to be a suicide, although some thought otherwise.

February 24, 1959: Three glowing UFOs were sighted by Captain Peter W. Killian and his American Airlines crew while flying a DC-6B nonstop from Newark to Detroit. The plane was approximately thirteen miles west of Williamsport, Pennsylvania, and flew at 8,500 feet. The UFOs continuously changed brightness, flashing "brighter than any star," with colors fluctuating from yellow-orange to a brilliant blue-white. The official Air Force explanation was that the crew actually saw "B-47 aircraft accomplishing night refueling from KC-97 tankers." Killian refused to believe the "official" explanation and told the press:

> *If the Air Force wants to believe that, it can. But I know what a B-47 looks like and I know what a KC-97 tanker looks like, and I know what they look like in operation at night. And that's not what I saw.*

The Killian UFO Incident is one of the most thoroughly investigated and controversial on record, considered, by some, to be a classic UFO event.

1959: An example of the scientific community's condescension and systematic censorship was best represented by a restricted newsletter from the Smithsonian Astrophysical Observatory, responding to "popular comments on UFOs":

> *It is exceedingly undesirable to be associated with these "sightings," or the persons originating them ... on no account should any indication be given to others that a discussion even remotely concerned with UFOs is taking place.*

April 1959: Considered to be the most outrageous UFO film of all time, the black-and-white science fiction–horror film *Plan 9 from Outer Space* was released, produced, written, and directed by Ed Wood. The film stars Gregory Walcott, Mona McKinnon, Tor Johnson, and "Vampira" (Maila Nurmi) and is narrated by Criswell. It also posthumously bills Bela Lugosi (before Lugosi's death in August 1956). Harry Medved and Michael Medved dubbed it "the worst film ever made" in their book *The Golden Turkey Awards*. The cult film had a bizarre religious connection, according to writer Mark Mancini:

> *The film, about aliens who try to conquer Earth by reanimating human corpses and turning them against the living, was given the working title* Grave Robbers from Outer Space. *But most of the movie's funding came from J. Edward Reynolds, a devout Southern Baptist, whose religious sensibilities were offended by the title. So, Wood changed it to* Plan 9 from Outer Space. *To further improve his relationship with the financier, Wood underwent a full-body baptism at Reynolds' church. Several cast members did likewise—including (Swedish wrestler Tor) Johnson, who pranked the minister by pretending to drown mid-ceremony.*

June 26–27, 1959: Anglican priest William B. Gill, with a mission in Boiani, Papas New Guinea, observed several UFOs on two consecutive evenings. They would later be assigned J. Allen Hynek's CE3/CE-III classification, as humanoid figures were observed, according to writer Bill Chalker:

> *About twenty-five natives, including teachers and medical technicians, also observed the phenomena. They "signaled" the humanoids and received an apparent response. This was one of sixty UFO sightings within a few weeks in the New Guinea area.*

May 18, 1959: G. George Adamski is invited by Queen Juliana and Prince Bernhard of the Netherlands to discuss extraterrestrial beings, raising a public stir. In a statement he wrote afterward in response to the fiercely critical newspaper reports, he said:

> *I am nothing but a common man, but the Queen is more than a symbol, as she represents the kind people of Holland before the world. And so, if any statement has to be made as to what*

has been said in her presence, she has the honor to make such, and not me.

The royal audience, scheduled to last forty-five minutes, went on for two hours, making Adamski twenty minutes late for his lecture in The Hague.

Adamski supposedly claimed a secret 1963 meeting with Pope John XXIII, as well. Arthur C. Clarke, the author of *2001: A Space Odyssey*, not only denounced Adamski's work but characterized his believers as "nitwits."

June 1, 1959: After George Adamski was invited to meet with Juliana, Queen of the Netherlands, a *Time* magazine article, "The Queen and the Saucers," said that the chief of staff for the Netherlands Royal Air Force reportedly referred to Adamski as "a pathological case," while a prominent newspaper bemoaned:

She had invited to the palace a crackpot from California who numbered among his friend's men from Mars, Venus, and other solar-system suburbs.

1959: Margaret Storm published *Return of the Dove,* a surreal novel about inventor genius Nikola Tesla. In the book, Tesla is described as having been born on a flying saucer en route from the planet Venus to Earth in 1856.

1959: During his "International Tour," hoaxer G. George Adamski claimed to have meetings with Pope John XXIII, President John F. Kennedy, and leaders from the United Nations. Pope John XXIII is believed to have appeared during the 1963 Sheppton mining disaster.

June 1959: After the Soviet Union launched Sputnik on October 4, 1957, the United States was under pressure to come from behind and win the "Space Race." One option was to establish a base on the moon, called Project Horizon. According to a one-hundred-and-eighteen-page monograph, produced by the US Army:

> *To be second to the Soviet Union in establishing an outpost on the moon would be disastrous to our nation's prestige and in turn to our democratic philosophy.*

September 19, 1959: Giuseppe Cocconi (1914–2008) and Philip Morrison (1915–2005) published their ground-breaking paper "Searching for Interstellar Communications," encouraging fellow astronomers to search specifically for radio signals sent from other planetary civilizations. Cocconi and Morrison believed the radio domain was the most efficient region of the electromagnetic spectrum for interstellar communications and recommended the 1,420 MHz (21 cm) line of atomic hydrogen. The last sentence of the Cocconi and Morrison paper, published in *Nature*, was a thought-provoking call for action:

> *The probability of success is difficult to estimate, but if we never search the chance of success is zero.*

October 28, 1959: In the "Space Race," the Soviet Union achieved two firsts by escaping Earth's gravity and making the first lunar impact. That same year, Luna 3 achieved another first after it photographed the moon's far side.

1959: Psychotherapist Carl Jung, a confessed skeptic in such matters, published Flying Saucers: a Modern Myth of Things Seen in the Sky, at the height of popular fascination with UFOs. The following abstract declared that:

> *Jung was nevertheless intrigued, not so much by their reality or unreality, but by their psychic aspect. He saw flying saucers as a modern myth in the making, to be passed down the generations just as we have received such myths from our ancestors. In this wonderful and enlightening book, Jung sees UFOs as "visionary rumors," the center of a quasi-religious cult and carriers of our technological and salvationist fantasies. Forty years later, with entire religions based on the writings of science fiction authors, it is remarkable to see just how right he has proved to be.*

1959: George Hunt Williamson published *Road in the Sky,* proposing that Peru's Nazca Plain's geometrical designs were built as landing strips for extraterrestrial UFOs. Williamson's theory pre-dated a similar one later proposed by Erich von Däniken.

1959 to 1985: Occultist and saucerian Riley Hansard Crabb took over as director of the Borderland Sciences Research Associates (BSRA), succeeding founder Meade Layne. Crabb was a prolific writer who theorized about everything from flying saucers and Forteana to radionics and subtle energy.

December 1959: Ray A. Palmer announced that flying saucers were not from outer space but came from secret Earth bases located under the north and south poles. Palmer contended that the Earth is shaped like a donut, with openings at both poles where the saucer people reside.

Chapter 14

The Moon Landing: 1960s

The psychedelic 1960s gave us The Byrds, *The Andromeda Strain*, the Men in Black, *The Jetsons*, *Stranger in a Strange Land*, Gabriel Green for President, the Kecksburg UFO, Lonnie Zamora, and Socorro.

January 1, 1960: Brinsley Le Poer Trench published *The Sky People*. According to the author, mankind was created by extraterrestrials and provided help by these benevolent elder brothers—ancient alien themes later echoed by Erich von Däniken and Graham Hancock. Trench suggests that there were many gods and godlike beings, long before Adam and Eve. "Human progress has been the gift of this inspired minority," as the front cover states.

1960: Project Ozma was the first in the modern era to probe the skies for evidence of extraterrestrial intelligence. Radio astronomer Frank D. Drake attempted to locate extraterrestrials by listening for narrow-band microwave radio waves coming from nearby star systems. The stars chosen by Drake for the first SETI search were Tau Ceti in the constellation Cetus (the Whale) and Epsilon Eridani in the constellation Eridanus (the River), each being approximately eleven light-years (sixty-four trillion miles) away. Drake's SETI project was named after the queen of L. Frank Baum's imaginary land of Oz—a place "very far away, difficult to reach, and populated by strange and exotic beings."

1960: Ufologist Gabriel Green, another of the alleged contactees, threw his hat into the race for US president, claiming to represent the Universal Flying Saucer Party. Green based his political philosophy on the "United World Universal Economics." He ran unsuccessfully for California's US Senate in 1962, claiming to have accumulated over 171,000 write-in votes. He published *Let's Face Facts about Flying Saucers* in 1972.

1960: Two French authors, Jacques Bergier and Louis Pauwels —interested in the occult, Nazis, UFOs, and H. P. Lovecraft— published *Morning of the Magicians*. They attempted to show that Lovecraft's vision of ancient astronauts could be correlated to the "occult" truths of Theosophy and the UFO movement. In 1964, Erich von Däniken simply appropriated this material wholesale for a magazine article. On the strength of the magazine article, he received a book deal for *Chariots of the Gods*.

1960: Molecular biologist-turned-exobiologist Joshua Lederberg (1925–2008) who won the Nobel prize at age thirty-three (for discoveries about the genetics of bacteria), explored the possibilities of extraterrestrial life. He wrote in the journal *Science* that:

> *Exobiology is no more fantastic than the realization of space travel itself, and we have a grave responsibility to explore its implications for science and for human welfare with our best scientific insights and knowledge.*

Lederberg is recognized for his work in microbial genetics, artificial intelligence, and the United States space program.

March 4, 1960: "The Monsters Are Due on Maple Street" aired on CBS's *The Twilight Zone*, written and narrated by Rod Serling. The episode is an interactive story about an alien invasion and the human inclination to find a convenient scapegoat. In 2009, *Time* named it one of the ten best *Twilight Zone* episodes, and it became a major influence on science fiction. Serling's closing narration explains that the tools of conquest do not necessarily come with bombs and explosions and fallout:

> *There are weapons that are simply thoughts, attitudes, prejudices ... to be found only in the minds of men. For the record, prejudices can kill ... and suspicion can destroy ... and a thoughtless, frightened search for a scapegoat has a fallout all of its own—for the children and the children yet unborn. And the pity of it is that these things cannot be confined to the Twilight Zone.*

March 7, 1960: The National Investigations Committee on Aerial Phenomena (NICAP), one of the largest flying saucer organizations, listed a UFO that was visible from Canada to Florida. It was described by observers as possibly three or four unknown craft flying in formation.

July 15, 1960: A declassified document, published by the National Archives of Australia, detailed a UFO sighting at Wewak, a British nuclear testing range about twenty-four kilometers from Maralinga Village in South Australia. The report cited multiple witnesses who saw a moving red light that was not believed explainable by any natural phenomena and was likely to be "either a cone from a satellite or a flying saucer."

January 1, 1961: Long John Nebel published *The Way Out World*, which included UFO contactees, a stage magician, the Shaver Mystery, Edgar Cayce, and much more, gleaned from Nebel's "twenty thousand hours of interviewing and research." Radio historian Michael C. Keith wrote that Nebel was regarded as one of after-hours radio's true pioneers:

> *Few people before or since have brought to all-night radio the kind of ingenuity, originality, and variety that Nebel did. He represents one of post-World War II radio's creative high points and another example of the special nature of overnight programming.*

July 1, 1961: The Aerial Phenomena Group, charged with investigating UFOs, was transferred from the Aerospace Technical Intelligence Center's (ATIC) assistant chief of staff to the jurisdiction of the Air Force Systems Command.

1961: G. George Adamski, with co-writer Desmond Leslie, published *Flying Saucers Farewell* despite continued criticism from scientific circles about his alleged contact with an alien Venusian.

July 1, 1961: Robert A. Heinlein published *Stranger in a Strange Land*, becoming his Hugo Award-winning all-time masterpiece and cult favorite. Heinlein's protagonist, Valentine Michael Smith, is a Martian sent to Earth and a stranger who must learn what it is to be a man:

> *But his own beliefs and his powers far exceed the limits of humankind, and as he teaches them about grokking and water-sharing, he also inspires a transformation that will alter Earth's inhabitants forever ...*

September 19, 1961: In one of the first abduction cases, American couple Barney and Betty Hill, returning from a vacation to Niagara Falls and Montreal, said they witnessed a UFO and experienced missing time—later claiming to have been abducted by extraterrestrials in a rural portion of New Hampshire. The incident came to be called the "Hill Abduction" and the "Zeta Reticuli Incident." With the aid of hypnosis, conducted by Boston psychiatrist Dr. Benjamin Simon, Betty was able to draw a star map she was shown aboard the UFO. Her map indicated the location of two stars, Zeta 1 and Zeta 2 Reticuli, the alleged home base of the aliens. The existence of these unknown planets was not confirmed by astronomers until 1969—eight years later. After being hypnotized, Barney Hill's horrifying experience was tape-recorded by Dr. Simon:

> *I could feel them examining me with their hands ... They looked at my back, and I could feel them touching my skin ... as if they were counting my spinal column ... and then I was turned over, and I was looked at ... My mouth was opened, and I could feel two fingers pulling it back ...*

The Hills' story was adapted into the best-selling 1966 book *The Interrupted Journey* and the 1975 television film *The UFO Incident*.

November 1961: During the Green Bank Conference, astronomer Frank Drake postulated his theoretical "Drake Equation," determining the likelihood of intelligent life in the universe. The Drake Equation, a roadmap to extraterrestrial life, sought to ascertain the potential number of technological civilizations in the galaxy. Drake's speculation about the existence of intelligent life elsewhere in the universe became known as astrobiology. Later, in the 1990s, he estimated that ten thousand planets possessed advanced civilizations in the Milky Way alone.

1962: WNBC offered Long John Nebel more than $100,000 per year to begin broadcasting from the station. He worked there until the station decided to switch to an all-rock format in 1973. Nebel refused to change the content of his show and resigned in protest.

1962: Kenneth Arnold, "the man who started it all," won the Republican Party's nomination for lieutenant governor of Idaho, losing in the general election. Fifteen years earlier, Arnold had seen nine "flying saucers" flying near Mount Rainier, which initiated a global hysteria.

1962: Gray Barker and Albert K. Bender published *Flying Saucers and the Three Men* under Barker's imprint, Saucerian Books. Bender said in March 1953 he had been approached by three Men in Black, who communicated with him telepathically and shared with him the origin of UFOs. The book proposed that the MIB were extraterrestrials and were described by Bender in terrifying language:

> *They floated about a foot off the floor ... They looked like clergymen but wore hats similar to the Homburg style. The faces were not clearly discernible, for the hats partly hid and shaded them ... The eyes of all three figures suddenly lit up like flashlight bulbs ... They seemed to burn into my very soul as the pains above my eyes became almost unbearable.*

Bender's mythology began to lose credibility as he spun his convoluted tale, layer upon layer, to his IFSB devotees. He said that the MIB were monstrous creatures in human disguise who came to Earth to extract seawater. They flew him to Antarctica, where he was threatened to stop researching and talking about the saucers.

1962: Hoaxer extraordinaire G. George Adamski announced that he would be attending an interplanetary conference held on the planet Saturn, mailing accounts of the meeting in June 1962.

September 12, 1962: Addressing students at Rice University, President John F. Kennedy declared, "We choose to go to the Moon," planning to land a man on the Moon before 1970.

September 23, 1962: With images of cartoonish flying saucers, the animated *The Jetsons* aired in prime time as an animated sitcom. It was Hanna-Barbera's Space Age counterpart to *The Flintstones*. It debuted as the first program broadcast in color on ABC, back in the early 1960s when only a handful of ABC stations were capable of broadcasting in color.

December 14, 1962: *Mariner* 2 became the first space probe to visit Venus, scientifically confirming that the planet's surface temperature was over 750 degrees F and measuring the solar wind, the constant stream of charged particles emanating from the Sun. Five years later, *Mariner* 5 followed up on *Mariner* 2's exploration of Venus with an even closer look.

January 1, 1963: Donald H. Menzel and Lyle G. Boyd published The World of Flying Saucers: a scientific examination of a major myth of the space age, espousing what astrophysicist Carl Sagan would label "our chauvinism," the theory that aliens would most likely resemble human beings. Menzel and Boyd wrote:

> *Whether from Venus, Mars, Saturn, or the planets of other solar systems [the space visitors'] physical appearance, cloth-*

ing, tastes in food, habits of thought, and ethical values usually seem indistinguishable from those of citizens (whether American, French, or Brazilian) who report the visitors.

Many contactees have described alien visitors as looking, speaking (sometimes telepathically), and dressing like us.

January 1, 1963: UFO debunker Donald Howard Menzel published *The World of Flying Saucers: A Scientific Examination of a Major Myth of the Space Age*, where he explained the definition of the "classic" UFO sighting:

A "classic," in the literature of flying saucers is a particularly dramatic UFO incident whose specific cause has not yet been found or, if found, cannot be absolutely proved from the evidence available. Lacking a completely airtight explanation, official investigators classify the case as Unknown. Saucer fans classify it as proof that flying saucers exist.

But, sidestepping his lesson in semantics, Menzel orchestrates a one-man demolition squad, systematically deconstructing just about every flying saucer story landing on his desk. Menzel objectively scolds:

Human beings now stand on the threshold of space. Visits to and from other worlds may occur in the future, bringing new facts and new interpretations of reality that we cannot now imagine. No evidence yet found indicates that such visits have begun. No fact so far determined suggests that a single unidentified flying object has originated outside our own planet.

1963: Robert Charroux, in his book *One Hundred Thousand Years of Man's Unknown History,* suggests that the biblical Ark of the Covenant was an electric condenser. Charroux attributes the idea to Maurice Denis-Papin, who published the original theory in 1948. In his *Chariots of the Gods*, Erich von Däniken usurped the aforementioned models twenty years later.

February 14, 1963: Old Testament scholar Michael S. Heiser (1963–2023) was born in Lebanon, Pennsylvania, and wrote over ten books about the Bible's spiritual realm. Heiser was an ardent critic of ancient astronaut theories and especially those promoted by Zechariah Sitchin. Heiser appeared in *Ancient Aliens Debunked* as a scholar on the Hebrew Bible and ancient Near Eastern texts.

April 1963: Dr. Allen Hynek, as quoted in *Yale Scientific Magazine:*

> *The surprising thing is the level of intelligence of the observers and reporters of UFO—certainly above average, and in some cases decidedly above average. The typical (UFO) witness is honest and reliable.*

April 7, 1963: Yale University's *Yale Scientific Magazine* was among those critical of the Air Force UFO investigations, charging:

> *Based on unreliable and unscientific surmises as data, the Air Force develops elaborate statistical findings which seem impressive to the uninitiated public, unschooled in the fallacies of the statistical method. One must conclude that the highly publicized periodic Air Force pronouncements based upon unsound statistics serve merely to misrepresent the true character of UFO phenomena.*

1963: Jacques Vallée co-developed the first computerized map of Mars for NASA.

September 30, 1963: The third episode of the classic *The Outer Limits* television show, "The Architects of Fear," offered a theme of mankind uniting against a common threat from outer space. In the episode, endemic Cold War fears of a nuclear holocaust prompt a cabal of scientists to decide that they must act to save the world—planning a fake alien invasion of Earth in an effort to unite all humanity against a perceived common enemy. The program's opening narration warned:

> *Is this the day? Is this the beginning of the end? There is no time to wonder. No time to ask why is it happening, why is it finally happening. There is time only for fear, for the piercing pain of panic. Do we pray? Or do we merely run now and pray later? Will there be a later? Or is this the day?*

1963: Massachusetts Institute of Technology meteorologist Edward Lorenz (1917–2008), a pioneer of chaos theory, coined the term "Butterfly Effect," suggesting that the flapping of a butterfly in Brazil might lead to huge outcomes in weather patterns across the globe. In his paper "Deterministic Nonperiodic Flow" Lorenz said:

> *Two states differing by imperceptible amounts may eventually evolve into two considerably different states ... If, then, there is any error whatever in observing the present state—and in any real system such errors seem inevitable—an acceptable prediction of an instantaneous state in the distant future may well be impossible ... In view of the inevitable inaccuracy and incompleteness of weather observations,*

> *precise very-long-range forecasting would seem to be nonexistent.*

Some ufologists have suggested a connection between Lorenz's theory and certain paranormal elements.

1963: Contactee luminary G. George Adamski boasted that he had received a "Golden Medal of Honor" from Pope John XXIII. Skeptics noted that the medal was actually a common tourist souvenir sold in tourist shops in Rome. Adamski claimed he met with the "Good Pope" at the request of the extraterrestrials, to offer him a liquid substance in order to save him from the gastric enteritis that he suffered from. Pope John XXIII died on June 3, 1963, of acute peritonitis. As an example of life after death, he is believed to have materialized in August 1963, during the Sheppton mining disaster.

1963: In an early suspected "crop circle" event, Patrick Moore described a crater in a potato field in Wiltshire, England. Moore believed it was caused by an unknown meteoric body, because, in nearby wheat fields, there were several circular and elliptical areas where the wheat had been flattened, referred to as "spiral flattening" by researchers.

October 17, 1963: The UN General Assembly, concerned about an arms control treaty governing outer space, unanimously adopted a resolution prohibiting the introduction of weapons of mass destruction in outer space. The legislation led to the Outer Space Treaty of 1967.

1963: Frank Scully published *In Armour Bright,* which included material about alleged flying saucer crashes and dead extraterrestrials. It was published by Chilton Books, with an introduction by talk show host Jack Parr.

January 1, 1964: *New York Times* science editor Walter Sullivan published *We Are Not Alone,* concluding:

> *The universe that lies about us, visible only in the privacy, the intimacy of night, is incomprehensibly vast. Yet the conclusion that life exists across this vastness seems inescapable. We cannot yet be sure whether or not it lies within reach, but in any case, we are a part of it all; we are not alone.*

Sullivan's book was awarded the 1965 International Nonfiction Prize. He also wrote Black Holes: The Edge of Space, The End of Time in 1979.

April 24, 1964: Police officer Lonnie Zamora observed a UFO and two humanoid beings on the outskirts of Socorro, New Mexico. He watched the UFO land and then take off. After the craft flew away, Zamora saw charred bushes and marks suggesting four landing pods. Zamora's report stated:

> *It looked at first like a car turned upside down. Thought some kids might have turned it over. Saw two people in white coveralls very close to the object. One of these persons seemed to turn and look straight at my car and seemed startled.*

The Lonnie Zamora UFO incident has been recognized by many researchers as a classic UFO case. Rupert Matthews, author of *Alien Encounters,* asserts that Zamora was an excellent witness who was highly respected by his colleagues:

> *Dr. Hynek of Project Blue Book was on the scene just two days later, and returned several times to check up on measurements, cross-examine Zamora and investigate further. His conclusion that a real, physical event of an unex-*

> *plained nature had taken place, lifted the reports of ufonauts out of the margins and into the mainstream.*

1964: The National UFO Conference was organized in Cleveland, Ohio. The co-founders were Clevelanders Rick Hilberg and Al Manak, and Al Greenfield of Atlanta, Georgia. Members of the Permanent Organizing Committee, well-known in ufological circles, have included Jim Moseley, Rick Hilberg, Karl Pflock, William Moore, Al Greenfield, Antonio Huneeus, Curt Sutherly, Timothy Green Beckley, Tom Benson, Matt Graeber, and Tim Brigham.

1964: The United States began its spacecraft exploration of Mars when it launched the *Mariner* 3 and 4 spacecraft. Although both missions launched successfully, the solar panels powering *Mariner* 3 did not deploy, and that mission ended up in solar orbit.

1964: Ufologist and abduction pioneer Budd Hopkins became interested in the UFO phenomenon after he and two others had a daylight UFO sighting near Truro, Massachusetts.

1964: *The Morning of the Magicians*, written by French journalists Louis Pauwels and Jacques Bergier and influenced by the research of Charles Fort, was released in the United States. The book was a cult classic with the French 1960–1970s New Age counterculture and pre-dated the ancient astronaut narrative of Erich von Däniken. Author Jason Colavito connected *The Morning of the Magicians* with the earlier writing of H. P. Lovecraft, in particular, *The Call of Cthulhu* (1928) and *At the Mountains of Madness* (1931).

January 1965: The Honorable John McCormack, Speaker of the House, addressed the UFO situation in *True Magazine:*

I feel that the Air Force has not been giving out all the available information on these Unidentified Flying Objects. You cannot disregard so many unimpeachable sources.

April 12, 1965: The California Institute of Technology announced evidence of extraterrestrial life when a radio survey detected emissions from a blazar-type quasar, designated CTA 102. Soviet theoretical radio astronomer Iosif S. Shklovsky believed that it could be a supercivilization seeking to draw attention to itself. Although it caused a global stir, CTA 102 turned out to be a false alarm after astronomers later identified the radio source as one of the many varieties of a quasar.

July 14, 1965: *Mariner 4* became the first successful flyby mission of Mars when it passed within 9,920 km of the Red Planet's surface and returned twenty-two close-up photos, revealing a heavily cratered surface. Instrumentation confirmed that Mars has an atmosphere composed primarily of carbon dioxide (CO_2). After its successful flyby of Mars, *Mariner 4* went into solar orbit.

July 15, 1965: The first image of Mars, a "color by numbers" representation of data, was sent to Earth by NASA's *Mariner 4* spacecraft and broadcast on television. In 1962, *Mariner 2* became the first spacecraft to visit another planet when it flew by Venus.

September 21, 1965: Rex Heflin, an Orange County highway department investigator, snapped four Polaroid photos of a metallic disc hovering above the Santa Ana Freeway. He took the photos near the Santa Ana Marine Corps Air Facility, estimating the craft to be about thirty feet in diameter and eight feet thick. Researchers considered the photograph to be genuine.

1965: Well-known dog trainer James W. Flynn of Fort Myers, Florida, was knocked unconscious for twenty-four hours by a hovering UFO while in the Everglades. The spacecraft blasted him with a "short beam of light" from the bottom of a bright yellow UFO that appeared to be around one hundred feet in diameter and thirty-five feet above the ground. Flynn lost vision in his right eye for several days. He complained of hearing loss and numbness in his arms.

September 3, 1965: Hitchhiker Norman J. Muscarello and Exeter, New Hampshire, police officers David Hunt and Eugene Bertrand claim to have separately witnessed a silent, round UFO, about ninety feet long. Bertrand described the UFO as:

> *This huge, dark object as big as a barn over there, with red flashing lights on it.*

The object was observed at an altitude of about one hundred feet and one hundred feet away from the observers. John G. Fuller published *Incident at Exeter* in 1978, to document the sightings. As recounted by Fuller, over sixty UFO sightings were witnessed by regular citizens and police officers in Exeter, over a period of several weeks in the fall of 1965. Fuller's book made the *New York Times* Best Seller list.

November 8, 1965: American columnist Dorothy Kilgallen (1913–1965), was found dead in her New York apartment, fully dressed and sitting upright in her bed. The police reported that she had died after taking a cocktail of alcohol and barbiturates. Ufologists quickly pointed out that one of her articles was about the 1946 Spitzbergen UFO crash—and that any further secrets about the Norwegian crash had died along with her.

December 9, 1965: A fireball streaked across northeastern North America with sightings reported as far apart as Indiana, New York, Virginia, and Ontario, and an acorn-shaped UFO crashed in the small western Pennsylvania town of Kecksburg in Westmoreland County. It became known as Pennsylvania's Roswell, and some believe that it was extraterrestrial.

But another theory attempting to explain the UFO was that Kosmos 96, a Soviet Union Venus space, probe crashed shortly after launch. Kosmos 96 was intended to make a flyby of Venus, and because it contained heat shield technology, it was able to survive reentry into the Earth's atmosphere and not burn up. The probe was able to maneuver while landing on Venus and may have attempted those movements over Kecksburg, giving the impression of a controlled UFO—or at least one theory has suggested.

December 15, 1965: Two US manned spacecraft, Gemini 6A and Gemini 7, maneuvered to within ten feet of each other while in orbit.

January 1, 1966: Daniel W. Fry published *The White Sands Incident*, purported as a "true" account of his ride in a flying saucer from the rocket-testing ground near White Sands, New Mexico, to New York. Fry said that the saucer made the trip in thirty minutes at eight thousand miles per hour. Fry, who claimed that he had earned a doctorate degree, failed a polygraph examination about his UFO encounter, while his 16 mm photos of the craft were called a hoax.

January 9, 1966: An Australian farmer from Tully, Queensland, witnessed a saucer-shaped craft rise forty feet from a swamp and then fly away. On investigating, he found a "saucer nest," a nearly circular area thirty-two feet long by twenty-five feet wide where the grass was flattened in clockwise curves, and the reeds uprooted from the mud. The Royal Australian Air Force concluded the "saucer nest" was most likely caused by natural causes, like a down draught, dust devil, or a waterspout.

February 8, 1966: *Look* magazine published former *Saturday Review* columnist John G. Fuller's article "Outer-Space Ghost Story" about the Exeter UFO sightings. It was reprinted in the May 1966 issue of *Reader's Digest*, and in the same year was expanded into Fuller's well-received book *Incident at Exeter*.

March 21, 1966: At least eighty-seven Hillsdale College co-eds and William Van Horn, the Hillsdale Michigan County Civil Defense director, witnessed a UFO that hovered over a swamp 1,500 yards from the New Women's Dormitory.

March 22, 1966: Frank Mannor, forty-seven, while sitting on his Dexter, Michigan, back porch with his nineteen-year-old son, sighted a UFO. The craft hovered just off the ground before rocketing off at their approach. The *CBS Evening News with Walter Cronkite* broadcast the photo on their March 24 program.

March 25, 1966: J. Allen Hynek, under extreme pressure from the Air Force and the "near hysteria" reports of unusual lights in separate areas of Michigan, held a press conference at the Detroit Press Club. In what would become one of his greatest missteps, Hynek claimed that the sighting was possibly the result of flares caused by the burning of gases bubbling up from the area's swamps—familiar to folklore as jack-o-lantern, fox fire, or will-o'-the-wisp:

> *It appears very likely, that the combination of conditions of this particular winter—an unusually mild one in this area—*

> *and the particular weather conditions were such as to produce this unusual and puzzling display of swamp gas.*

1966: Michigan congressman and House Minority Leader Gerald Ford disagreed with the "swamp gas" theory, demanding a congressional investigation. Hynek used the occasion to argue for an extensive, transparent study of UFOs—marking his first public break from the Air Force.

1966: Walter Cronkite anchored a 1966 CBS report titled, "UFO: Friend, Foe or Fantasy?" which featured J. Allen Hynek's Dexter, Michigan "swamp gas" theory.

March 23, 1966: Eddie Laxton, an electronics instructor at Sheppard Air Force Base, observed a silvery, fish-shaped UFO with a "normal-sized" occupant dressed in "ordinary military work clothes." The sighting occurred on Highway 70, near the Texas-Oklahoma state line. Laxton said that the inscription *"tl-41"* was etched on the craft.

April 22, 1966: Infamous debunker Philip J. Klass believed that many UFOs sighted near high-tension power lines may have been electricity-generated lightning. He published his theory in an article titled "Plasma Theory May Explain Many UFOs" in *Aviation Week & Space Technology.*

August 1966: UFO conspiracy theorist John Lear piloted a Learjet carrying the rock band The Byrds. The flight trip inspired them to write a song about the plane—"2-4-2 Foxtrot (The Learjet Song)," which sampled Lear's voice as he speaks over the radio.

September 1966: The folk-rock group The Byrds released "Mr. Spaceman" as the third single from their album *Fifth Dimension.* Upon its release, the music press coined the term "space rock" to describe it, although the song has also been cited by critics as one of the earliest examples of country rock. Written by Byrds member Jim McGuinn, the song was—along with "5D (Fifth Dimension)"—one of two science-fiction-themed songs on the *Fifth Dimension* album. Initially conceived as a "melodramatic screenplay," the song soon evolved into a whimsical meditation on the existence of extraterrestrial life.

1966: Carl Sagan, addressing the American Astronomical Society (AAS), postulated that the Earth may have been visited by various extraterrestrial beings, perhaps as many as ten thousand times. He said:

> *It is not out of the question that artifacts of these visits still exist, or even that some kind of base is maintained (possibly automatically) within the solar system to provide continuity for successive expeditions.*

The AAS was founded in 1899 and spearheaded by the efforts of astrophysicist George Ellery Hale (1868–1938), best known for his discovery of magnetic fields in sunspots, and a prominent figure in the construction of several world-leading telescopes.

1966: John G. Fuller published the best-selling book The Interrupted Journey: Two Lost Hours Aboard a UFO: The Abduction of Betty and Barney Hill, detailing the alleged abduction and missing time of Betty and Barney Hill on September 19, 1961—one of the first reports of its kind. Fuller also wrote the UFO book Incident at Exeter.

1966: Brinsley Le Poer Trench's *The Flying Saucer Story* provided an interesting description of "Angel Hair," which seemed to resemble the alien "goo" inspiring 1958's *The Blob*:

> *What is Angel Hair? What do we know about it? We know that this stringy fibrous substance has been frequently linked with UFOs, and that it generously drapes itself about the countryside, on telegraph wires, hedges, trees, fields, and all over the place. We know that it becomes gelatinous and evaporates shortly after touching the ground, and that when someone picks it up and it touches the skin, the substance disappears!*

Trench was the chairman of the International Committee of Sky Scouts.

March 24, 1966: The *CBS Evening News* with Walter Cronkite broadcast an exclusive photograph of a suspected UFO taken by police chief Robert R. Taylor on Frank Mannor's Dexter, Michigan, farm.

May 16, 1966: Hillsdale County civil defense director William Van Horn issued a twenty-four-page report challenging the Air Force conclusion that "swamp gas" caused the Hillsdale (Michigan) College UFO sightings in March 1966. Van Horn argued that conditions at the time were too windy for swamp gas to form and that a chemical analysis disclosed an abnormally high amount of radiation and the element boron in both the water and the soil.

July 26, 1966: The Lost Creek Saucer sighting, purported to be film footage of an actual flying saucer, was actually a hoax brainstormed by Gray Barker and James Moseley. As Mosely drove his vehicle, Barker filmed a ceramic "boogie" saucer that John Sheets dangled on a fishing pole in front of the car. Moseley played the film during his UFO lectures, while Barker sold copies of the footage via his mail-order film business. Moseley later wrote:

In addition to showing the film on New York–area television and at one of the Saucer News monthly lectures, I incorporated it and the story behind it into my American Program Bureau talk. I had decided I needed a "prop" for my lectures.

1966–1968: The US Air Force commissioned the Condon Committee, conducted by scientists at the University of Colorado, to study the UFO problem and make a report. The program, intended to be a lengthier scientific inquiry than Project Blue Book, was led by physicist Edward U. Condon. The results of the two-year, nine-hundred-and-sixty-five-page study, *Scientific Study of Unidentified Flying Objects*, (better known as the Condon report), recommended that the Air Force end Project Blue Book—which it did on December 17, 1969. Dr. Edward U. Condon, the project director, reported:

Our general conclusion is that nothing has come from the study of UFOs in the past twenty-one years that has added to scientific knowledge. Careful consideration of the record as it is available to us leads us to conclude that further extensive study of UFOs probably cannot be justified in the expectation that science will be advanced thereby.

The Condon report was immediately available to the public, and (like the Robertson Panel) concluded that UFOs posed no threat to the US and that most sightings could be easily explained. The government never allowed the Robertson Panel, the Condon Committee, or even Project Blue Book to review sensitive UFO sightings that may have contained classified information, as suggested by writer Becky Little:

If true, this would not necessarily mean the government had information about extraterrestrials it wanted to conceal. In

> *some cases, the government may have been trying to cover up its activities. Since Project Blue Book's end, the CIA has admitted that more* than half *of the UFO reports the government received in the late 1950s and into the '60s were related to secret U-2 and OXCART spy flights by the US government.*

Kevin D. Randle observed that the Condon report rejected the idea of UFOs:

> *The Condon Committee found that not only did UFOs not pose a threat to national security, one of the Air Force's requirements for the inquiry, but, more outrageously, nothing of scientific importance could be learned by studying them. Skeptics have cited this investigation as if it is the final word on UFOs since it was released.*

November 2, 1966: Woodrow Derenberger claimed that, while driving home from Parkersburg, West Virginia, he encountered a large gray UFO and a "spaceman" named "Indrid Cold." Fortean researcher John A. Keel later promoted the contactee story in *The Mothman Prophecies.*

November 22, 1966: Prof. Marsico Genovese, who teaches Greek in Tijuana, Mexico, claimed he was taken to Mars on a flying saucer. Genovese predicted that two Earth-based UFOs would come to Miami Beach—a flight that would take only about twenty minutes.

January 25, 1967: Betty Andreasson, of South Ashburnham, Massachusetts, after regressive hypnosis, claimed she was abducted by extraterrestrials who took her aboard their craft, where she was probed by needles. She said she was transported to another world, where she spoke with an entity identified as

Quazgaa and met a being whom she saw as God. In 1979, Raymond Fowler wrote the first of four books discussing what became known as the "Andreasson Affair."

January 30, 1967: In a typewritten statement, nine years after the Trindade Island UFO incident, Almiro Baraúna described a UFO sighting at a cove on Trindade Island, about eight hundred miles from the coast of Espirito Santo:

> *Instantly, everybody that was at the deck of the ship, around fifty people, started looking at a strange saucer-shaped silvery object which moved from the sea towards the island.* The *object did not emit any noise, it was luminous and shifted sometimes fast, then slow, moved up and down smoothly, and when speeding it left a phosphorescent white trail that six pictures, two of them were lost due to the pandemonium created at the deck, the other four pictures show the object at the horizon, on a reasonable sequence, approaching the island and at the hillside, and finally disappearing, moving away.*

Baraúna affirmed that almost all the ship crew saw the UFO, and they were unanimous in their reports to the Brazilian Navy Secret Service.

February 6, 1967: Zanesville, Ohio, barber and amateur astronomer Ralph Ditter reported to the media that he took Polaroid photographs of a UFO described as "an object from a solar system other than our own."

February 19, 1967: Dr. James E. McDonald, professor of meteorology at the University of Arizona, claimed that flying saucers "may very well be visitors from outer space—spying on the Earth." In an article published in the *Enquirer*, he said:

> *The US Air Force has been scandalously blinding the public as to what is really going on in the skies. The Air Force investigations have been absurd, superficial, and incompetent. There is strong evidence that these objects are extraterrestrial vehicles. And scientists all over the world had better stop accepting the ridiculous Air Force reports and start investigating the problem themselves at once. The matter is urgent.*

1967: After one year of intense investigation, John Keel abandoned the extraterrestrial visitation hypothesis, after:

> *... my own field investigations disclosed an astonishing overlap between psychic phenomena and UFOs ... The objects and apparitions do not necessarily originate on another planet and may not even exist as permanent constructions of matter. It is more likely that we see what we want to see and interpret such visions according to our contemporary beliefs.*

Keel concluded that the ultimate solution to the UFO problem would involve a complicated system of new physics related to theories of the space-time continuum. Similar conclusions about UFOs were also shared by J. Allen Hynek, Jacques Vallée, and Carl Jung.

May 20, 1967: While prospecting for quartz and silver, Stefan Michalak saw two cigar-shaped UFOs, about the size of a large private aircraft, in Manitoba's Falcon Lake Woods. The objects were glowing with a stunning purple illumination. Believing it was a secret US military craft, he began to investigate but was struck in the chest by a blast that pushed him backward and set his shirt and cap ablaze. He ripped away his burning garments and was treated at a hospital for chest and stomach burns that later turned into raised sores with a grid-like pattern. For weeks afterward, Michalak suffered from diarrhea, headaches, and blackouts. The unexplained Falcon Lake event is believed to be Canada's most famous UFO encounter.

June 27, 1967: Columnist Drew Pearson, in an article titled "Thant Views UFOs As Problem for UN," made a controversial remark about United Nation's Secretary General U Thant:

> *Interestingly, U Thant has confided to friends that he considers UFOs the most important problem facing the United Nations, next to the war in Vietnam.*

June 29, 1967: Gabriel Kozora, using a Polaroid camera, took photos of a flying saucer-shaped object near New Castle, Pennsylvania. Kozora said the UFO was about sixty feet long.

1967: The folk rock band The Byrds, considered the originators of "space rock," celebrated the original view that CTA 102 was a sign of extraterrestrial intelligence in their song "C.T.A.-102." The song was included in their album *Younger Than Yesterday*.

1967: Ted Bloecher observed in his *Report on the UFO Wave of 1947*, that infamous pilot Kenneth Arnold described the Mount Rainier airborne disks as flying:

> *In a diagonally stepped-down, echelon formation, the entire assemblage stretched out over a distance that he later calculated to be five miles.*
>
> *The objects seemed to be flying on a single, horizontal plane, but they also weaved from side to side, occasionally flipping and banking—darting around, like the tail of a Chinese kite. They moved in unison. They didn't seem to be piloted.*

1967: Brinsley Le Poer Trench founded Contact International, a worldwide UFO organization with members in thirty-seven different countries. He published a variety of books, including some that moved from ufology to the consideration of the ancient astronaut hypothesis. Trench was the former editor of *Flying Saucer Review*.

August 8, 1967: Three circular formations, suspected to be connected to UFOs, were found in a field in Duhamel, Alberta, Canada. The Defense investigators concluded that the circles were artificial but were unable to explain how they were made, or who might have made them.

September 7, 1967: One classic and well-documented case of cattle mutilation involved "Lady," a horse discovered dead and partially skinned at a ranch near Alamosa, Colorado—the animal's brain, lungs, heart, and thyroid appeared to have been surgically removed, as well as its spinal column. Witnesses also observed three orange rings flying in a triangular formation at incredible speeds, far beyond any military capabilities, leading to speculations that UFOs were involved. Lady's owner, Mrs. Berle Lewis, was convinced of what she had seen:

> *I really believe that a flying saucer had something to do with Lady's death.*

October 4, 1967: Residents of Shag Harbour, Nova Scotia, watched as a light dropped from the sky, hovered over the water, then disappeared into the harbor. Many eyewitnesses who saw the light assumed a plane had gone down, while others believed it was a UFO. No wreckage was ever found, and no planes were reported missing.

October 10, 1967: The Outer Space Treaty, also known as the Treaty on Principles Governing the Activities of States in the Exploration and Use of Outer Space, Including the Moon and Other Celestial Bodies, was one of the United Nations' most significant treaties of the twentieth century. The Outer Space Treaty established the framework of the present legal regime of outer space and celestial bodies and created the foundations of international regulation of space activities.

November 16, 1967: Field technician Robert Rinker, from the Chalk Mountain laboratory weather station, accidentally discovered a photograph of a UFO on a roll of film he had taken. Rinker sent it to the University of Colorado for examination.

December 3, 1967: Ashland, Nebraska, police officer Sgt. Herb Schirmer, after viewing an oval-shaped metallic UFO, agreed to undergo hypnotic regression. Dr. Leo Sprinkle believed that Schirmer was likely missing "time" or stored memories of the encounter. Marcus Lowe, writing for *UFO Insight,* observed:

> *Once inside the other-worldly craft, several beings would greet (Shirmer). They looked, however, exactly the same as any human being on Earth. Each adorned a uniform that itself had a strange "snake insignia" on it. Given the later, and to some outlandish, claims of reptilian aliens—who can shapeshift into a human form no less—this claim back in the late-1960s connecting a reptilian symbol to extra-terrestrial entities is perhaps of interest.*

Schirmer's account was investigated by the Condon Committee on December 11 and 12, 1967. In the summary of the report, the committee investigator noted the aspect of missing time:

> *Mr. Schirmer felt perhaps he had not been conscious during a period of approximately twenty minutes while he was observing the UFO.*

He said that the beings were about four and a half to five feet tall, wearing close-fitting uniforms with both boots and gloves. Although based on Venus or Saturn, they were from another galaxy and were attempting to keep the people of Earth from destroying the planet. Schirmer's credibility was questioned in the final Condon report, indicating that he was "a young man who has a number of possible psychological problems."

1967: John A. Keel popularized the term "Men in Black" after an article he wrote for the men's adventure magazine *Saga* was published. Keel's piece was titled "UFO Agents of Terror."

December 15, 1967: With an introduction by John Keel, Gray Barker published his book *They Knew Too Much About Flying Saucers,* in his fringe publishing house, Saucerian Press, recounting the Men in Black phenomenon. Barker described Albert K. Bender's MIB visitors as:

> *Three men in black suits with threatening expressions on their faces. Three men who walk in on you and make certain demands. Three men who know that you know what the saucers really are!*

December 15, 1967: The Silver Bridge, which connected Point Pleasant, West Virginia, with Gallipolis, Ohio, collapsed during rush hour, plunging thirty-one vehicles into the icy Ohio River. Forty-six people died in the disaster, documented in John A. Keel's *The Mothman Prophecies.* Some allege that a winged creature was seen on the bridge just before its collapse.

January 1, 1968: Howard V. Chambers, in his book *The Facts on the Flying Saucer Controversy,* pivoted off the Roswell and Kenneth Arnold sightings to conclude:

> *And even if every case previous to the 1947 classics is written off, still there is a startling statement which must stand. During the course of the past twenty years, there have been significant UFO sightings over every major European city, over every major American city, over major military installations throughout Asia and Europe, and over every major American strategic Air Command and nuclear installation.*

March 3, 1968: In what was called "a massive sighting," several witnesses described a cigar-shaped UFO with windows on the side. Officials quickly explained that the anomaly was the reentry and breakup of the Soviet Union's Zond IV spacecraft.

March 1968: The US Army accidentally killed more than four thousand five hundred sheep while clandestinely testing nerve agents. The sheep convulsed and collapsed near Utah's Dugway Proving Ground, a US Army facility established to test chemical and biological weapons. Government officials refused to acknowledge the secret biological weapons tests until 1998 and were suspected to be behind the 1970s cattle mutilations as well.

April 1, 1968: *Life* magazine published an eight-page article, "A Well-witnessed Invasion by Something," almost two weeks after the Dexter, Michigan, "swamp gas" incident. An angry Frank Mannor was quoted as saying:

> *I'm a simple fellow. But I seen what I seen and nobody's going to tell me different. This wasn't no old foxfire or hullabillusion. It was an object.*

April 26, 1968: The United States exploded a 1.3 megaton nuclear device called "Boxcar" beneath the Nevada desert.

1968: James Moseley sold *Saucer News* (which he had published since 1954) to Gray Barker. Moseley then published *Saucer Cruise, Saucer Booze,* and *Saucer Jews* (dedicated to his lifelong friend Gene Steinberg). He decided on *Saucer Smear,* which became the longest continuously published UFO journal in the world, "Dedicated to the highest principles of UFOlogical journalism."

June 1, 1968: Arthur C. Clarke, the author of the landmark *2001: A Space Odyssey*, addressed the UFO mystery in his book *The Promise of Space*:

> *Whether their explanation is psychological or physical, they constitute one of the most remarkable phenomena of modern times. Unfortunately, it has become extraordinarily difficult to arrive at the truth in this matter; seldom has any object been so investigated with fraud, hysteria, credulity, religious mania, incompetence, and most of the other unflattering human characteristics.*

Clarke felt there would be fewer UFO sightings around today "if reason, or even elementary common sense, were in better supply."

July 29, 1968: Physicist James E. McDonald addressed the United States Congress's UFO hearing, stating that:

> *UFOs are entirely real and we do not know what they are, because we have laughed them out of court. The possibility that these are extraterrestrial devices, that we are dealing with*

> *surveillance from some advanced technology, is a possibility I take very seriously.*

July 4, 1968: Oscar Iriart, fifteen, sighted a UFO and two humanoids in fields near his home in Sierra Chica, in southwestern Argentine. Iriart was riding horseback when he saw two humanoids slightly over six feet tall, with sparse hair and unblinking deep-set eyes. They wore red turtleneck sweaters, and Iriart could see through their transparent legs. One of the humanoids gave him a message that read:

> *You are going to see the world. F. Saucer.*

July 29, 1968: Physicist James E. McDonald submitted "Statement on UFOs" to the House Committee on Science and Astronautics, Symposium on Unidentified Flying Objects. In his statement, McDonald made the following remarks:

> *The scientific world at large is in for a shock when it becomes aware of the astonishing nature of the UFO phenomenon and its bewildering complexity. I make that terse comment well aware that it invites easy ridicule; but intellectual honesty demands that I make clear that my two years' study convinces me that in the UFO problem lie scientific and technological questions that will challenge the ability of the world's outstanding scientists to explain—as soon as they start examining the facts. ... the scientific community ... has been casually ignoring as nonsense a matter of extraordinary scientific importance.*

September 1968: Stanley Kubrick, who directed *2001: A Space Odyssey*, told *Playboy* magazine:

I will say that the God concept is at the heart of 2001—but not in any traditional, anthropomorphic image of God. I don't believe in any of Earth's monotheistic religions, but I do believe that one can construct an intriguing scientific definition of God.

1968: Paranormal investigators Timothy Green Beckley and Jim Moseley were involved in possibly the most legendary MIB photo ever taken. After receiving calls for help from Mary Robertson, the wife of prominent ufologist and secretary of the National UFO Conference Jack Robertson, Beckley and Moseley drove over to Jersey City, New Jersey, in an unannounced trip, attempting to catch the MIB, who had been harassing the Robertsons. As documented by Justin Bamforth:

Sure enough, as they approached the building, standing in the recessed part of the building was the black-clad individual, just as Mary had described. As Moseley drove down the street, Beckley took a pic of the MIB. He then took a second pic of the vehicle that the guy had presumably arrived in—a classic black Cadillac, to which most MIBs of that time had been seen driving.

The shadowy figure was dressed in classic MIB attire—a dark suit, black hat, and sunglasses—and just standing there, in a doorway, rigidly.

November 1968: The Condon Committee released their report on UFOs to the Air Force, who publicly released it in January 1969. The report concluded that little, if anything, had come from the study of UFOs in the past twenty-one years and that further extensive study of UFO sightings was unwarranted. It also recommended that the Air Force special unit Project Blue

Book be discontinued. It did not mention CIA participation in the Condon Committee's investigation but concluded:

> *On the basis of present knowledge, the least likely explanation of UFOs is the hypothesis of extraterrestrial visitations by intelligent beings.*

1968: Carl Sagan became a professor at Cornell University and also director of the Laboratory for Planetary Studies. He was well known as a pioneer in the field of exobiology—the study of the possibility of extraterrestrial life—and was among the first to determine that life could have existed on Mars.

January 6, 1969: Former US president Jimmy Carter, who was at the time governor of Georgia, saw a UFO while waiting to address the local Lions Club. Several people also witnessed the craft, Carter recalled:

> *I am convinced UFOs exist because I've seen one. It was a very peculiar aberration, but about twenty people saw it. It was the darnest thing I've ever seen. It was big; it was very bright; it changed colors; and it was about the size of the moon. We watched it for ten minutes, but none of us could figure out what it was.*

February 1, 1969: In an article published in the *Saturday Review*, Dr. Edward U. Condon, professor of physics and astrophysics, and the person in charge of the government's UFO investigation, strongly recommended that teachers should refrain from giving students credit for schoolwork based on their reading of UFO articles:

> *Teachers who find their students strongly motivated in this direction should attempt to channel their interests in the direction of serious study of astronomy and meteorology and in the direction of critical analysis of arguments for fantastic propositions that are being supported by appeals to fallacious reasoning or false data.*

April 26, 1969: American physicist Edward Condon, of the infamous Condon report, while addressing the American Philosophical Society, associated UFO studies with "pseudo-sciences" and urged that:

> *Publishers who publish or teachers who teach any of the pseudosciences as established truth should, on being found guilty, be publicly horsewhipped, and forever banned from further activity in these usually honorable professions.*

1969: Jacques Vallée concluded that the prevailing extraterrestrial hypothesis was limiting, as it ignored significant data. He began exploring the cohesions between UFOs, cults, religious movements, demons, angels, cryptid sightings, and psychic phenomena, detailed in his third book, *Passport to Magonia: From Folklore to Flying Saucers.*

May 12, 1969: Michael Crichton published his classic sci-fi, techno-thriller *The Andromeda Strain*, about the outbreak of a deadly extraterrestrial microorganism that appeared to have killed everyone in Piedmont, Arizona. *The Andromeda Strain* appeared on the *New York Times* Best Seller list and was made into a film in 1971.

May 31, 1969: MUFON, Inc., was initially established as the Midwest UFO Network after a schism with the defunct Aerial Phenomena Research Organization. MUFON was founded in Quincy, Illinois, by Allen R. Utke, Walter H. Andrus Jr., John F. Schuessler, and others. The organization is frequently criticized for focusing on pseudoscientific practices, conspiracy theories, and unscientific methodology.

July 20, 1969: Neil Armstrong, a thirty-eight-year-old civilian research pilot, became the first human to step on the moon. He and Buzz Aldrin walked around for three hours, performing experiments. They picked up bits of moon dirt and rocks. They left a US flag on the moon and a sign. On July 24, all three astronauts (Armstrong, Aldrin, and Michael Collins) returned to Earth safely. As Armstrong stepped off the ladder and planted his foot on the moon's powdery surface, he spoke his famous quote:

> *That's one small step for a man, one giant leap for mankind.*

1969: The location of Zeta 1 and Zeta 2 Reticuli, the home base of the extraterrestrials who allegedly abducted Barney and Betty Hill in 1961, was confirmed by astronomers eight years later. With the aid of hypnosis, Betty was able to draw a star map of the two (unknown at the time) planets she was shown aboard the UFO.

December 17, 1969: Air Force's Project Blue Book (1952–1969) officially discontinued research investigations. Critics have charged that the real goal of the combined Robertson Panel, the Condon Committee, and Project Blue Book was to assuage public concern about them rather than to explain them. Blue Book personnel concluded:

> *Little, if anything has come from the study of UFOs in the past twenty-one years that has added to scientific knowledge,*

> *and further extensive study of UFO sightings is not justified in the expectation science will be advanced.*

1969: The US Air Force abandoned its twenty-one-year-old UFO investigation. The programs included Project Sign (1947–1948), Project Grudge (1949–1951), and Project Blue Book (1952–1969). Of the 12,097 UFO sightings investigated, 90 percent were explained as planes, satellites, balloons, or various natural phenomena. Although many sightings are explainable as natural or artificial phenomena, the remaining ten percent would dominate the ongoing debate and prove to be the most puzzling.

Chapter 15

Cattle Mutilations: 1970s

THE DISCO ERA of the 1970s brought about Pascagoula, *The Mothman Prophecies*, *Future Shock*, *The Andromeda Strain*, *Pioneer 10*, and J. Allen Hynek addressing the United Nations.

1970: John A. Keel published *UFOs: Operation Trojan Horse: The Classic Breakthrough Study of UFOs*, explaining that UFOs are produced by "ultra-terrestrials"—beings with the ability to manipulate matter and human senses. As he revisits *The Mothman Prophecies* and the collapse of the Silver Bridge, Keel also speculates about God as "a pure energy state" and the Devil as a Lovecraftian creature that dwelt on earth "before man arrived or was created." According to the *Daily Telegraph:*

> *In his much-acclaimed second book,* UFOs: Operation Trojan Horse, *Keel suggested that many aspects of modern UFO reports, including humanoid encounters, often paralleled ancient folklore and religious visions, and directly linked UFOs with elemental phenomena.*

Keel believed that, in the past, the "ultra-terrestrials" manifested themselves as fairies, demons, and other anomalies, and concluded:

Our skies have been filled with "Trojan horses" throughout history, and like the original Trojan horse, they seem to conceal hostile intent.

1970: Futurist Alvin Toffler published the international bestseller *Future Shock*, warning of "information overload" and "too much change in too short a period of time." The book became a bestseller and has sold over six million copies. Toffler argued that society is undergoing a revolution from an industrial society to a "super-industrial society."

Toffler's "Death of Permanence" depicted a post-industrial society marked by a transient culture where everything ranging from goods to human relationships will be temporary. His later variations of the theme included The Third Wave and Powershift.

1970: George D. Fawcett, founder and vice-president of the Florida UFO Study Group, responded to news that the Air Force was dropping its twenty-one-year-old investigations of UFOs. He cited the closure of Project Sign (1948), Project Saucer (1949), Project Grudge (1950), and Project Blue Book (1969) and remarked:

> *The Air Force is trying to get rid of its number one public relations problem after making a mess of the flying saucer problem for over two decades. Global investigations are now needed with the United Nations to be utilized as a "world-wide UFO clearing house" for the global reports.*

March 1970: In his article titled "Flying Saucers: The Money Making Myth," Xavier F. Aguilar of Donora, Pennsylvania, leveled charges against an unnamed Kenneth Arnold in Ray Palmer's *Flying Saucer Magazine*. Aquilar charged:

> *I therefore surmise that this individual saw nothing, but instead, fabricated the whole incident as part of a long-range plan to become a celebrity and to produce a substantial amount of wealth from the subject of flying saucers ... the money-making myth.*

1970: West Virginia ufologist Gray Barker published *The Silver Bridge: The Classic Mothman Tale*. The book linked the collapse of the Silver Bridge in Point Pleasant, West Virginia, with the appearance of an alleged paranormal creature known as Mothman. Five years later, John Keel published his well-received *The Mothman Prophecies*.

February 9, 1971: The crew of Apollo 14 returned to Earth after man's third landing on the Moon.

March 12, 1971: The American science fiction thriller *The Andromeda Strain* is released. The film was based on the 1969 novel by Michael Crichton and directed by Robert Wise. In the film, an elite team of scientists discovers a microscopic alien organism that wiped out an entire town in Arizona. The greenish, throbbing life form is assigned the code name "Andromeda." Inhaled through the lungs, Andromeda kills biological life almost instantly via a blood clot in the brain. The film starred Arthur Hill, James Olsen, Kate Reid, and David Wayne. According to reviewer Chris Galloway:

> *Before he created* Westworld *and* Jurassic Park, *Michael Crichton first blurred the line between science fiction and*

science fact with his breakout success The Andromeda Strain. *Two years after the novel's publication, Robert Wise* (The Haunting) *directed the film adaptation, a nail-biting blend of clinically realized docudrama and astonishing sci-fi visuals that ushered in a new subgenre: the killer virus biological thriller.*

July 26, 1971: *Apollo 15*, the ninth crewed mission in the United States' Apollo program and the fourth to land on the Moon, was successfully launched but ended in controversy. In an ongoing attempt to unravel the origin of our solar system, *Apollo 15* astronauts (Commander David Scott, James Irwin, Alfred Worden) brought one hundred and seventy pounds of rocks and surface material from the Moon's Mare Imbrium, the largest impact crater on the near side of the Moon. Some of these rocks were dated as 3.9 billion years old.

Apollo 15 ended in negative publicity after it was revealed that the crew had carried unauthorized postal covers to the lunar surface, some later sold by a West German stamp dealer, Hermann Sieger. The astronauts were called before a closed session of a Senate committee, were reprimanded for poor judgment, and did not fly in space again.

1971: One of the best pictures of a possible flying saucer was taken by Sergio Loaiza flying over Costa Rica. Loaiza, an aerial photographer, was photographing the terrain as part of a study by the National Geographic Institute. His hundred-pound camera took dozens of photos at twenty-second intervals from ten thousand feet in the air. Experts have concluded that the image, between 120 and 220 feet wide, was not caused by trick photography or double exposure. In the recent *New Yorker* article "How the Pentagon Started Taking UFOs Seriously," *New York Times* reporter Leslie Kean said, "This photograph of a UFO may be the most extraordinary one ever released by government officials."

1971: In an article titled, "The Problem with Witness Reliability," the British UFO Research Association listed a number of variables that would prompt individuals to falsely claim to see a UFO. One of these, "notoriety," may comprise lonely and inadequate persons. BUFORA observed that "neurotic and egotistical individuals may be tempted to fabricate a colorful UFO in order to win a measure of public attention for themselves":

> *This is probably not often attempted, for in the main the UFO witness is more likely to attract kicks than kudos and find himself branded as a liar or a lunatic. Personal contact with a witness will usually reveal to an experienced interviewer whether this rather pathetic expedient to bask in the limelight has been resorted to.*

1971: Jim Moseley (1931–2012), best known as the editor of *Saucer Smear*, became permanent chairman of the National UFO Committee. Mosely addressed all the previous NUFOC conventions and was a frequent guest on countless radio and television shows. From 1966 to 1974 he was a popular speaker on the US college lecture circuit.

November 2, 1971: Woodrow Derenberger published *Visitors from Lanulos*, which claimed that, while driving home from Parkersburg, West Virginia, he encountered a "spaceman" named "Indrid Cold." Fortean researcher John A. Keel wrote the book's foreword and later promoted the story in *The Mothman Prophecies*. *Visitors from Lanulos* became among the rarest of "contactee" books. Before its reissue, only a half-dozen copies remained in the world's library system, with the rest trading for thousands of dollars each.

November 14, 1971: *Mariner 9* became the first spacecraft to enter into orbit around another planet—Mars, unfortunately during a planet-wide dust storm.

March 3, 1972: NASA's space probe *Pioneer 10* completed the first mission to Jupiter and was the first of five artificial objects to achieve the escape velocity needed to leave the solar system. Between July 15, 1972, and February 15, 1973, it became the first spacecraft to traverse the asteroid belt.

Pioneer 10 carried a plaque with diagrams of the solar system and its location relative to fourteen pulsars. The expectation is that intelligent beings would be able to interpret the diagram to determine the position of the Sun—and thus, Earth—at the time of launch relative to the pulsars.

The plaque was designed by Cornell astronomers Carl Sagan and Frank Drake to inform other intelligent lifeforms of our existence, appearance, and location in the universe. The aluminum plaque was constructed of a complex alloy that could have been produced only by relatively advanced technology. According to Elizabeth Howell:

> *The plaque depicts two nude figures—a man and a woman—along with diagrams of the solar system and the sun's position in space. It was intended to serve as a map to Earth for any extraterrestrials who might be curious about who made the spacecraft.*

Pioneer 10 was a spectacular success and notched a series of firsts unmatched by any robotic spacecraft. Initially designed for a twenty-one-month mission to fly by Jupiter, the probe lasted more than thirty years.

November 2, 1971: A sixteen-year-old boy from Delphos, Kansas, heard a rumbling sound in his backyard and spotted an illuminated object seventy-four feet away. Upon investigating the event, the boy and his parents discovered a glowing ring of soil and surrounding trees that glowed. Analysis of the soil proved that it had been baked as if by intense microwave radiation.

January 1, 1972: Christian author Clifford A. Wilson published *Crash Go the Chariots!: An alternative to Chariots of the Gods,* claiming that von Däniken grossly misrepresented data in his book that inspired a cult following.

1972: J. Allen Hynek published *The UFO Experience: A Scientific Inquiry*, which provided the best scientifically accepted definition of a UFO:

> *The reported perception of an object or light seen in the sky or upon the land the appearance, trajectory, and general dynamic and luminescent behavior of which do not suggest a logical, conventional explanation and which is not only mystifying to the original percipients but remains unidentified after close scrutiny of all available evidence by persons who are technically capable of making a common sense identification, if one is possible.*

The UFO Experience is most famous for introducing the "Close Encounter" classification: A Close Encounter of the First Kind entails the spotting of an unidentified aircraft; the Second Kind includes accompanying physical effects, like the sudden malfunctioning of equipment; and the Third Kind includes the sighting of life forms on or near the aircraft. Hynek's book inspired Stephen Spielberg's 1977 sci-fi epic *Close Encounters of the Third Kind.*

1972: Hynek also explained that a little-known group of scientists were all working toward a common goal:

> *There is truly a growing "Invisible College" of scientifically and technically trained persons who are intrigued by the UFO phenomenon and who, if provided with opportunity, time, and facilities, are most willing to undertake its serious study. They represent an international group ready to accept the challenge of the UFO.*

1972: Arthur C. Clarke won the Nebula Award of the Science Fiction Writers of America in 1972, 1974, and 1979.

January 5, 1973: NBC-TV aired *In Search of Ancient Astronauts*. In the following two days, Bantam Books sold more than a quarter of a million copies of Erich von Däniken's *Chariots of the Gods*.

March 19, 1973: Germany's *Der Spiegel* interviewed South American explorer Juan Moricz, who called Erich von Däniken a liar. In von Däniken's *The Gold of the Gods* (1972), the commercially successful hoaxer claimed that Moricz documented a gigantic tunnel system under Ecuador and Peru containing vast gold treasures.

1973: After reports of cattle mutilations began to proliferate, some suggested that UFOs or cults might be involved. Nevertheless, among ranchers, the most common theory was that the mutilations might be part of a secret government program testing biological weapons. Ranchers reported seeing unmarked helicopters near the crime scenes and even being chased away by the aircraft. In a few cases, incensed ranchers shot at government helicopters.

August 30, 1973: A bizarre wave of UFO sightings was reported in twenty-two different towns in Georgia, a pattern that would be repeated in other states and in a similar manner.

September 3, 1973: Chester Tatum, publisher of the *Sowega Free Press*, used a Polaroid camera to shoot a photo of an alleged UFO in the skies of South Georgia, seen by several witnesses.

1973: Astronomer Gerald Hawkins of Boston University, in his book *Beyond Stonehenge*, studied the lines of Nazca. Hawkins concluded that the solar, lunar, and stellar alignments were no better than what would be expedited by chance, refuting the theory that the lines represented a gigantic astronomical calendar.

1973: Under hypnosis, Texan Judy Doraty recalled being abducted and witness to the mutilation of a cow. Linda Moulton Howe filmed the hypnosis session that suggested the presence of extraterrestrial mutilators. Howe's 1989 book was titled *An Alien Harvest: Further Evidence Linking Animal Mutilations and Human Abductions to Alien Life Forms*.

October 11, 1973: Calvin Parker, nineteen, and Charles Hickson, forty-seven, while fishing in Pascagoula, Mississippi, claimed that they were abducted by three five-foot-tall, gray-skinned creatures and medically examined. According to writer Alexandra Kennan, Parker recalled that, without saying a word, the creature:

> *... put its left hand on his jaw, and opened his mouth. "That's when she took her right hand and started running it down my throat, and I started gagging. She had scratched it up real bad, and it was bleedin', it was a darn mess." It pulled its hand back out; Parker had the impression that it didn't want to hurt him anymore. Then, it made a groan from deep within its*

> *throat. "I don't know if you ever heard a alligator's matin' call, where they vibrate the whole air around you, but that's how it sounded."*

October 18, 1973: Edward Deutsch claimed that his car was buzzed and turned around by a UFO described as "being round with flashing lights and about as big as a large tractor-trailer tire." Deutsch, forty-seven, from Catawissa, Pennsylvania, said the craft hovered over his car at a height of about one hundred feet:

> *It was right above the car, going round and round, and I could hear a humming sound. When I got to the top of the mountain, it lit up the whole car and before I knew what happened, the car was turned around and I was headed back home.*

October 25, 1973: Researcher Stan Gordon documented an early report of a simultaneous UFO and Bigfoot sighting. Approximately fifteen individuals witnessed a large red ball descend near a farm in Uniontown, Pennsylvania. From the illumination of the craft, they were able to see two tall, apelike creatures with glowing eyes. The creatures were heard making crying sounds, and the air was filled with the smell of "burning rubber." The sighting took place in Chestnut Ridge, an area of numerous paranormal incidents.

1973: Carl Sagan, in *The Cosmic Connection: An Extraterrestrial Perspective*, disagreed with what he called the "chauvinism" theory, suggesting that extraterrestrials would resemble humans:

> *The most likely circumstance is that extraterrestrial beings will look nothing like any organisms or machine familiar to us.*

Discover Magazine placed the book as number thirteen in a list of the "25 Greatest Science Books of All Time."

November 3, 1973: *Mariner 10* was launched and was the first probe sent to study Mercury. Using a "gravitational sling-shot" technique, *Mercury 10* used the gravity of Venus to reach Mercury. *Mercury 10*'s closest flyby of Venus was on February 5, 1974, and Mercury on March 16, 1975. *Mariner 10* returned over 2,700 pictures during its three Mercury flybys that covered nearly half of the planet's surface, filled with Moon-like craters.

December 3, 1973: *Pioneer 10* reached its closest approach to Jupiter, at a range of 132,252 kilometers (82,178 mi). Onboard instruments were used to study the asteroid belt, Jupiter's environment, the solar wind, and cosmic rays.

1973: MUFON, Inc., changed its name to the Mutual UFO Network after its expansion to other states and countries.

1973: J. Allen Hynek formed the Center for UFO Studies (CUFOS) to further legitimize the field of "ufology." CUFOS was the first research facility established by a scientist dedicated to the collection, investigation, and analysis of UFO reports. The organization enjoyed some successes in its early years, leading investigations of reported sightings while fostering working relationships with law enforcement agencies.

December 22, 1973: The *Kansas City Times,* investigating an outbreak of cattle mutilations, reported:

> *Two points confounding investigators have been the absence of blood and footprints. Even on warm days, with the carcass freshly killed, there has been no bleeding on or around the animal. Some believe the cattle were drained of blood. No human tracks have been detected near each mutilation, even in fresh snow.*

January 1, 1974: Jack Stoneley, with A. T. Lawron, published Is Anyone Out There?—posing the perpetual question about extraterrestrial life and concern about man's rapid advances in technology:

> *With each recent decade his technological evolution has accelerated at such an explosive rate that even the most conservative observers accept that the next one hundred years —a mere moment in the galactic time scale—must produce social and scientific innovations beyond our wildest dreams— or, perhaps, nightmares.*

February 1974: Josef F. Blumrich published *The Spaceships of Ezekiel*, depicting several encounters with UFOs allegedly observed by the prophet Ezekiel. Blumrich was chief of NASA's systems layout branch at the Marshall Space Flight Center's program development office. Other researchers have pointed out that although he wrote about Ezekiel, Blumrich did not know Hebrew and was not a biblical scholar. He had no academic background in theology, religion, history, or archaeology.

August 2, 1974: At the thirty-second World Science Fiction Convention in Washington, DC, Arthur C. Clarke, best known for the novel and movie 2001: *A Space Odyssey*, won the Hugo Award for his novel *Rendezvous with Rama*.

1974: Florida ufologist Robert Spencer Carr charged that the Air Force was hiding "two flying saucers of unknown origin" inside Wright-Patterson's Hangar 18. Twelve alien beings had autopsies performed on them, according to a high-ranking military source. Carr's disclosure was widely reported in the media, including the *Tampa Tribune*.

August 1974: In a Playboy interview, Erich von Däniken admitted that his ancient astronaut "theory" was not original and that at least three other researchers, Louis Pauwels, Jacques Bergier, and Donald Keyhoe, had earlier reached the same erroneous conclusions.

1974: A remarkable number of UFOs, Bigfoot sightings, and animal mutilations were centered in Pennsylvania. Filmmaker Linda Moulton Howe observed:

> *Everything seemed concentrated in Pennsylvania, a huge focus for this odd activity. Why, I don't know.*

September 1974: In her Redbook article titled "UFOs: Visitors from Outer Space," American cultural anthropologist Margaret Mead (1901–1978) argued that the UFO phenomena represented a tangible entity, not some abstract construct demanding our unwavering faith. Dismissing the question, "Do you believe in UFOs?" she wrote:

> *Belief has to do with matters of faith. It has nothing to do with the kind of knowledge that is based on scientific inquiry. We should not bracket UFOs with angels and archangels, devils, and demons. But this is just what we are doing when we ask whether people "believe" in UFOs—as if their existence were an article of faith. Do people believe in the sun or the moon or the changing seasons or the chairs they are sitting on?*

Mead argued that most people continue to frame the UFO question around their personal belief system rather than looking to the scientific community for answers to this phenomenon.

1974: The National UFO Reporting Center was founded by noted UFO investigator Robert J. Gribble and is independent of all other UFO-related organizations. Their website has operated continuously since 1994. The center's primary function over the past five decades has been to:

> *Receive, record, and to the greatest degree possible, corroborate and document reports from individuals who have been witness to unusual, possibly UFO-related events.*

The center has processed over 170,000 reports and makes available to the public all of its data. It has distributed information to thousands of individuals. It is a nonprofit Washington State corporation.

October 10, 1974: Dr. Robert Spencer Carr, a former government researcher, told reporters at a press conference that two crashed UFOs are being stored in a secure area of Wright-Patterson Air Force Base, Dayton, Ohio. Twelve blue humanoids, who supposedly died of decompression, after their crafts landed in the Mojave Desert in the early 1950s, are also stored at the facility.

Carr said that the CIA withheld information about the crash from the public for fear of the psychological effect on the people. Carr said that in 1952, the government paid an unidentified company $50,000 to conduct a psychological-sociological study, which determined that the public could not handle the shock of such a report, and as a result, it has been considered "top secret" until now.

October 25, 1974. Carl Higdon, forty-one, went hunting in the Medicine Bow National Forest in Wyoming's Carbon County, where he met an alien called "Ausso," described as a humanoid figure in a skin-tight black one-piece outfit that looked "like straw was growing out of his head."

Ausso said he had come to Earth also to hunt deer. Higdon was drugged with four pills and found himself in a transparent cubicle with his arms and legs tied with ribbon-like material. His abduction was documented in *Alien Abduction of The Wyoming Hunter: First person story of Carl Higdon,* written by Higdon's wife, Margery.

November 12, 1974: Over forty-three hours, thousands of Carbondale, Pennsylvania, residents viewed a suspected UFO emitting light at the bottom of a silt pond. Officials later determined that the incident was a hoax. The object turned out to be a railroad trainman's lantern. A local newspaper article revealed:

> *The incident was marked with so much realism that when a Carbondale policeman arrived at the scene, the lantern was floating on the surface of the pond, and at least four shots were fired at the floating object on Saturday night.*

November 16, 1974: The world's largest radio telescope was constructed in Arecibo, Puerto Rico. The 450,000-watt transmitter began sending a deliberate signal, the most powerful radio signal ever sent from Earth. Cornell University astrobiologist Frank Donald designed and implemented the Arecibo message (with 1,679 bits of data), meant to demonstrate human technological achievement. It was broadcast into space to the globular cluster, Messier 13, about 25,000 light-years from Earth, but scientists believe it may take 24,000 years for the impulses to be received.

December 24, 1974: The *National Enquirer* carried the front-page headline "1st Evidence That Beings from Outer Space Have Visited Us." The misguided article said that Swiss electronics engineer Heinrich Gosswiler recognized certain Santa Barbara, California, rock paintings as a "complex scientific diagram." The Quechan Indians of southern California explained, however, that the paintings communicated messages between one hunting party to another and not from man to outer space.

December 14, 1974: Reviewing the NBC one-hour special *UFO's: Do You Believe?,* Associated Press television writer Jay Sharbutt described the show as:

> *A tedious rehash of those UFO stories you tend to find in yellowing magazines in barbershops where one can still get a haircut for two bucks or less.*

January 1, 1975: In their book *UFOs: What on earth Is happening? The Coming Invasion,* theologists John Weldon and Zolo Levitt boldly assert:

> *It is high time that we all realize that there exists a spiritual world. This world, not perceptible by our senses moves along parallel to our earthly existence and affects us profoundly all the time. This parallel world, as we are styling it, is a very full world, occupied by a variety of beings and entities rather like the world we can see.*

The authors believe that UFOs are extra-dimensional beings that are beyond our current scientific understanding but can be explained through biblical narratives of fallen angels and demons.

January 1, 1975: Forty-eight years ago, writing the foreword to *The New UFO Sightings*, researcher Brad Steiger summed up the UFO narrative in a comprehensive and profound paragraph, going far beyond the "mechanical spaceships from other planets" theory:

> *Others, equally strong in their convictions, believe that the UFOs are from other dimensions and that the spaceships are not mechanical, but pure energy. Some contend further that the UFOs are not inhabited by alien beings but that the UFOs are themselves the beings. Some look upon the UFO occupants as space brothers keeping an eye on things here on troubled earth.*

UFO theories remain diverse and prolific; however Steiger's conclusion, already visited by Charles Fort, is the most troubling, theorizing that:

> *Perhaps we are the property of the space people and that we are being shepherded, just as farmers keep cattle, sheep, and pigs—until they are ready for market!*

January 1, 1975: In *The New UFO Sightings*, authors Glenn Mc Wane and David Graham ask that, if UFOs are not physical phenomena, could they be mental apparitions or hallucinations? The authors admit that most ufologists react violently to such suggestions:

> *There is no conclusive proof that the UFO is always physical phenomena. It could on occasion be another manifestation of psychological forces, or even spiritual forces. Some photographs of UFOs appear to indicate that UFOs may not be solid at all and may be an unknown form of energy.*

1975: The Robertson report—which the CIA didn't release publicly until 1975—suggests "mass hysteria" over UFOs could lead to "greater vulnerability to possible enemy psychological warfare."

March 28, 1975: Arizona senator Barry Goldwater, the chairman of the US government's Senate Intelligence Committee, supposedly wrote to UFO researcher Shlomo Arnon:

> *The subject of UFOs is one that has interested me for some long time. About ten or twelve years ago I made an effort to find out what was in the building at Wright-Patterson Air Force Base where the information is stored that has been collected by the Air Force, and I was understandably denied this request. It is still classified above Top Secret.*

April–October 1975: Nearly two hundred cases of cattle mutilation were reported by Denver, Colorado's local CBS affiliate KMGH-TV. The bizarre story was voted by the Colorado Associated Press as the state's number one story. Colorado's then-senator Floyd Haskell asked the FBI to get involved in what many believed to be a paranormal/UFO event.

1975: Fortean researcher John A. Keel published his book *The Mothman Prophecies: A True Story*, which investigated UFO sightings and paranormal events surrounding the West Virginia Silver Bridge collapse. Like Edgar Rice Burrows marketing his Tarzan "franchise," Keel worked hard to further promote his book. He had it republished in 1991 and turned into a motion picture in 2002, celebrated by review sites such as Bookotron.com:

> *He's Philip K. Dick in a pork-pie hat, chasing down winged creatures, men in black, prophetic dreams, and problematic phones. Keel's book is based on actual events, events that were documented by others and experienced by many. But what John Keel* brings to the party *is something unique: his "Our Haunted Planet" hypothesis, and something not so unique, but something that's a lot of help when you're describing reality—a sense of humor. He's also a skilled story-teller, not a cut-and-dried documentarian.*

June 7, 1975: William Spaulding, head of Ground Saucer Watch (GSW), convinced that the CIA was withholding major files on UFOs, wrote to the agency requesting a copy of the Robertson Panel report and all records relating to UFOs.

1975: Colorado Sheriff George A. Yarnell of Elbert County, a rural area south of Denver, questioned about the widespread cattle mutilations, told the *New York Times*:

> *I've been around cattle all my life and I can sure tell whether it's been done by coyote or a sharp instrument.*

1975: Carl Sagan won a Pulitzer Prize for his book *The Dragons of Eden*. He reached international acclaim after his television series *Cosmos*, one of the most watched shows in public television history, was seen by more than five hundred million people in sixty different countries.

1975: French author and ancient astronaut advocate Jean Sendy published The Moon: Outpost of the Gods: Evidence of

Ancient Astronaut Voyages to Our Satellite (New York: Berkley Publishing) claiming that the interstellar visitors who founded Earth's civilizations also set up bases on the Moon. Sendy said:

> *If exploration of the moon reveals no trace of the earlier presence of astronauts, the hypothesis of this book will be disproved.*

Ignoring Project Apollo, which landed the first humans on the Moon on July 20, 1969, Sendy further insisted that the synchronous rotation of the Moon was created by ancient astronauts.

1975: Jacques Vallée published the original version of The Invisible College: What a Group of Scientists Has Discovered About UFO Influences on the Human Race. Vallée and J. Allen Hynek referred to themselves as the "Invisible College," a group of scientists, known to each other, who believed that their UFO investigations were either extraterrestrial or interdimensional. The "Invisible College" is an old idea that comes from the seventeenth-century British philosopher Francis Bacon and was meant to describe the work of scientists that challenged contemporary beliefs of the church. Vallée's book was the result of international researchers actively investigating UFO cases and exchanging data, as he explained:

> *I believe that a powerful force has influenced the human race in the past and is again influencing it now. Does this force represent alien intervention, or does it originate entirely within human consciousness? This is the question that forms the basis of the work of the Invisible College of UFO researchers.*

August 4, 1975: Dr. Thor Heyerdahl, the ethnologist and experimental archeologist, invited to respond to Erich von Däniken's criticism about his Easter Island findings, submitted the following to author Ronald Story for his book *The Space Gods Revealed*:

> *We the scientists are to be blamed for not speaking up, the uninformed laymen are to be blamed for not using their own common sense, and commercial writers like von Däniken are to be blamed for not telling their readers that they are selling them entertaining fiction and not popular-science books.*

August 1975: Colorado senator Floyd K. Haskell addressed the FBI, on over one hundred and thirty reports of cattle mutilations throughout Colorado and other western states:

> *The Colorado Bureau of Investigation has verified that the incidents have occurred for the last two years in nine states. The ranchers and rural residents of Colorado are concerned and frightened by these incidents. The bizarre mutilations are frightening in themselves: in virtually all the cases, the left ear, rectum and sex organ of each animal have been cut away and the blood drained from the carcass, but with no traces of blood left on the ground and no footprints.*

October 20, 1975: *The UFO Incident* premiered on American television screens, recounting the legendary abductions of Betty and Barney Hill on September 19, 1961. The low-budget special, based on John G. Fuller's 1966 book, *The Interrupted Journey*, was timely, as about a dozen well-attested abduction cases had already been investigated by ufologists. The program starred James Earl Jones and Estelle Parsons and was directed by Richard A. Colla—and pre-dated Stephen Spielberg's multimillion-dollar *Close Encounters of the Third Kind* by several years.

November 5, 1975: After a group of loggers witnessed a bright crimson light in Arizona's White Mountains, Travis Walton went out for a closer look. Pushed to the ground by a blue-green energy beam, his co-workers escaped in terror, informing the police that Walton had been abducted by a flying saucer. For the next five days, Walton remained missing, and the loggers were accused of murder. When he was found alive, Walton was unable to account for the missing time. The science fiction film *Fire in the Sky* is based on Walton's ordeal.

December 15, 1975: J. Allan Hynek and Jacques Vallée co-authored *The Edge of Reality: A Progress Report on Unidentified Flying Objects*, asserting that UFOs represent an unknown but real phenomenon, and a domain of nature as yet unexplored. On that note, Vallée observed that both scientists and witnesses to UFOs are reluctant to come forward:

> *Because their life is going to change. There are cases where their house is broken into. People throw stones at their kids. There are family crises—divorce and so on ... You become the person who has seen something that other people have not seen. And there is a lot of suspicion attached to that.*

January 1, 1976: Ronald Story published *The Space-Gods Revealed: A Close Look at the Theories of Erich von Däniken*. Reviewed in *Time* magazine, R. Z. Sheppard described Story's book as "a coherent and much-needed refutation of von Däniken's theories." Sadly, Story's science-based book, with a foreword by Carl Sagan, was unable to attract the masses who salivated at Erich von Däniken's plagiarized and pseudoscientific babble.

January 1, 1976: Ancient astronaut theorist Zecharia Sitchin, among the first to suggest that extraterrestrials played a significant role in ancient human history, published *The 12th Planet*, aggressively advertised as:

> *The product of more than thirty years of meticulous research treats as fact, not myth, the tales of Creation, the Deluge, the Tower of Babel, and the Nefilim who married the daughters of man.*

Although rejected by scientists and historians who dismiss them as pseudoscience and pseudohistory, Sitchin's books have sold millions of copies and have been translated into over twenty-five languages.

April 30, 1976: Temple University's Dr. David M. Jacobs, author of *The UFO Controversy in America* (1975), presented a paper at the Chicago CUFOS conference, defending the extraterrestrial hypothesis:

> *I have seen no substantial evidence to suggest that the old-fashioned extraterrestrial hypothesis is untenable. It still seems to explain the vast majority of data we have encountered. The new theories about the origins, purposes, and psychic components of UFOs have tended to place the extraterrestrial theory in disfavor without really offering a shred of evidence to disprove or discount it. I believe that it would be a fundamental mistake to abandon the nuts and bolts hypothesis without first proving it to be unfeasible.*

1976: Former US Navy midshipman Bill Kaysing self-published the book *We Never Went to the Moon: America's Thirty Billion Dollar Swindle*. Kaysing proposed the conspiracy theory that the six Apollo moon landings, which took place between 1969 and 1972, were hoaxes, and that the photographs released by NASA documenting them were faked.

April 3, 1976: Luis Barroso Fernandez claimed that he had been attacked and abducted at Quixada, Brazil. Afterward, he reported diminished mental health when a UFO hit him with a powerful, blinding light beam. Much of the account comes from Luis's son, Francisco Leonardo Barroso, who said that his father was left with reddened skin and diminished mental cognition. The Barroso case is a classic study of the alarming aftereffects of UFO close encounters and became the basis for the film *Area Q*. Francisco Leonardo Barroso told reporters:

> *I have no ill will against the extraterrestrials, as there were other similar cases to that of my father's. It was an accident. It could happen to me, to you, or to anyone else. My father was among the first to undergo such an experience. To see that story in the film is admirable, as he really went down in history.*

July 20, 1976: The anticipated *Viking* landing on Mars was met with a fever pitch of excitement, with some predicting the possibility of actually finding extraterrestrial life. Among those was Carl Sagan, who looked forward to encountering, via *Viking*, visible, "perhaps floating creatures."

Viking I touched down symbolically on the seventh anniversary of the Apollo 11 Moon landing. *Viking I* was the first successful Mars lander in history. It took several spectacular images of Mars's Olympus Mons, one of the largest volcanoes in the solar system and about two and a half times larger than Mount Everest.

1976: Ancient astronaut theorist Zecharia Sitchin published *The 12th Planet* (Ishi Press, 1976). The introduction to his "groundbreaking, best-selling series—millions of copies sold worldwide," explained the premise of Sitchin's book:

> *By weaving together the biblical narrative with Sumerian and Babylonian clay-tablet texts, it challenges the established notions of the origins of Earth and mankind and offers a compelling alternative history and prehistory of both.*

August 7, 1976: *Viking* 2 entered into Mars orbit, and the lander set down in the Utopia Planitia region of Mars at 47.97°N, 134.26°E, on September 3, 1976. *Viking* 2 was launched on September 9, 1975.

1976: Author Ronald Story founded the original UFO Encyclopedia Project, which resulted in the writing of his classic book *Encyclopedia of UFOs* (1980). Story has worked as a consultant on the television series *Ancient Aliens*.

December 13, 1976: In a keynote speech at the Radio Television News Directors Association convention in Bal Harbour, Florida, Walter Cronkite denounced a *National Enquirer* article titled "Top TV Newscaster Walter Cronkite: I'm Convinced UFOs Exist." The article included "a fascinating UFO sighting that Cronkite and several network executives supposedly made." According to an article in the Milwaukee *Journal*, Cronkite called it "a total lie from beginning to end."

January 1, 1977: In *UFO: Flying Saucers Over Britain,* science journalist Robert Chapman revealed what he perceived to be the secret of George Adamski's popularity:

> *Adamski was so damnable normal and this was the overall impression I carried away. He believed he had made contact with a man from Venus, and he did not see why anyone should disbelieve him. I told myself that if he was deluded he was the most lucid and intelligent man I had met.*

1977: Alien abduction researcher John Edward Mack became the head of Psychiatry at Harvard Medical School. He won the Pulitzer Prize for his book *A Prince of Our Disorder*, his biographical study of the life of British officer T. E. Lawrence that same year.

1977: J. Allen Hynek inspired Stephen Spielberg's sci-fi epic *Close Encounters of the Third Kind*, serving as advisor. His "Close Encounter" classification of sightings. Hynek even made a brief cameo in the film as a scientist.

The title is derived from ufologist J. Allen Hynek's classification of close encounters with extraterrestrials, in which the third kind denotes human observations of extraterrestrials or "animate beings."It was a critical and financial success, eventually grossing over $300 million worldwide. It received numerous awards and nominations at the 50th Academy Awards, the 32nd British Academy Film Awards, the 35th Golden Globe Awards, and the 5th Saturn Awards, and has been widely acclaimed by the American Film Institute.

February 18, 1977: The space shuttle *Enterprise*, sitting atop a Boeing 747, went on its maiden flight over the Mojave Desert.

1977: While working on Project Blue Book, J. Allen Hynek discovered how normal the people who reported seeing UFOs tended to be. He recalled in his book *The Hynek UFO Report*:

> *The witnesses I interviewed could have been lying, could have been insane, or could have been hallucinating collectively—but I do not think so.*
>
> *Their standing in the community, their lack of motive for the perpetration of a hoax, their own puzzlement at the turn of events they believe they witnessed, and often their great reluctance to speak of the experience—all lend a subjective reality to their UFO experience.*

1977: In another example of ancient alien psychobabble, writer Alex Saunders introduced his article "A Super Technological World," published in Ray Palmer's *Search Magazine*, with a personal insight:

Several of my articles that have appeared in Palmer Publications have discussed something of tremendous interest to me. Namely, the possible existence in outer space of supertechnological races. And when I say "super," I mean just that. Alien races that, having evolved eons before Man, are ahead of him in science and technology by, not thousands or millions of years, but literally Billions!

January 1, 1978: Travis Walton publishes *The Walton Experience* (Berkley) recollecting his alleged alien abduction and five harrowing days of his disappearance in Arizona's White Mountains. His story was later made into the 1993 motion picture *Fire in the Sky*. Walton graphically described his horrible abduction and ordeal:

> *I looked at the vague but reassuring forms of the doctors around me. Abruptly my vision cleared. The sudden horror of what I saw rocked me as I realized I was definitely not in a hospital. I was looking square into the face of a horrible crea-*

> *ture ... with huge, luminous brown eyes the size of quarters! I looked frantically around me. There were three of them! Hysteria overcame me instantly.*

January 16, 1978: NASA named thirty-five candidates to fly on the space shuttle, including Sally K. Ride, who became America's first woman in space, and Guion S. Bluford Jr., America's first black astronaut in space.

January 18, 1978: A military police officer shot an extraterrestrial being in the Pine Barrens surrounding New Jersey's Fort Dix, according to the book *Strange Craft: The True Story of an Air Force Intelligence Officer's Life with UFOs* (Bayshore, 1978). According to the account:

> *In the freezingwinter darkness of that day in January 1978, a bipedal creature, described as about four feet in height and grayish-brown in color, with a "fat head, long arms and slender body," was shot to death with five rounds fired from a service member's .45-caliber (military issue M1911A1) handgun.*

A cleanup crew from Wright-Patterson Air Force Base allegedly flew in to retrieve the body.

1978: Project Stargate began to investigate if psychics could perform "remote viewing" and "see" events from great distances. This secret program, which involved the military and the paranormal, was later declassified.

1978: Brad Steiger published *Alien Meetings* (Ace Books) documenting a muddle of convoluted paranormal themes, including numerous extraterrestrial encounters, but with scant reference data.

June 2, 1978: The British-produced film *Capricorn One* was released. The science-fiction thriller is about a reporter discovering that a supposed Mars landing has been faked, revealing a conspiracy involving governmental and corporate interests. It was written and directed by Peter Hyams and stared Elliott Gould, James Brolin, Sam Waterston, Hal Holbrook, and O. J. Simpson. Jack Kroll, writing for *Newsweek*, said:

> Capricorn One *is just too dumb to be fun. We know too much about space shots, astronauts, and moonwalks to swallow the dopey implausibility with which writer-director Peter Hyams tells his story of how sinister forces fake the first manned landing on Mars ... But Brolin, Waterston, and Simpson are just jump-suited dummies. O.J. displays more style, wit, and grace in a one-minute Hertz commercial than he's allowed to show in this entire flick.*

July 25, 1978: The *Viking* 2 orbiter ran out of attitude-control gas and was deactivated on August 7, 1980. The *Viking 1* orbiter was utilized as a communication relay to shut the lander down.

1978: French UFO researcher Michel Monnerie published *And what if UFO's don't exist?* suggesting that the study of UFOs should be conducted by psychologists and sociologists rather than physicists and astronomers. Monnerie is regarded as a pioneer of the psychosocial hypothesis (PSH), intimating that many UFO experiences are triggered by an external stimulus producing projections of mental images and materials that the contactee holds significant.

1978: Ufologist Stanton T. Friedman interviewed Major Jesse Marcel, who was involved with the original 1947 Roswell incident. Marcel believed the military had covered up the recovery of an alien spacecraft, and over the years, additional witnesses added to the story.

November 27, 1978: J. Allen Hynek delivered a presentation on UFOs to the United Nations:

> *In conclusion, Mr. Chairman, let me once again clearly state that it is my considered opinion, as a scientist who has devoted may years to its study, that the UFO phenomenon is real and not the creation of disturbed minds, and that it has both grave and important implications for science and for the political and social well-being of the peoples of this earth. It is therefore, in my opinion, worthy of cognizance by the United Nations Organization, and worthy of study as a phenomenon. I distinguish sharply here, as do my colleagues, between any given theory of the UFO such as, for example, that they originate in some specific solar system, and the phenomenon itself, a situation which would put the cart before the horse.*

October 21, 1978: Frederick Valentich, while embarking on a solo nighttime flight in a Cessna 182, from Melbourne, Australia, to King's Island, witnessed a UFO, with four bright lights, passing about one thousand feet above him. Valentich radioed Melbourne Flight Control:

> *It seems to be playing some game with me. It's not an aircraft. It's flying past. It has a long shape. Cannot identify more than that ... It's coming for me right now.*

Despite an extensive search, authorities never found any evidence of Valentich or his Cessna. His last message was:

> *Unknown aircraft is now on top of me.*

The Valentich event shares similarities with the 1948 Thomas Mantell, Kentucky Air National Guard, Incident.

January 1, 1979: Jacques Vallée published *Messengers of Deception: UFO Contacts and Cults.* Vallée believes that some agency—either UFO cultists or aliens—with some kind of "control system" has been "staging" thousands of technologically complex, essentially "fake" UFO sightings around the world with the pointed intention of manipulating and guiding man in a very specific trap—trust and belief in benevolent space brothers:

> *I believe that UFOs are physically real. They represent a fantastic technology controlled by an unknown form of consciousness ... they may not be from outer space.*

January 18, 1979: As a member of the House of Lords, ufologist Brinsley Le Poer Trench introduced a serious debate on UFOs. This historic occasion was the first in which the subject was discussed by the British Parliament.

April 20, 1979: US attorney R. E. Thompson and US senator Harrison Schmidt held a public meeting about cattle mutilations. The well-attended meeting included controversial attendee Paul Bennewitz, who later espoused the "Dulce War" and an alleged underground alien-human base.

1979: UFO researcher Robert Todd obtained AFR 200-2, a declassified Air Force Intelligence document, which offered intriguing data on a suspected retrieval program. Dated November 3, 1961, the document stated in part:

> *In addition to their staff duty assignments, intelligence team personnel have peacetime duty functions in support of such*

> *Air Force projects as Moondust, Bluefly, and UFO, and other AFCIN directed quick reaction projects which require intelligence team operational capabilities ... Unidentified Flying Objects (UFO): Headquarters USAF has established a program for investigation of reliably reported unidentified flying objects within the United States.*

1979: After thousands of reported cattle mutilations, causing millions of dollars of livestock losses, the FBI finally opened an investigation into a number of bizarre and unexplainable cases that were witnessed on New Mexico's Indian lands. The bovine corpses' ears, eyes, udders, anuses, sex organs, and tongues had routinely been removed, seemingly with a sharp, clean instrument. Their carcasses had been drained of blood, and no tracks or footprints were found in the vicinity.

1979: Based in Alexandria, Virginia, the Fund for UFO Research (FUFOR) was created to:

> *Further the scholarly research of UFOs and the extraterrestrial hypothesis (ETH), and secure the release of allegedly classified US government documents pertaining to these.*

According to its promotional material, FUFOR has provided over $700,000 in research grants and supported numerous UFO-related investigations, including investigations into the secrecy behind the MJ-12 papers and the US Air Force's Project Blue Book.

Dr. Thomas E. Bullard of the University of Indiana became the first recipient of the Award for Distinguished UFO Research from FUFOR. Bullard authored a three-hundred-and-fifty-page study of abduction cases and, in 2010, published *The Myth and Mystery of UFOs.*

1979: Explosive engineer Philip Schneider, who worked for the US government, with a high-level security clearance, claimed that he participated in the building of a "secret underground base," in Dulce, New Mexico, the tribal headquarters of the Jicarilla Apache Reservation. He revealed that a battle between aliens and humans left sixty humans dead and injured countless aliens.

1979: Theoretical physicist John Archibald Wheeler addressed the American Association for the Advancement of Science (AAAS), requesting it to expel parapsychology, which had been admitted ten years earlier at the request of Margaret Mead, from its ranks. Wheeler called parapsychology "pseudoscience" that lacked earnest research and convincing testing. He argued that, if scientifically authentic, at least a few so-called psi effects could be demonstrated. Wheeler's request was turned down, and the Parapsychological Association remained a member of the AAAS.

1979: In his book *Broca's Brain: Reflections on the Romance of Science*, Carl Sagan suggested that he and Soviet astrophysicist Iosif Shklovsky, co-authors of *Intelligent Life in the Universe* (1966), may have inspired the wave of 1970s ancient astronaut books. Sagan castigated "paradoxers" like Erich von Däniken, who promoted these ideas not as guarded speculations but as "valid evidence of extraterrestrial contact."

Chapter 16
Majestic 12: 1980s

This decade gave us the UK's Rendlesham Forest Incident, the Cash-Landrum Case, and cattle mutilations as described in *A Strange Harvest*.

January 1, 1980: Former United States Air Force pilot Wendelle C. Stevens (1923–2010) and Lee Elders published a book called *UFO: Contact with Pleiades, Volume 1*, that investigated the assertions of Swiss farmer Billy Meier, who claimed he was in contact with aliens from the Pleiades star cluster and had the photographs to prove it.

During his fifty-year career, Stevens, a prominent UFO research pioneer, amassed one of the world's largest collections of UFO photographs. According to the *BBC*, Stevens's book subjected Meier's photographs to quasi-scientific tests:

> *Drawing upon early digital technology, these were designed to determine the photographs' veracity. Stevens concluded that the photographs weren't doctored.*

January 15, 1980: The FBI closed its inquiry into the spate of mysterious cattle mutilations that took place in Colorado and on New Mexico's Indian lands. The bureau issued a statement, concluding that:

> *None of the reported cases has involved what appear to be mutilations by other than common predators.*

1980: The Roswell Incident was published by Charles Berlitz and William L. Moore. More than seventy witnesses were located and interviewed in this first attempt to analyze the 1947 events.

1980: The Royal Canadian Mounted Police blamed widespread cattle mutilations on an unidentified cult, while Iowa's Department of Criminal Investigations asserted that the mutilations were Satanic in nature.

May 1, 1980: Ronald Story edited the ambitious Encyclopedia of UFOs after founding the original UFO Encyclopedia Project in 1976. Encyclopedia of UFOs contains more than three hundred and fifty articles, illustrated with two hundred and forty photographs. The book offers detailed analyses of UFO sightings and government involvement.

May 5, 1980: Myrna Hansen claimed that, while driving with her son near Eagle Nest, New Mexico, they witnessed two large, silent UFOs approximately the size of Goodyear blimps hovering over a meadow. After contacting ufologist Paul Bennewitz, she was hypnotized by psychologist Leo Sprinkle. Hansen reported being abducted by aliens, given a surgical implant, and taken to an underground base with body parts floating in vats. Hansen's recollections would later evolve into the legend of Dulce Base.

May 25, 1980: Linda Moulton-Howe's Emmy award-winning TV documentary *Strange Harvest* was aired. It investigated hundreds of cattle mutilations throughout North America, including Canada down to Texas, New Mexico, and Arizona. Typically, what appears to be laser-like surgery removes the entire contents of eye sockets, ears, flesh from the mouth and jawbone, udders, reproductive organs, and rectal area.

July 1980: *Hangar 18* was released, indirectly promoting the legendary status of the Wright-Patterson Air Force Base and ongoing stories of UFOs and alien humanoids. The science-fiction film was directed by James L. Conway and starred Darren McGavin, of *The Night Stalker* fame, and Robert Vaughn and Gary Collins.

November 1980: During an evening stroll outside his home village of Burneside, in the English Lake District, Mario Luisi saw a UFO about the size of a helicopter. He also saw two humanoids, about six feet tall, wearing dark, skintight clothing with strange lapel badges. The aliens told Luisi that they came in peace but that he must never reveal the strange symbols on the ship, nor those on their badges.

November 28, 1980: Police constable Alan Godfrey claimed to have experienced missing time after witnessing a UFO that looked like a metallic spinning top with windows. He later revealed, after regressive hypnosis, that he had been abducted by eight small "robots" who gave him a medical examination. The incident occurred while Godfrey was on duty in the north of England.

1980: The Aerial Phenomena Research Organization (APRO) expressed caution about the well-publicized mutilation of the horse "Lady," and a possible-UFO connection:

> *APRO does not claim that Lady was killed by "flying saucer people," but rather that she died in a very strange manner and that her death has yet to be satisfactorily explained.*

December 26, 1980: The high-profile Rendlesham Forest Incident took place between the twin bases of RAF Bentwaters and Woodbridge, now recognized as the UK's most famous sighting. Military witnesses observed a metallic probe suspended in a yellow mist, with a pulsating blue and red circle of light. The UFO's triangular landing gear left three impressions on the ground that were visible the next day. In an obvious cover-up, the soldiers were allegedly threatened by officials and ordered to sign documents that vowed silence.

December 29, 1980: Referred to as the Cash-Landrum Case, researcher Bob Pratt described it as one of the "most important UFO cases in the history of ufology." According to *Grunge* reporter William J. Wright, the Cash-Landrum UFO incident, which took place outside of Houston, Texas, has baffled UFO researchers for three decades:

> *A textbook example of a close encounter of the second kind, as defined by ufology pioneer Dr. J. Allen Hynek, the Cash-Landrum incident left its three primary witnesses with physical evidence of their encounter in the form of blistered skin, sores, nausea, and, in the case of Betty Cash, a life of deteriorating health and cancer.*

Cash and Landrum described the UFO as being a silver-colored diamond-shaped craft with a string of round blue lights, that hovered about sixty yards from their car.

1980: Linda Moulton Howe produced the documentary *A Strange Harvest*, suggesting unusual wounds found on cattle are the work of extraterrestrials who harvest body parts required for their survival or research. Howe believed that the US government was complicit.

1981: Linda Moulton Howe's documentary *A Strange Harvest* received a Regional Emmy award for Audio Achievement. Howe stated:

> *I am convinced that one or more alien intelligences are affecting this planet.*

1981: Denver-based journalist Linda Moulton Howe was invited to Albuquerque, New Mexico's Kirtland Air Force Base and shown the "Briefing Paper for the President of the United States of America." She was warned not to duplicate these MJ-12 documents listing details of UFO crashes and recovered aliens. The papers revealed a treaty between extraterrestrials and the US government, which allegedly allowed the aliens to abduct humans and livestock to study and manipulate the DNA of Earth primates to produce *Homo sapien hybrids*.

December 2, 1981: In a letter written to US Senator Pete Domenici, Paul Bennewitz revealed details about the 1979 "Duce War," which allegedly pitted humans against aliens:

> *Sometime late '79 or first of '80 an argument ensued over weapons and the military abandoned* [*Dulce base*]*; the final circumstance of the men unknown ...*

Bennewitz claimed to have specific information about underground alien bases located in Northern New Mexico on the Jicarilla Apache Reservation, 4.5 miles northwest of Dulce, New Mexico. He claimed that the aliens were providing the US military with advanced technology.

November 2, 1982: Three experienced Airforce pilots, including Airline Captain Julio Miguel Guerra, witnessed a UFO near the Ota Airbase over the skies of Portugal. The Portuguese Air Force chief of staff took the unusual decision to release all files to UFO investigators in an effort to clarify events. Guerra, who was serving as a flight instructor for the Portuguese Air Force, recalled:

> *At various times the object had been very close to me and I was able to verify that it was round with two halves like two tight-fitting skullcaps. I carefully looked at the lower one, which seemed to be somewhere between red and brown, with a hole or dark spot in the center.*

The UFO circled Guerra's DHC-1 Chipmunk for fifteen minutes, with a speed estimated at over three hundred miles per hour and a size of about eight to ten feet. Officials concluded that the object was not an observational balloon.

August 12, 1983: Al Bielek claimed that he and his brother were projected into the future and dropped into the middle of the Montauk Project's Camp Hero. Bilek said they served aboard the USS *Eldridge*, in 1943, during the Philadelphia Experiment, and that after the USS *Eldridge* broke through the space-time continuum, it opened up a wormhole to the future. Bielek also revealed that his real name was Edward Cameron and that he and his brother, Duncan, were crewmembers on the *Eldridge* when they were in their twenties.

December 6, 1984: Before his death at age, fifty-nine, Gray Barker wrote a final book about the Men in Black, called *MIB: The Secret Terror Among Us*.

4: *The Philadelphia Experiment*, a motion picture about the 1943 secret government experiment aboard the destroyer USS *Eldridge*, was released. It starred actor Michael Pare and contained a graphic scene of two sailors embedded into the ship's steel hull, alive and in horrible pain. Al Bielek claimed that after seeing the film for the first time, repressed memories were triggered, alerting him that he had served aboard the Eldridge.

December 11, 1984: TV producer Jaime Shandera claimed he was sent two documents stamped TOP SECRET. One was dated September 24, 1947, and signed by President Harry Truman, and the other, dated November 18, 1952, was addressed to President Dwight Eisenhower from Admiral Roscoe H. Hillenkoetter, a former director of the CIA. Truman's purported document was a classified executive order authorizing Secretary of Defense James Forrestal to establish Majestic 12 (MJ-12), tasked with investigating the Roswell crash.

January 1985: In an official statement, the Air Force responded to continued stories of the mysterious Hangar 18 and the retrieval of UFOs and alien humanoids:

> *Periodically, it is erroneously stated that the remains of extraterrestrial visitors are or have been stored at Wright-Patterson Air Force Base. There are not now, nor have there ever been, any extraterrestrial visitors or equipment on Wright-Patterson Air Force Base.*

The Air Force did admit that a "Building 18" exists on the base.

1985: HBO presented a special about UFOs on their *America Undercover* series and devoted fifteen minutes to the Hudson Valley sightings when thousands saw large, low-flying UFOs. The book *Night Siege: The Hudson Valley UFO Sightings* was published in 1987. According to reviewer Brian Patterson:

> *New Year's Eve 1982 marked the beginning of one of the most puzzling UFO cases in recent times: the Hudson Valley "siege." The siege begot over seven thousand sightings of a boomerang-shaped craft or crafts moving silently through the sky over New York and Connecticut between 1982 and 1995.*

Patterson observed that the UFO sightings, investigated by Dr. J. Allen Hynek and others:

> *Somehow went largely untouched by the local authorities and the national media ...*

1985: In Westmoreland County, part of Pennsylvania's bizarre Chestnut Ridge, seventeen cows had their tails, ears, and teats removed, and a hole eight inches in diameter cleanly sliced into their chests, as documented by TV producer Linda Moulton Howe in her Emmy-winning film, *An Alien Harvest*.

1985: Researcher Ray Boeche filed a Freedom of Information request for more data on the Kecksburg, Pennsylvania, UFO incident. Thirty pages of vague data were received with a memo stating that a three-man team had been dispatched to Acme, Pennsylvania, to pick up the object that started the fire.

December 17, 1985: The legendary aerospace pioneer Kelly Johnson published his autobiography, *Kelly: More Than My Share of it All*. He is celebrated for his leadership of the Skunk

Works and development of the U-2 and SR-71 spy plane stealth technology.

December 26, 1985: Horror writer Whitley Strieber claimed that he was abducted from his upstate New York cabin by nonhuman beings he called "the visitors." *Communion* (1987), his first non-fiction book, told of his experience and made the *New York Times* Best Seller list (non-fiction), with more than two million copies sold. Strieber wrote four additional autobiographies: *Transformation* (1988); *Breakthrough: The Next Step* (1995); *The Secret School* (1996); and lastly, *Solving the Communion Enigma: What Is to Come* (2011).

January 24, 1986: The unmanned NASA spacecraft *Voyager 2* flew closely past Uranus, the seventh planet from the Sun. *Voyager 2* discovered eleven additional moons to the five already known, and a system of faint rings around the gas giant. At its closest, the spacecraft came within 81,500 kilometers (50,600 miles) of Uranus's cloud tops. *Voyager 2*'s itinerary has taken the spacecraft to Jupiter (1979), Saturn (1981), and Uranus. The spacecraft was launched on Aug. 20, 1977, to study the outer planets.

January 28, 1986: The space shuttle *Challenger* exploded seventy-three seconds after liftoff from Cape Canaveral, Florida, killing all seven of its crew members.

April 26, 1986: The world's worst nuclear accident occurred at the Chernobyl plant in Ukraine.

1986: George Clinton Andrews published his book *Extra-Terrestrials Among Us*, claiming to have a decade's worth of research into the Dulce Base legend, as well as Fortean themes such as weird objects falling from the sky and spontaneous human combustion.

July 18, 1986: *Aliens*, a classic science fiction-horror film, was released to huge commercial success. It starred Sigourney Weaver and was directed by James Cameron. A laserdisc version, with seventeen restored minutes, was being sold for one hundred dollars in 1992.

November 17, 1986: Captain Kenju Terauchi, while piloting Japan Airlines Flight 1628, witnessed several UFOs that followed his Boeing 174-200F cargo aircraft for about four hundred miles. The sighting occurred over Anchorage on a return flight from Paris. The objects appeared to be twice the size of their aircraft. Captain Terauchi described the craft:

> *The thing was flying as if there was no such thing as gravity. It sped up quickly, stopped, then flew at our speed, in our direction, so that it appeared to be standing still. The next instance, it changed course like it had overcome gravity, which is impossible for a normal plane to do.*

1986: Arthur C. Clarke, author of the novel and movie *2001: A Space Odyssey*, became Grand Master of the Science Fiction Writers of America.

February 1987: Whitley Strieber published his widely read book *Communion: A True Story*, his firsthand account of an extraterrestrial encounter and alleged abduction. Strieber's experience, and subsequent episodes of missing time, took place in a cabin in upstate New York. The book was later made into a film directed by Philippe Mora, starring Christopher Walken and Lindsay Crouse.

May 29, 1987: Author William Moore and TV producer Jaime Shandera, waiting for over two years, made their alleged TOP SECRET MJ-12 documents public. Moore coauthored The

Roswell Incident, and ufologist Stanton T. Friedman was involved in the controversial revelation. Shandera claimed to have received a secret packet about Operation Majestic 12. The packet, mailed in a brown paper wrapper with 35 mm film, allegedly revealed information about the 1947 Roswell crash.

The documents, subjected to intense scrutiny by researchers, including Jacques Vallée and Philip Klass, are believed to have been falsified. One observation was that the 1947 document was written on a Smith Corona typewriter not manufactured until 1963.

November 10, 1987: Horror master Stephen King published *The Tommyknockers*, a science fiction novel based upon H. P. Lovecraft's short story "The Colour out of Space." The book is about the residents of Haven, Maine, who gradually fall under the influence of a long-buried alien spacecraft buried in the woods.

1987: Intruders: The Incredible Visitations at Copley Woods, written by alien abduction researcher Budd Hopkins, becomes a New York Times bestseller and the subject of a CBS miniseries starring Richard Crenna.

1987: *Communion* by Whitley Strieber details the author's harrowing experience of coming face-to-face with alien life, and his supposed abduction, while spending Christmas with his family in a cabin in upstate New York. Like Sheppton's David Fellin, Strieber took and passed a lie detector test and got a statement from a psychiatrist attesting to his sanity. Arguably the most widely read firsthand account of an encounter with life from another planet.

December 29, 1987: UFO conspiracy theorist John Lear posted a statement to *ParaNet*, an early paranormal bulletin board, claiming that the US government has an association with extraterrestrials and was secretly "promoting" films like *E.T.: The Extra-Terrestrial* and *Close Encounters of the Third Kind* to influence the public to view extraterrestrials as benevolent "space brothers." Lear also referenced the secret government committee Majestic 12, who made a treaty with Gray aliens, but were later deceived by the aliens.

January 20, 1988: The Knowles family, while driving across the Nullarbor, Australia's enormous 77,200 square-mile stretch of arid land, encountered the blinding lights of an egg-shaped UFO that lifted and suspended their car in the air. Four indentations were discovered on the car. The event was witnessed by others.

March 12, 1988: *Missing Time*, released by Ballantine Books, is Budd Hopkins's narrative about alien abductions. He described how the "victims" retained no memory of these traumatic experiences:

> *All traces of the trauma were effectively erased from their memory. Yet, under hypnosis, many abductees were able to recall in vivid, convincing detail, the harrowing experiments that left mysterious scars on their bodies, the eerie interiors of UFOs where they were held captive, and the astonishing faces of their alien hosts.*

1988: Paul Bennewitz wrote a paper titled "Project Beta," detailing how the New Mexico secret Duce Base might be successfully attacked. Bennewitz claimed that in 1980, he filmed UFOs over the Manzano Weapons Storage Facility.

1988: After he watched the movie *The Philadelphia Experiment* (1984), Al Bielek, fifty-seven, claimed an overwhelming sense of *déjà vu*. Regressive hypnosis techniques unlocked repressed memories about his extensive involvement in the Philadelphia Experiment and a secret government mind-control program called the Montauk Project. Bielek believed that his memory had been wiped clean by the CIA's MK-Ultra techniques to maintain the secrecy of the program. Bielek also said that he and his brother were crewmembers on the USS *Eldridge* in 1943 when they were in their twenties.

October 14, 1988: CBS TV aired a two-hour documentary titled *UFO Coverup?* It was hosted by former *M.A.S.H.* actor Mike Farrell, who noted:

> *Having been associated with a number of things contrary to government policy, I am a very firm believer in the fact that there are people in the government who believe the people of the United States aren't mature enough to handle the facts in a given situation. They arrogate to themselves the right to determine for everyone what facts will be released.*

January 1, 1989: TV producer and Emmy award winner Linda Moulton Howe published *An Alien Harvest: Further Evidence Linking Animal Mutilations and Human Abductions to Alien Life Forms*, with the foreword written by Jacques Vallée. Howe eventually concluded—after researching hundreds of cases—that extraterrestrials were likely involved.

February 1, 1989: UFO debunker Philip J. Klass, in the preface to his scathing *UFO Abductions: A Dangerous Game*, made his view clear:

> *The public has been hoodwinked and brainwashed. I can assure you that there is absolutely no scientifically credible physical evidence to indicate that Earth is being visited by extraterrestrials—let alone that they are abducting people.*

Questioning the claims of Betty and Barney Hill, Betty Andreasson, Whitley Strieber, and other celebrated abductees, Klass also warns about the dangers of using hypnotherapy to unlock these experiences.

1989: Stanford-educated author Linda Moulton Howe, in her book *An Alien Harvest: Further Evidence Linking Animal Mutilations and Human Abductions to Alien Life Forms*—after researching more than one thousand animal mutilation cases, concluded that extraterrestrials were likely involved. Moulton Howe won an Emmy award for her 1980 documentary *A Strange Harvest.*

1989: Budd Hopkins founded the nonprofit Intruders Foundation, based in Manhattan, to help "provide sympathetic help, understanding, and personal investigation for those reporting UFO abduction experiences." Hopkins believed that aliens, or "visitors," as he preferred to call them, were practicing a form of extraterrestrial eugenics, aiming to regenerate their declining race by crossbreeding with *Homo sapiens*.

May 4, 1989: The NASA spacecraft *Magellan* was launched from the space shuttle. *Magellan* reached Venus in 1990 and orbited the planet for four years, revealing that the planet has a volcanic landscape. Magellan was the fifth successful NASA mission to Venus, ending an eleven-year gap in US interplanetary probe launches.

July 1, 1989: Ufologist William L. Moore delivered what has become a legendary lecture at the Las Vegas MUFON Symposium. Facing criticism about the authenticity of the MJ-12 documents, Moore made a shocking confession that he had been recruited by the US government, tasked with spreading falsehoods to Paul Bennewitz and others. Moore claimed that other ufologist also spread disinformation about UFOs:

> *I would play the disinformation game, get my hands dirty just often enough* [*while trying*] *to learn as much as possible about who was directing it and why.*

Moore confessed that he'd attempted to force Paul Bennewitz into a mental breakdown by feeding him false information. Bennewitz, who espoused the "Duce War" narrative, between humans and aliens, was admitted to the mental health unit of Presbyterian Anna Kaseman Hospital. He died in 2003.

1989: Las Vegas KLAS investigative reporter George Knapp interviewed Bob Lazar, who claimed to have worked in a secret underground lab called S4, eight miles south of the main Area 51 base. Lazar claimed he had helped reverse engineer extraterrestrial technology from several disc-shaped craft and also saw medical photographs of small alien humanoids.

August 25, 1989: NASA's *Voyager* 2 made a close flyby of Neptune, giving scientists their first close-up of our solar system's eighth planet. Neptune marked the end of the Voyager mission's Grand Tour of the solar system's four giant planets—Jupiter, Saturn Uranus, and Neptune. The planet was wrapped in teal-and-cobalt-colored bands of clouds, the blue indicating the presence of methane. *Voyager* 2 discovered six new moons and four rings and completed a close flyby of Neptune's largest moon, Triton.

September 20, 1989: The NBC television show *Unsolved Mysteries* broadcast a program based on William Moore and Stanton Friedman's investigation into the Roswell Incident. After thirty-nine years, this single program catapulted Roswell into the minds of the general public. An updated version aired on September 18, 1994.

November 29, 1989: A wave of numerous UFO sightings was seen near the border between the Netherlands and West Germany. Individuals, including police officials, reported seeing flying platforms scanning the surface with huge search-lights and dancing lights. The sightings were confirmed by "radar blips on the screens."

1989: Former civilian mortician Glenn Dennis provided a detailed personal account, claiming that alien autopsies were carried out at the Roswell base in 1947. Dennis claimed that he had been threatened by the military to keep quiet.

1989 to 1993: Valentina De Andrade created the 1980s Superior Universal Alignment UFO cult in a remote part of Brazil. She claimed to receive messages from extraterrestrials that Jesus was an alien, and He was going to send a spacecraft to save true believers from the End Times. She preached that she received a message from aliens asserting that all male children born after 1981 were evil and needed to be sacrificed to the alien overlords. She was able to manipulate several highly respected citizens into murdering at least nineteen boys between the ages of eight and thirteen.

Part Four

Chapter 17
The New Frontier: 1990s

Yet another decade of weird anomalies—Al Bielek and the Montauk Project, the Heaven's Gate mass suicide, J. Antonio Huneeus, the Ariel School children, and *Stranger in a Strange Land.*

January 3, 1990: Robert A. Heinlein's *Stranger in a Strange Land* was re-released thirty years after its original publication and two years after the author's death. The fifty-thousand-word extended edition is based on the original manuscript. *Kirkus* said the novel, about the Martian Valentine Michael Smith, deserves to be called a "classic":

> *Now, is a human raised to adulthood by Martians, his viewpoints completely alien. This is the mechanism for Heinlein's Swiftian examination of human culture, politics, religion, and customs, starting with Michael's puzzlement and ending with his founding of a religion/discipline combining Martian wisdom and Michael's understanding of what human nature really is.*

January 13, 1990: Al Bielek told an audience at the Mutual UFO Network Conference that the Philadelphia Experiment was real, and that he and his brother, Duncan, served aboard the ship during the incident. Bielek said that Nikola Tesla had designed the "equipment" that caused the USS *Eldridge* to break out of space-time and open up a wormhole. Bielek claimed that he and his brother were projected into the future and, on August 12, 1983, were transported into the middle of the Montauk Project's Camp Hero.

1990: Ufologist Steven M. Greer founded the Center for the Study of Extra-Terrestrial Intelligence (CSETI) to create a research-based initiative to contact extraterrestrial civilizations. CSETI defined CE-5, or Close Encounters of the Fifth Kind, as human-initiated communication with extraterrestrial life.

1990: Howard Blum published *Out There: The Government's Secret Quest for Extraterrestrials.* Blum believed that the government had sent undercover agents to befriend and mislead Paul Bennewitz using counterfeit documents. Bennewitz was later admitted to a psychiatric unit for observation.

1990: Investigative reporter J. Antonio Huneeus received the Ufologist of the Year award at the National UFO Conference in Miami Beach and the Courage in Journalism award at the 2007 X-Conference in Gaithersburg, Maryland. He co-authored the Laurance Rockefeller-funded *UFO Briefing Document: The Best Available Evidence* and edited the book *A Study Guide to UFOs, Psychic & Paranormal Phenomena in the USSR.*

August 4, 1990: Two hikers near Calvine in Scotland took photographs of a mysterious, one-hundred-foot craft hovering in the middle of the sky. The two hikers watched the diamond-shaped metallic craft for ten minutes before it shot up vertically out of sight. A thirty-year rule meant the incident was due to be declassified in January 2020, but the Ministry of Defense blocked release until 2072 without explanation. Some believe The Calvine Incident is one of the most fascinating of all the UFO mysteries from that period and question the government's motives.

September 19, 1990: Robert Stack and the crew of *Unsolved Mysteries* flew into Kecksburg, Pennsylvania, to film an episode about the mysterious UFO crash in December 1965. The producers created a replica spaceship that looked just like an acorn and interviewed Stan Gordon. The story was listed as Episode # 3.1. Later, the Sci-Fi Channel filmed a documentary titled *The New Roswell: Kecksburg Exposed*, hosted by Bryant Gumbel, former host of *Today* and *The Early Show*.

December 29, 1990: In an international example of cattle mutilation, the dismembered corpse of a cow was discovered at a farm in Saga, Japan. Half of the tongue was missing, and the teats were cored out from the udder.

July 9, 1991: Sappho Henderson provided a witnessed affidavit claiming that her husband, former World War II pilot Oliver Wendell "Pappy" Henderson, flew the Roswell UFO wreckage to Wright Field in Dayton, Ohio. Sappho attested that her husband described the beings as:

> *Small with large heads for their size. He said the material that their suits were made of was different than anything he had ever seen. He said they looked strange. I believe he mentioned that the bodies had been packed in dry ice to preserve them. He was not aware of the book* [The Roswell Incident] *that*

> *had been published about this event at the time he told me this.*

Sappho, one of three individuals who provided personal affidavits, also stated:

> *I have not been paid or given anything of value to make this statement, which is the truth to the best of my recollection.*

1991: British cosmonaut Dr. Helen Sharman completed an eight-day space mission aboard Russian space station Mir. At twenty-seven, she became the first British cosmonaut in space and a national hero. Dr. Sharman told *Observer Magazine* that it is without a doubt that "all sorts of forms of life are alive in the universe—but perhaps they are so different from humanity." She added:

> *Aliens exist, there's no two ways about it ... there are so many billions of stars out there in the universe that there must be all sorts of forms of life ... Will they be like you and me, made up of carbon and nitrogen? Maybe not. It's possible they're right here right now, and we simply can't see them.*

September 15, 1991: Benjamin John Stankey Jr., founder of the New Jersey UFO Psychic Phenomena Metaphysical Association, told a gathering of his followers that he was a reincarnated alien sent to teach metaphysics and spiritual truths. The doctor of metaphysics said:

> *I've been ridiculed, even called satanic, heretical, and other things, but in the final analysis, in terms of the truth, I think I'm going to have the last laugh.*

September 16, 1991: Betty Hill, the nation's most recognized abductee, announced she is retiring from further public appearances. Hill, seventy-two, confessed that she is "disappointed in the way the UFO field is headed" and was critical of the paranormal community:

> *If you don't know the answers to something, you can always dream them up, whether they are true or not. A lot of the UFO field certainly is not sticking to facts.*

October 1991: Linda Moulton Howe was the supervising producer and original concept creator for *UFO Report: Sightings*, which became the paranormal *Sightings* series on Fox. *Sightings* ran from 1992 to 1998 and produced several specials and a film, *Sightings: Heartland Ghost.*

1991: Artists Doug Bowers and Dave Chorley, of Southampton, England, confessed to having made more than two hundred crop circles since the late 1970s with nothing more complex than ropes and wooden boards. They had initially been inspired by a 1966 account of a UFO sighting near Tully, Queensland. They faked another crop circle design for journalists to prove how easy the procedure was. The British "crop circle fad," and UFO connection, ended around 1993.

October 1, 1991: Former *New York Times* reporter Howard Blum published *Out There*, revealing the existence of a "UFO working group" that met deep within the Pentagon, in a bunker known as the Tank. Blum claimed that the group was organized by the Defense Intelligence Agency in 1987, after a UFO flew across US airspace, accelerating in a way that would be theoretically impossible for an earthly craft. The clandestine group was tasked with the mission to determine whether extraterrestrial life exists.

January 8, 1992: More than two hundred people near Scranton, Pennsylvania, viewed anomalous flashing lights in the skies above Newton Township. The lights were videotaped and later broadcast on *CBS News*.

1992: The former USS *Eldridge* (DE-173), believed to have been connected to the secret 1943 Philadelphia Experiment, was sold for scrap. At the time, the destroyer had been transferred to Greece, where it was redesignated as the HS *Leon* (D-54).

1992: Preston B. Nichols's self-published book *The Montauk Project: Experiments in Time* involved the alleged abduction of orphans and runaways who were subjected to physical and psychological torture. Nichols's book also described experiments in mind control and telepathy, opening space-time portals to other dimensions, and contact with alien life.

According to the bizarre narrative, the American military has been conducting experiments in psychological warfare on the eastern end of Long Island as far back as the mid-1980s, financed by Nazi gold recovered during World War II.

April 15, 1992: US Geological Survey geophysicist John S. Derr said that some UFO sightings are caused by "earthquake lights"—basketball-sized, glowing spheres of electricity that are identical to ball lightning but are generated by the crushing of rock or changes in groundwater flow as underground stress accumulates in the months before an earthquake. Derr said:

> *The typical report is an orange ball of light, although some are blue-white and some tend toward greenish. they just float along through the air. Some people feel spooked. Some people feel awed.*

Derr presented his findings, using a computerized list of UFO sightings reported throughout New Mexico during 1951 and 1952, at the Seismological Society of America's annual Santa Fe, New Mexico, meeting.

May 15, 1992: American psychologist Kenneth Ring published *The Omega Project: Human Evolution in an Ecological Age,* a book that dealt with near-death experiences, abductions and UFO encounters. Rink co-founded the International Association for Near-Death Studies (IANDS) and was the founding editor of the *Journal of Near-Death Studies.*

1992: Writing for *Mysteries of Mind, Space & Time,* in an article titled "The UFO Paradox," writer Hilary Evans threw cold water on any suggestions that the space brothers walk among us:

> *Although the number of potential sources of life in the Universe is virtually infinite, the probability of any civilization being at a stage of development appropriate for space travel is very small. The fact that no solid evidence has been found for the extraterrestrial hypothesis is discouraging. Although it is the best available explanation, it remains no more than speculation.*

1992–1998: The paranormal *Sightings* series on Fox ran from 1992–1998. Ufologist Linda Moulton Howe was credited as the supervising producer and original concept creator.

1992: Former *Fate* editor Jerome Clark authored the comprehensive, multivolume *The UFO Encyclopedia: The Phenomenon from The Beginning.* (Omnigraphic Books, 1992). *Library Review* observed that:

> *A respected UFO authority provides a much-needed update on the [UFO] field with this new encyclopedia ... [it] is the most thorough treatment yet of this puzzling phenomenon ... the [encyclopedia] should be considered by larger public and academic libraries.*

1992: David Jewitt and his PhD student Jane Luu discovered the first of over one thousand more small planets that they named "trans-Neptunian objects." Using the International Astronomical Union's new planetary definition, Pluto, once considered our ninth planet, was downgraded to a TNO or dwarf planet in 2006.

March 12, 1993: The science fiction thriller *Fire in the Sky* was released. Directed by Robert Lieberman, it was based on Travis Walton's book *The Walton Experience*, which describes an extraterrestrial abduction and missing time in Arizona's White Mountains. The film stars D. B. Sweeney as Walton, and Robert Patrick as his best friend and future brother-in-law, Mike Rogers. James Garner, Craig Sheffer, Scott MacDonald, and Peter Berg also star.

Fire in the Sky grossed $19.9 million domestically on a $15 million budget and received mixed reviews. It was nominated for four Saturn Awards.

March 1993: Rep. Steven H. Schiff (R-NM) asked the Air Force to declassify all material relating to the Roswell crash. Air Force officials referred Schiff to the National Archives, which promptly told Schiff it had no information.

August 6, 1993: Ron Rummel, publisher of *Alien Digest*, was found dead in a park in Portland, Oregon; his death was ruled a "suicide." Rummel's magazine published revolting issues, including the alien/human relationship and the use of humans for food and recyclable body parts.

August 1993: Longtime UFO skeptic Philip Klass, interviewed in *Omni* magazine, addressed the Hudson Valley boomerang-shaped UFO sightings, witnessed by thousands of observers:

> *I've been investigating UFO reports for seventeen years and have yet to find an indication of the unknown or extraterrestrial phenomenon. It would take a lot to convince me, but it could be that for the first time in seventeen years this is an unexplainable case.*

October 1993: Congress terminates the Search for Extraterrestrial Intelligence (SETI), a massive program that for decades scoured the heavens with a vast array of radio telescopes in search of alien communication.

1993: Steven M. Greer founded the Disclosure Project, requesting the public disclosure of the government's knowledge of UFOs, extraterrestrial intelligence, and advanced energy and propulsion systems. The program would grant amnesty to government whistleblowers willing to violate their security oaths by sharing classified information. Greer discussed his program on Larry King's TV special *The UFO Coverup?* in October 1994.

October 1993: After Rep. Steven H. Schiff (R-NM) asked the General Accounting Office to look for Roswell documents, the Air Force claimed that the Roswell debris was part of Project Mogul—an experiment aimed at detecting future Soviet nuclear blasts by monitoring sound waves in the high atmosphere using airborne balloons and sensors.

January 1, 1994: David Ritchie published the book *UFO: The Definitive Guide to Unidentified Flying Objects and Related Phenomena*. According to *Booklist:*

> *Ritchie rejects the view that extraterrestrials are visiting Earth. Knowledge of surrounding planets indicates none can support life even remotely similar to Earth, the distances to other solar systems are too vast for visitors, and no solid evidence has ever been discovered to support the existence of life beyond Earth. He does believe UFOs are real but relies on paranormal or spiritual explanations.*

Ritchie views flying saucers as a psychological and spiritual phenomenon and cites similarities between accounts of UFO pilots with demonic visitations.

1994: Longtime UFO researcher Karl Pflock published *Roswell in Perspective*, presenting the initial results of his UFO investigations. The book-length monograph was published by the Fund for UFO Research.

March 14, 1994: Seven years after the release of the original MJ-12 documents, ufologist Don Berliner received an undeveloped roll of 35 mm film, with purported copies of pages from a "Top Secret/MAJIC/Eyes Only" special operations manual (SOM 1-01) informing military retrieval units how to recover crashed saucers. SOM 1-01, purportedly printed in April 1954, contained many flaws. The document stated that crashed ET craft should be sent to "Area 51 S-4" in Nevada. But that portion of the Nellis Air Force Base was not given the name "Area 51" until several years after SOM 1-01 was printed. It has been denounced as "counterfeit."

1994: The US Air Force conceded that the Roswell "weather balloon" was a bogus cover story deflecting attention from the wreckage from the covert Project Mogul. The crashed Project Mogul spy device was a connected string of high-altitude balloons equipped with microphones, designed to monitor the Soviet government's attempts at testing their atomic bomb.

June 1994: A Chinese lumberjack claimed that a ten-foot female alien had sex with him in midair while his wife slept below them. The alleged abduction became known as the "Meng Zhaoguo Incident," where a shimmering UFO appeared on the mountainside near the semi-mountainous town of Wuchan, near Phoenix Mountain. Meng said that he was hit by a surge of electricity and knocked out, leaving him with no memory of the missing time. According to Chen Yanchun, director of the UFO Society of China, Meng was with thirty men, who took him back to their quarters after he lost consciousness.

1994: *Invasion of the Body Snatchers,* the 1956 science-fiction horror film, was selected for preservation in the United States National Film Registry by the Library of Congress for being "culturally, historically, or aesthetically significant." The black-and-white film was based on Jack Finney's 1954 novel, *The Body Snatchers,* about an extraterrestrial invasion.

1994: After an interview about alien abductions, parapsychologist and broadcaster Jeffrey Mishlove stated that John Mack seemed "inclined to take these [abduction] reports at face value." Mack replied by saying:

> *Face value I wouldn't say. I take them seriously. I don't have a way to account for them.*

September 13, 1994: In Chacon, New Mexico, Larry Gardes was hunting for a bear in a remote part of the county. Gardes, who may have been the first to actually witness a cattle mutilation, saw a dead cow and heard a whirring sound like that made by a welder's torch. Another cow was hovering through the air, just slightly above the ground. The cow, bawling and struggling, was being dragged into the forest, as if it were being pulled by a gravitational force. Gardea instinctively raised his rifle and shot twice toward the sound. The sound ceased, and the cow got away.

September 16, 1994: Considered one of the largest mass sightings of UFOs in history, sixty-two young students outside a school in rural Ruwa, Zimbabwe, reported seeing a strange, silver craft come down from the sky and land in a nearby field by a clump of trees. According to *Daily Hampshire Gazette* writer Steve Pfarrer:

> *Then, the students said, one or more humanoid creatures, dressed in what seemed like skin-tight black and making odd movements, approached them; some of the students said the creatures seemed to communicate with them telepathically, transmitting a message of concern about the damage human beings were doing to the Earth.*

September 30, 1994: The American comedy-drama biopic *Ed Wood* is released. The Oscar-winning film was produced and directed by Tim Burton and starred Johnny Depp. It depicts Wood's creation of *Plan 9 from Outer Space*. The film won two Academy Awards: Best Supporting Actor for Martin Landau (as Bela Lugosi) and Best Makeup for Rick Baker, who designed Landau's prosthetic makeup.

1994: The Office of the Secretary of the Air Force released the results of its Roswell investigation. Their conclusion was that witnesses had been mistaken about an alleged flying saucer crash in New Mexico, in 1947, and the retrieval of alien bodies.

November 1994: Researcher John Mack traveled to Zimbabwe to interview the Ariel School children. Mack was convinced the children's testimony was authentic, though some critics claimed he had coached some of the responses. The UFO incident created a negative professional backlash for Mack.

July 29, 1995: As expected, Rep. Steve Schiff (R-New Mexico), said a General Accounting Office report he had requested about the Roswell Incident showed that important documents were missing:

> *Documents that could have provided more information were destroyed. The military cannot explain who destroyed them or why.*

July 1995: *Galileo* was the first spacecraft to enter into orbit around Jupiter. Over an eight-year period, it made extensive observations of the planet, including significant data on the planet's weather.

August 28, 1995: *Fox Television* aired a documentary titled *Alien Autopsy: Fact or Fiction*, hosted by Jonathan Frakes, that claimed to show footage of an alleged postmortem of Roswell's UFO's "extraterrestrial" occupant. *Time* magazine declared that the film had sparked a debate "with an intensity not lavished on any home movie since the Zapruder film," and, writing for *LiveScience,* Mindy Weisberger described the procedure:

> *In the autopsy footage, a lifeless humanoid figure lies on a table; a gaping wound can be seen on its right leg. It has a rounded trunk and belly, bulbous, dark eyes and a hairless head that's much larger than the average human skull. Figures clad head-to-toe in white protective suits circle the "corpse" and perform a methodical dissection.*

The seventeen-minute black-and-white film supposedly depicted a secret physical autopsy of an alien retrieved by the US military.

September 1995: Al Bielik and Phil Schneider participated in the Preparedness Expo in Orange County, California. They delivered personal accounts of the Philadelphia Experiment, the Montauk project, and the Dulce Wars. Schneider was prepared to leak vital information to the public but was killed in what appeared to be a military-style execution.

December 7, 1995: *Galileo*, an American robotic space probe, became the first spacecraft to enter into orbit around an outer plant, Jupiter. *Galileo* was delivered into Earth orbit on October 18, 1989, by space shuttle *Atlantis*.

January 10, 1996: UFO researcher Dr. Karla Turner died of an unidentifiable and unexpected cancer. Her friend Phil Schneider believed that she had been threatened for investigating alien abductions and the so-called MAAR (Malevolent Alien Abduction Research.)

January 11, 1996: Whistleblower Phil Schneider was found dead in his apartment with surgical tubing wrapped around his neck in a military-style execution. He had previously lectured at the Preparedness Expo, where he claimed the New World Order is connected to extraterrestrial biological entities and world domination.

1996: During NASA's mission STS-80, astronaut Story Musgrave recorded a craft emerging out from nowhere over Puerto Rico with a speed of six hundred and eighty miles per second, that disappeared into deep space. Researchers view this as evidence of documented extraterrestrial activities.

February 27, 1996: *Kidnapped by UFOs? The True Story of Alien Abductions* was presented on *Nova.* Narrated by Joe Morton, the program featured famed abductees Betty and Barney Hill, Budd Hopkins, John E. Mack, and Carl Sagan. The program's official description read:

> *Debunking the alien abduction concepts and practices for more earth-bound common sense explanations in a format of critical analysis that, in the end, lets you decide. Are alien abductions plausible in light of these new findings?*

1996: During an interview with PBS, Harvard Professor and abductee researcher John Mack stated:

> *There are aspects of this which I believe we are justified in taking quite literally. That is, UFOs are in fact observed, filmed on camera at the same time that people are having their abduction experiences ... It's both literally, physically happening to a degree; and it's also some kind of psychological, spiritual experience occurring and originating perhaps in another dimension.*

Mack suggested that the experience of alien contact itself may be more transcendent than physical in nature—yet nonetheless real—which set him apart from many of his contemporaries, such as Budd Hopkins, who advocated the physical reality of aliens.

January 1, 1997: *The Day After Roswell*, written by United States Army Colonel Philip J. Corso, with help from William J. Birnes, was published as a tell-all memoir a year before Corso's death. Corso claims that he was assigned to a secret government program that provided extraterrestrial materials recovered from the crashed Roswell spacecraft to private industry to reverse engineer them for corporate use. Writing for *UFO Digest*, Robert L. Mason allowed Corso little credibility as he held back no punches:

> *Above, I mentioned the possibility that Col. Corso is a liar, plain and simple. Perhaps that is a bit harsh. I'll give him the benefit of the doubt and say that his book,* The Day After Roswell, *impresses me as the deluded ramblings of an old man.*

March 26, 1997: The San Diego County Sheriff's Department discovered the bodies of thirty-nine members of the Heaven's Gate cult who had committed mass suicide. Heaven's Gate was led by Bonnie Nettles (1927–1985) and Marshall Applewhite (1931–1997) and was described as a UFO religion. The central philosophy of Heaven's Gate was that followers could transform themselves into immortal extraterrestrial beings by rejecting their human nature, and they would ascend to heaven, referred to as the "Next Level" or "the Evolutionary Level Above Human."

June 24, 1997: On the fiftieth anniversary of the Roswell UFO crash, the Air Force released a two-hundred-and-thirty-one-page report claiming that the alleged "alien bodies" were crash test dummies.

The official explanation was that life-size dummies were used during a series of experiments in the 1950s. The dummies, dressed in Air Force flight suits, were dropped from high-altitude balloons to determine if astronauts could survive such a drop. According to AP writer, Robert Burns:

> *The majority of the dummies—which had skeletons of aluminum or steel, skin of latex or plastic, cast aluminum skulls, and instrument cavities in their torsos and heads—landed outside military bases in eastern New Mexico, near Roswell.*

July 11, 1997: *Contact,* based on Carl Sagan's 1985 novel, was released. Directed by Robert Zemeckis, it starred Jodie Foster, Matthew McConaughey, James Woods, and Angela Bassett. The film grossed over $171 million worldwide. It won the Hugo Award for Best Dramatic Presentation and several Saturn Awards. Reviewer Germain Lussier noted the film's "captivating depiction of the eternal struggle between science and religion":

> *The argument is the core of the film and, frankly, not subtle in the least, but it fascinated me.* Contact *takes the two equally compelling sides of the argument and personifies them with Jodie Foster's scientist Ellie Arroway and Matthew McConaughey's religious scholar Palmer Joss. Science demands proof, but religion makes it okay to believe without proof.*

1997: The NASA/ESA *Cassini-Huygens* spacecraft was launched, believed to be history's most successful planetary mission. The joint mission opened the likelihood of extraterrestrial life in places that were previously thought to be completely unlikely.

July 23, 1997: Philip J. Corso was a guest on Art Bell's late-night radio show, where he elaborated upon his Roswell story and alleged involvement with reverse engineering extraterrestrial technology. Corso died of a heart attack less than a year later.

1997: An abridged, one-volume edition of Jerome Clark's *The UFO Encyclopedia: The Phenomenon from The Beginning,* retitled *The UFO Book: Encyclopedia of the Extraterrestrial,* was published by Visible Ink Press as a trade paperback.

1998: Karl Pflock, author, consultant, and UFO researcher, was named Ufologist of the Year by the National UFO Conference. His articles on UFOs have appeared in such journals as *Fortean Times, Omni,* the *International UFO Reporter,* the *Anomalist, Fate,* and the *MUFON UFO Journal.* Pflock is a member of the Permanent Organizing Committee of the National UFO Conference and author of *Roswell in Perspective* and the definitive *Roswell: Inconvenient Facts and the Will to Believe.*

1998: Jerome Clark's *The UFO Book: Encyclopedia of the Extraterrestrial* won the Benjamin Franklin Award in the Science/Environment category sponsored by the Independent Book Publishers Association.

March 1998: Australian researcher Warren Aston published an article about the Wartena Incident in *UFO Magazine.* Udo Wartena witnessed a large, one-hundred-foot-wide, disc-shaped object. He communicated with two humanoids, who asked if their ship could take water.

1998: Government officials acknowledged the secret US Army biological weapons tests that accidentally killed more than four thousand sheep while clandestinely testing nerve agents. The sheep convulsed and collapsed near Utah's Dugway Proving Ground, a US Army facility established to test chemical and biological weapons. Farmers believe that the government is behind the 1970s cattle mutilations as well.

June 1, 1999: The song "Aliens Exist" was released by the rock band Blink-182 from their multiplatinum studio album *Enema of the State* (1999). The silly tune, about the existence of extraterrestrials, includes references to CIA interference and Majestic 12. It was written by guitarist Tom DeLonge, with additional songwriting credit to bassist Mark Hoppus. DeLonge's company, To the Stars, was instrumental in the 2017 release of military footage of unidentified aircraft, prompting the Pentagon to formally establish the All-domain Anomaly Resolution Office.

1999: The French government published a study concluding that the United States government has withheld evidence that proves the existence of UFOs and extraterrestrials.

1999: Often mistaken by some to have been a UFO, the high-altitude Lockheed SR-71 Blackbird spy plane was grounded after flying NASA's final mission. The USAF permanently retired it in 1998, while NASA operated the final two airworthy Blackbirds for one more year.

August 5, 1999: Jerome Clark and co-author Loren Coleman published *Cryptozoology A to Z: The Encyclopedia of Loch Monsters, Sasquatch, Chupacabras, and Other Authentic Mysteries of Nature* with nearly two hundred entries, and, as *Salon* observed:

> *Show a touchingly supportive nature for a subject often criticized for lack of scientific rigor.*

Chapter 18

Beyond the Cosmos: 2000s

THE UNIVERSE of ufology continued to expand with the USS *Nimitz* sighting, Kecksburg, *Pioneer 10*, Jason Colavito, Walter Haut, as well as *Ancient Aliens*, the alien autopsy, and the "Fake Moon Landing."

January 5, 2000: In an area of Southern Illinois known as the St. Clair Triangle, several eyewitnesses, including police officer Ed Barton, reported seeing a massive triangle-shaped craft as large as a football field. The silent craft had two floors and brightly lit windows and was approximately one thousand feet above the ground. The sighting was documented by various news outlets, including "UFOs Over Illinois" on the *Discovery Channel* and Darryl Barker's independent documentary titled *The Edge of Reality: Illinois UFO January 5, 2000.*

November 7, 2000: Harvard professor John Mack's second (and final) book on the alien encounter experience, *Passport to the Cosmos: Human Transformation and Alien Encounters* (Three Rivers Press, 1999), provided a philosophical treatise connecting the themes of spirituality and modern worldviews. It also represented the culmination of his work with the "experiencers" of alien encounters, to whom the book is dedicated.

December 1, 2000: James R. Lewis, who specializes in New Age religions, published *UFOs and Popular Culture* (Santa Barbara: ABC-CLIO, 2000), which straddled the UFO line between logic and hysteria. As noted in Thomas E. Bullard's forward:

> *Whether UFOs crumble into a collection of conventional occurrences or exist as an independent phenomenon, no one can hope to study UFOs without recognizing the role of human beliefs and concerns in UFO lore.*

May 2001: Ufologist Steven M. Greer held a press conference at the National Press Club in Washington, DC, demanding that Congress hold hearings on "secret US involvement with UFOs and extraterrestrials." The conference featured twenty retired Air Force, Federal Aviation Administration, and intelligence officers. In 1990, Greer founded the Center for the Study of Extraterrestrial Intelligence (CSETI).

June 1, 2001: UFO researchers Karl Pflock and Jerry Pournelle published the definitive *Roswell: Inconvenient Facts and the Will to Believe.* It was published in the US by Prometheus Books and in France by O.P. Editions. The authors, after an exhaustive investigation and citing formerly classified records, conclude that no alien craft or bodies were ever found at Roswell—proving that the US government has absolutely no physical evidence of aliens.

2001: Old Testament scholar Dr. Michael S. Heiser challenged Zecharia Sitchin to a debate over Sitchin's translations of the Sumerian texts. Sitchin believed that the Sumerians actually witnessed these events, while Heiser dismissed the texts as myth and allegory. Heiser convinced George Noory to arrange for a debate on *Coast to Coast AM* and later founded the website *SitchinIsWrong.com*.

July 14, 2001: Just after midnight, drivers on the New Jersey Turnpike pulled alongside the road and, for fifteen minutes, stared in disbelief at the sight of strange orange-and-yellow lights in a V formation over the Arthur Kill Waterway between Staten Island, New York, and Carteret, New Jersey. The New York Strange Phenomena Investigators (NY-SPI) claimed to receive FAA radar data that validated the UFO sightings from that night.

January 24, 2002: *The Mothman Prophecies* film was released, based on alleged paranormal events that occurred between November 1966 and December 1967 in Point Pleasant, West Virginia. Directed by Mark Pellington, the film starred Richard Gere, Debra Messing, and Laura Linney. Roger Ebert's lukewarm review said:

> *John A. Keel has written a book about Mothman, and now here is this movie. The "true story" part involves the possible existence of Mothman; the human characters are, I believe, based not on facts but on an ancient tradition in horror movies, in which attractive people have unspeakable experiences.*

2002: James Moseley and Karl Pflock co-authored *Shockingly Close to the Truth—Confessions of a Grave Robbing UFOlogist*, published by Prometheus Books.

2002: Leslie Keane was asked by the SCI-FI Channel to spearhead a Freedom of Information Act (FOIA) initiative attempting to acquire documentation of the Kecksburg case. In 2003 Keane was in Washington, DC, as a plaintiff in a federal

FOIA lawsuit against NASA, which continued to stonewall and withhold documents.

January 23, 2003: At a distance of twelve billion kilometers (80 AU) from Earth, radio communications with *Pioneer 10* ended because of the loss of electric power for its radio transmitter, supplied by four radioisotope thermoelectric generators that provided one hundred and fifty-five watts at launch. According to *Solar System Exploration*, *Pioneer 10* scored six firsts unmatched by any other robotic spacecraft to date:

> *First spacecraft placed on a trajectory to escape the solar system into interstellar space*
>
> *First spacecraft to fly beyond Mars*
>
> *First spacecraft to fly through the main asteroid belt*
>
> *First spacecraft to fly past Jupiter*
>
> *Crossed the orbit of Neptune to become the first human-made object to go beyond Neptune*
>
> *First spacecraft to use all-nuclear electrical power*

January 2003: Following Art Bell's retirement, George Noory became the nighttime host of *Coast to Coast AM*. According to Arbitron:

> *Noory hosts the nationally syndicated program* Coast to Coast AM*, which is heard by millions of listeners on over six hundred stations across North America and is the most listened-to radio show in the nighttime time period.*

Bell announced his retirement in 2007 but occasionally served as a guest host. Classic episodes of *Coast to Coast AM* are heard in some radio markets on Saturday nights under the name *Somewhere in Time hosted by Bell.*

2003: *Aviation Week & Space Technology*, in commemoration of the hundredth anniversary of the Wright brothers, ranked aeronautical engineer Kelly Johnson eighth on its list of the top one hundred "most important, most interesting, and most influential people" in the first century. Johnson played a major role in the Skunk Works' development of the secret U-2 spy plane, which some assert has been misinterpreted as UFOs.

April 19, 2023: Sean M. Kirkpatrick, director of the All-domain Anomaly Resolution Office (AARO) testified before the Senate Armed Services Committee hearings, downplaying rampant reports of UAP sightings:

> *I want to underscore today that only a very small percentage of UAP reports display signatures that could reasonably be described as anomalous.*

2003: A lawsuit was filed against NASA to release the Kecksburg UFO documents from the military investigation. A NASA spokesperson told the Associated Press that a Russian satellite, not a UFO, was discovered on the site.

2003: Local WHJB radio station news director John Murphy produced a radio documentary titled *Object in the Woods*. And although he claimed to be the first to see the object, that has not been authenticated.

March/April 2003: In *Skeptical Inquirer*'s article titled "Lessons of the 'Fake Moon Flight' Myth," UFO debunker and scientist scholar James Oberg argued that many of the "Fake Moon Landing" stories have been born out of cultural and political hatred:

> *Resentment of American cultural and political dominance clearly fuels other "disbelievers," including those political groups who had been hoping for a different outcome to the Space Race—for example, many Cuban schools, both in Cuba and where Cuban schoolteachers were loaned, such as Sandinista Nicaragua, taught their students that Apollo was a fraud.*

Oberg wrote that this apparently widespread counterculture heresy "looked like a shriveling leftover of the original human inability to accept the reality of revolutionary changes."

2004: The National Institute for Discovery Science (NIDSci), a privately financed research organization founded by billionaire Robert Bigelow, disbanded.

June 4, 2004: NASA's twin rovers, *Spirit* and *Opportunity,* landed on opposite sides of Mars. Their ninety-day mission was to find evidence of water and to see if the Red Planet could ever have supported life. Both rovers outperformed their expectations.

2004. Senior defense and intelligence officials testified before Congress that the list of cataloged UAP sightings had since grown to four hundred, but many remain beyond explanation.

November 14, 2004: A US Navy strike group detected an unknown craft on radar one hundred miles southwest of San Diego. Two FA-18F fighter jets from the aircraft carrier USS *Nimitz* saw what appeared to be churning water, with a shadow of an oval shape underneath the surface. Then a Tic Tac-shaped object appeared above the water briefly. Strike Fighter Squadron 41 attempted to intercept the craft, but it accelerated away and moved at three times the speed of sound and more than twice the speed of the fighter jets. It had no visible markings to indicate an engine, wings, or windows, and infrared monitors didn't reveal any exhaust. Writer Greg Daugherty called this one of the best-documented and most baffling UFO sightings of the twenty-first century:

> *Witnesses included highly trained military personnel—among them several deeply experienced radar operators and fighter pilots—who, at the time of the sightings, was at the controls of arguably the most advanced flight technology ever created. And yet none can explain what they saw.*

The white craft was described as forty feet long, shaped like a Tic Tac candy, and with no wings or apparent means of propulsion.

2004: Navy commander and pilot David Fravor, while on a routine training exercise over the Pacific Ocean, shot the now widely circulated footage of a "Tic Tac," also identified by radar controllers. The object was observed close to the ocean surface, moving erratically like a "ping pong ball" that travelled more than sixty miles in less than a minute, and was capable of aerial maneuvers far beyond the technical limitations of modern aircraft. Fravor, when asked during a 2023 public congressional hearing why UAPs are a national security threat, said:

> *The controller told us that these objects had been observed for over two weeks coming down from over 80,000 feet, rapidly descending to 20,000 feet, hanging out hours and then going straight back up. The technology that we faced was far superior than anything that we had.*

2004: Jason Colavito's article in *Skeptic* magazine charged that Erich von Däniken borrowed many concepts from *Le Matin des Magiciens* (*Morning of the Magicians*)—a book that was heavily influenced by H. P. Lovecraft's Cthulhu Mythos. Colavito concludes that the core of the ancient astronaut hypothesis originated from "The Call of Cthulhu" and "At the Mountains of Madness."

2004: Retired US Navy fighter pilot Alex Dietrich described seeing a highly unusual object off the coast of Southern California after a colleague spotted something "roiling water below us." Dietrich described what has been called "one of the most compelling accounts of a UAP encounter":

> *It was this sort of roundish, oblong shape, and it didn't have any apparent flight control surfaces. It seemed to be bouncing around and changing course very quickly and in a way that we would not have been able to maneuver our own aircraft or certainly to keep up.*

February 8, 2005: Greg Bishop published the book *Project Beta: The Story of Paul Bennewitz, National Security, and the Creation of a Modern UFO Myth,* which documented the Air Force campaign of disinformation perpetrated against electrical physicist Paul Bennewitz. According to Bishop, researcher William Moore was hired by Air Force intelligence agents to keep tabs on Bennewitz, and in return, they provided Moore with classified UFO material.

June 29, 2005: The science fiction action thriller film *War of the Worlds*, based on Wells's novel, was released. The film was directed by Steven Spielberg and starred Tom Cruise, Dakota Fanning, and Tim Robbins, with narration by Morgan Freeman. The film grossed over $603 million worldwide, making it the fourth most successful film of 2005. It also earned Academy Awards nominations for Best Visual Effects, Best Sound Mixing, and Best Sound Editing.

November 7, 2005: Jason Colavito published *The Cult of Alien Gods: H. P. Lovecraft And Extraterrestrial Pop Culture*, connecting the influential science-fiction of horror writer H. P. Lovecraft (1890–1937) to the popular ancient aliens pseudoscience of Erich von Däniken, Graham Hancock, and Zecharia Sitchin.

2006: The International Astronomical Union (IAU) downgraded Pluto from a planet to a trans-Neptunian object. The essential determining factor was that a planet must dominate its orbital zone—clearing out other bodies in its orbit, gathering them, capturing them, or expelling them elsewhere. Pluto did not demonstrate orbital zone dominance.

May 1, 2006: Martin J. Sherwin and Kai Bird publish their Pulitzer Prize-winning book, *American Prometheus: The Triumph and Tragedy of J. Robert Oppenheimer,* which revisits the buildup to the Manhattan Project and the "father of the atomic bomb." Oppenheimer was a brilliant physicist and one of the iconic figures of the twentieth century.

2006: Responding to charges that the *Fox Television* documentary titled *Alien Autopsy: Fact or Fiction* was an elaborate hoax, sculptor and special-effects designer John Humphreys claimed that he crafted the alien in the autopsy footage and also appeared in the film as one of the pathologists, as reported by *Live Science*. The well-publicized documentary alleged to show footage of a postmortem of Roswell's "extraterrestrial" occupant.

November 7, 2006: Twelve United Airlines employees aboard Flight 446 witnessed a dark gray metallic craft hovering over gate C17 at Chicago's O'Hare Airport. The craft, shaped like a saucer, remained in the air for about five minutes before shooting upwards and creating a hole in the clouds. The Federal Aviation Administration dismissed the sighting as a "weather phenomenon" and chose not to investigate because the craft was not detected on radar.

December 8, 2006: Carl Sagan's *The Cosmic Connection: An Extraterrestrial Perspective* was placed at number thirteen in a list of the "25 Greatest Science Books of All Time" by *Discover* magazine:

> *(Sagan) also championed the search for extraterrestrial life and argued for the likelihood of planets around other stars two decades before they were discovered. The TV series* Cosmos *brought Sagan to the masses, but the adventure began here.*

2007: Stephen Spielberg's 1977 sci-fi epic *Close Encounters of the Third Kind* was deemed "culturally, historically, or aesthetically significant" and chosen for preservation in the library "for all time," by the United States Library of Congress. The film also received nominations for four Golden Globes and eight Academy Awards.

2007: Before his death in 2005, public relations officer Lieutenant Walter Haut left a sworn affidavit only to be opened after he passed away. Haut had written the original press release announcing that, in 1947, a flying disc had been found near Roswell, New Mexico. Haut claimed that the weather balloon explanation was a cover story and that the actual object found by the military was stored in the base's hangar. Haut said he was escorted into Roswell's Building 84, where he saw a metallic egg-shaped object and four-foot-tall aliens with large heads. He added there were actually two crash sites. In his affidavit, Haut concluded:

> *I am convinced that what I personally observed was some kind of craft and its crew from outer space.*

Haut explained that his press release was a cover story created to divert the public's interest from the second and more important crash site.

October 2007: After a federal Freedom of Information Act lawsuit, NASA was required to provide hundreds of new documents on the Kecksburg, Pennsylvania, UFO incident and pay plaintiff Leslie Kean's attorney's fees. NASA completed its search in 2009.

2007: Harry Reid joined his colleagues Ted Stevens, a Republican from Alaska, and Daniel Inouye, a Democrat from Hawaii, to invest $22 million in a clandestine Pentagon Defense Department operation called the Advanced Aerospace Threat Identification Program (AATIP). The program investigated military reports of UFOs and other inexplicable aerial objects. According to Reid:

> *They had many sightings, hundreds and hundreds of these sightings. I didn't know if it would be 20 or 40. I was stunned—it was hundreds of them.*

Tasked with investigating UAPs, the multiyear program was officially acknowledged in 2017, although the Pentagon said it had been shut down in 2012.

January 8, 2008: Countless residents of Stephenville, Texas, reported white strobe lights above Highway 67, with an estimated span of one mile long and a half mile wide. The objects silently traveled about three thousand miles per hour.

June 15, 2008: Stanton T. Friedman published *Flying Saucers and Science: A Scientist Investigates the Mysteries of UFOs: Interstellar Travel, Crashes, and Government Cover-Ups,* compiled over forty years of research obtained from his career as a nuclear physicist and lecturer. He explains, in plain terms, that UFOs are not only possible but probable, and concludes:

> *The evidence that planet Earth is being visited by intelligently controlled extraterrestrial spacecraft is overwhelming. In other words, some UFOs are ET spacecraft. Most are not—I don't care about them.*

September 15, 2008: The Roswell Legacy: The Untold Story of the First Military Officer at the 1947 Crash by Jesse Marcel Jr. and Linda Marcel. Major Jesse Marcel put his time in as an intelligence officer for the 509th Bomber Group. While he cemented his name in history for being part of the military group that dropped the atomic bomb on Japan, he made his mark even more indelible in Roswell, New Mexico. On record as being the first military officer to report to the scene of the now infamous Roswell crash, his firsthand account of his discoveries there is detailed by his son in The Roswell Legacy.

March 8, 2009: *Ancient Aliens* was broadcast as a two-hour documentary special. *Ancient Aliens: The Series* aired for three seasons as a flagship series on *History* from 2010 to 2012. The program, narrated by Robert Clotworthy, explores pseudoscientific and pseudohistorical topics, such as Atlantis and other lost ancient civilizations, extraterrestrial contact and ufology, and popular conspiracy theories in a noncritical documentary format.

The series has been criticized for promoting unorthodox or unproven hypotheses as fact and, according to Smithsonian, overwhelming the viewer with "fictions and distortions." The official promotional description read:

> Ancient Aliens *explores the controversial theory that extraterrestrials have visited Earth for millions of years. From the age of the dinosaurs to ancient Egypt, from early cave drawings to continued mass sightings in the US, each episode in this hit HISTORY series gives historic depth to the questions, speculations, provocative controversies, first-hand accounts, and grounded theories surrounding this age-old debate. Did intelligent beings from outer space visit Earth thousands of years ago?*

The program is narrated by Robert Clotworthy and features producer Giorgio Tsoukalos, writer David Childress, and journalist Nick Pope.

April 1, 2009: Author Jeff Allan Danelek published *The Great Airship of 1897: A Provocative Look at the Most Mysterious Aviation Event in History*, speculating that an unknown individual from San Francisco invented and tested the mystery airship widely seen passing slowly over California cities, sparking a media frenzy. Danelek believes these experimental flights formed the basis for wild newspaper accounts from the era, ending abruptly in mid-April 1897, suggesting that the craft may have met with disaster, effectively ending the mystery.

June 18, 2009: The NASA robotic spacecraft Lunar Reconnaissance Orbiter was launched—described as a detailed mapping program essential for planning future missions to the Moon. It sent back valuable photographs of the Moon's lunar surface, including formations of hundreds of new craters, safe landing sites, potential resources, and the radiation environment.

June 24, 2009. Anomalist Books published ufologist-abduction researcher Budd Hopkins's book *Art, Life and UFOs*.

Chapter 19
Worlds Without End: 2010s

In this decade, it all came back full circle, with *Midnight in the Desert*, *The Man from Mars*, James W. Moseley, Zecharia Sitchin, Diana Pasulka, and Pentagon and congressional promises of transparency and full disclosure.

2010: Astrophysicist Stephen Hawking, in a series for the Discovery Channel documentary, warned that humans should refrain from sending messages into space because they might attract the wrong sort of attention:

> *If aliens visit us, the outcome would be much as when Columbus landed in America, which didn't turn out well for the Native Americans.*

Hawking said it was "perfectly rational" to assume intelligent life exists elsewhere but warned that aliens might simply raid Earth for resources, then move on. Rather than actively trying to communicate with extraterrestrials, humans should do everything possible to avoid contact, he advised.

April 2, 2010: The iconoclastic radio personality Joey Reynolds left WOR-710 AM after a spectacular fourteen-year run (1996–2010). The last song he played was Lou Christie's "Beyond the Blue Horizon." Reynolds was replaced by George Noory's *Coast to Coast AM*, an enormously popular national show that dabbled in UFOs, extraterrestrial beings, and paranormal themes.

July 29, 2010: Mark Pilkington, contributing editor to *Fortean Times,* published *A Journey into Disinformation, Paranoia, and UFOs,* based on interviews with intelligence agents, scientists, psychics, and UFO hunters—and victims and scammers. The book was adapted into the 2013 documentary *Mirage Men.* According to the *Washington Post*:

> *Ultimately it is persuasive, if not definitive. In Pilkington's telling, UFO stories are "weapons of mass deception," used in bureaucratic battles to discredit competing agencies or protect real secrets. This is the stuff of normal power politics.*

August 2010: The fantastic account of Brazilian photographer Almiro Baraúna, who claimed to have photographed a sequence of a flying disc off the coast of Trindade Island, was debunked by the prime-time television program *Fantástico.* Baraúna, who passed away in 2000, only received a short segment on the program, consisting of the sound bite of a woman called Emília Bittencourt. Her secondhand confession alleged the photos were actually two cooking tablespoons, joined together, using a home refrigerator as the backdrop. Ufologists like physicist Dr. Bruce Maccabee and researcher Antonio Huneeus, however, contend that the Trindade photos are genuine.

2010: The *Coast to Coast AM* radio show presented Zecharia Sitchin with a lifetime achievement award. Sitchin, a frequent guest on the program, was a proponent of the ancient astronaut hypothesis, with his books selling millions of copies.

October 27, 2010: Folklorist Dr. Thomas E. Bullard of the University of Indiana published *The Myth and Mystery of UFOs* (University Press of Kansas, 2010). Bullard's book integrated the spectrum of alien visitations and abductions, advanced technologies, governmental conspiracies, varieties of religious salvation, apocalyptic fears, and other paranormal experiences. Reviewer Kevin D. Randle had this to say:

> *Thomas (Eddie) Bullard's book,* The Myth, and Mysteries of UFOs, *is one that walks the fine line between over-the-top scholarship and bottom-of-the-barrel trash. His is a book that belongs on everyone's shelf because of the scholarship and the readability.*

Bullard also authored a recognized three-hundred-and-fifty-page study of abduction cases.

October 30, 2010: According to Pennsylvania UFO/Bigfoot researcher Stan Gordon, not everything mandates an extraterrestrial or science-fiction origin. Writing in his book *Silent Invasion:*

> *Many UFO sightings were artificial or natural objects that looked strange under certain conditions. Many flying saucers or UFO reports were just bright meteors, planets, stars, satellites, and sometimes just lights reflecting off meandering birds and insects. Other strange events quite often could be explained as well.*

July 2011: The New Hampshire Division of Historical Resources marked the site of Barney and Betty Hill's alleged abduction by extraterrestrials with a historical marker. The roadside marker was erected on Daniel Webster Highway (Route 3) in Lincoln, New Hampshire, to commemorate the incident.

August 2011: NASA's Juno mission spacecraft began its five-year journey to explore Jupiter, arriving on the planet in July 2016. The probe will continue to explore the planet until September 2025 or until the spacecraft's end of life.

October 10, 2011: Al Bielek passed away at the age of ninety-five. Bielek claimed that he was involved with the 1943 Philadelphia Experiment and, that during the 1970s, had been a program director with the Montauk Project.

2011: Director Byron Haskin's 1953 adaptation of H. G. Wells's sci-fi novel *War of the Worlds* was selected for preservation in the National Film Registry by the United States Library of Congress, which deemed it "culturally, historically, or aesthetically significant."

2012: After NASA released detailed images of its *Curiosity* robotic rover on Mars, conspiracy theorists concluded that two visible crumbling pyramids indicated a lost civilization on the Red Planet and proof of alien life.

2011: The Discovery Channel's *Ancient Aliens* investigated the Kecksburg 1965 UFO incident, also known as Pennsylvania's Roswell.

February 22, 2012: The science-fiction action-adventure film *John Carter* marked the hundredth anniversary of the character's first appearance in 1911. The film was directed by Andrew Stanton and starred Taylor Kitsch in the title role. The film was based on Edgar Rice Burrough's *A Princess of Mars* (1912), the first book in the influential Barsoom series of novels.

The character has appeared in novels and short stories, comic books, television shows, and films.

2012: The Pentagon's Advanced Aerospace Threat Identification Program, a $22 million, multiyear program that began in 2007 to investigate UAPs, was defunded.

2012: Annie Jacobsen's *Area 51: An Uncensored History of America's Top Secret Military Base* (Boston: Back Bay Books) offers another version of the Roswell story. Jacobsen suggests that the aliens were malformed teenagers who were hideously modified, short-statured, and big-headed with odd large eyes. The Soviet Union's Joseph Stalin had arranged for the infamous Joseph Mengele to surgically mutilate some children so that they looked like aliens and then placed them into the remote-controlled craft. This was a Soviet attempt to fake an alien invasion after the example of *The War of the Worlds*. But the vehicle crashed, and the Roswell legend was born—according to the author.

2013: Fred Nadis published a biography of Ray A. Palmer, titled *The Man from Mars: Ray Palmer's Amazing Pulp Journey*. In 1945, Palmer, as editor of *Amazing Stories,* published a story by Berwick, Pennsylvania's Richard Sharpe Shaver, who believed that humanity was being controlled by an evil ancient subterranean race. For the next four years, "Shaver Mysteries," presented as "true" accounts, dominated the magazine but:

> *brought howls of outrage from fans who felt he was encouraging crackpots from the lunatic fringe.*

March 3, 2013: *The Astounding UFO Secrets Of James W. Moseley: Includes The Full Text Of UFO Crash Secrets At Wright Patterson Air Force Base* was published by James W.

Mosely and edited by Timothy Green Beckley. Mosely was ufology's most fascinating character—a debunker, hoaxer and Kokopelli-like trickster. His book, believed to have been ghost-written by Gray Barker, includes a paranormal smorgasbord of Roswell, contactees, Adamski, and UFOs from Antarctica, all as perceived by the court jester of ufology.

June 27, 2013: On the twenty-fifth anniversary of Bob Lazar's explosive interview with KLAS investigative reporter George Knapp, *Open Minds Radio* host Alejandro Rojas, attempting to get an interview, was presented with this polite refusal:

> *Sorry, Mr. Lazar no longer involves himself in matters related to the topic of UFOs.*
>
> *He hasn't followed the topic in about ten years and does not lecture on anything other than basic science and energy technologies.*
>
> *His companies are involved in several Military contracts and he is a science and technology consultant to Raytheon weapon systems.*
>
> *For these reasons, he avoids "rocking the boat" and generally keeps his distance from the topic.*

2013: Art Bell started a new nightly show, *Art Bell's Dark Matter*, on Sirius XM Radio, which aired for six weeks. Bell was the founder and the original host of the popular radio program *Coast to Coast AM*.

2013: Linda Moulton Howe appeared on a panel at the UFO Disclosure press event held at the National Press Club and reiterated Einstein's "wormhole theory":

Alien technology appears so advanced that space and time could be bent by outer space travelers, therefore allowing extraterrestrials to visit Earth.

August 2013: The US government officially acknowledged the existence of Area 51, the secret US Air Force military installation located at Groom Lake in southern Nevada. The installation has been the focus of numerous conspiracies involving extraterrestrial life, though it's only confirmed use is as a flight testing facility. Its existence was only officially acknowledged by the CIA in August 2013, and four months later, President Obama became the first US president to mention Area 51 publicly.

2013: The unmanned spacecraft *Chang'e* 3 made a soft landing on the lunar surface. China became the third nation, after the United States and the former Soviet Union, to reach the moon.

2013: Jan Harzan became MUFON's executive director. In his bio, Harzan described seeing a UFO as a child, which came within thirty feet before "shooting off over the horizon with no visible means of propulsion other than making a humming noise." During his tenure, Harzan, who previously worked in an executive management capacity for IBM, oversaw the creation of an online case management system to improve UFO reporting and data archiving.

2013: An article titled "Chariots of the Frauds: The Real Erich von Däniken" was published by Jason Colavito, who charged that von Däniken plagiarized *Morning of the Magicians*, written by French authors Jacques Bergier and Louis Pauwels, which led to von Däniken's book deal for *Chariots of the Gods*. Despite a pattern of "borrowing" ideas from earlier writers, von

Däniken enjoyed unprecedented success, fostering the ancient astronaut pseudoscience industry.

August 24, 2014: A copy of *Action Comics #1*, graded 9.0 by CGC, was sold on eBay for USD$3,207,852. It was the first comic book to have sold for more than $3 million for a single original copy and featured the superhero Superman.

October 20, 2014: Ufologist and high-ranking member of MUFON Raymond E. Fowler published *The Andreasson Affair: The True Story of a Close Encounter of the Fourth Kind*, about the abduction of New England housewife Betty Andreasson Luca. The book, which sold millions of copies, was originally published in 1979, with the foreword written by Dr. Allen J. Hynek. Author Whitley Strieber observed:

> *Something extraordinary happened to Betty Andreasson. Maybe she encountered non-human visitors or maybe something even more strange. Whatever the origin of her experience, her immensely powerful story awed me. Its rich and provocative imagery will remain with me forever.*

2014: Researcher Nick Redfern published *For Nobody's Eyes Only: Missing Government Files and Hidden Archives That Document the Truth Behind the Most Enduring Conspiracy Theories*, investigating previously hidden government files about the Roswell UFO crash and notable figures like President John F. Kennedy and Princess Diana.

2015: Art Bell returned to radio with a new show, *Midnight in the Desert*, which was available online via TuneIn as well as some terrestrial radio stations. He retired on December 11, 2015, citing security concerns. According to Heather Wade, his life had been threatened.

2015: Experimenting with the Laser Interferometer Gravitational-Wave Observatory (LIGO), scientists detected gravitational waves and proved that Einstein was right. They were able to catch high-frequency waves, quick "chirps" that come from specific moments when relatively small black holes and dead stars crash into each other. Researchers hope that the study of these specific gravitational waves will reveal more about the biggest objects in our universe. The LIGO concept tested a component of Albert Einstein's 1915 theory of general relativity, the existence of gravitational waves, and promises to open new doors to "cosmic archaeology," tracking the history of black holes and galaxies.

July 15, 2016: The Netflix TV series *Stranger Things* premiered. The science-fiction horror program is believed to have been inspired by the Montauk Project and purported time travel, and mind-control experiments.

August 13, 2016: John Higgs, investigating futurist H. G. Wells's "extraordinary insight," wrote that, as early as 1913:

> *Wells saw the coming century clearer than anyone else. He anticipated wars in the air, the sexual revolution, motorised transport causing the growth of suburbs and a proto-Wikipedia he called the "world brain." He foresaw world wars creating a federalized Europe ... In his novel* The World Set Free, *he imagined an "atomic bomb" of terrifying power that would be dropped from aeroplanes.*

Wells's utopian vision has been recognized by individuals, including Brian Aldiss, who called him the "Shakespeare of science fiction," and Charles Fort, who described him as a "wild talent."

August 17, 2016: Paranormal author Maxim W. Furek was interviewed by Heather Wade on *Midnight in the Desert* about the Sheppton Mythology and Richard Sharpe Shaver's UFO connection. Both Furek and Shaver were born in Berwick, Pennsylvania. Wade had replaced the legendary Art Bell, who was initially going to do the interview. At the time, Bell's life was being threatened, and he had gone underground. His location was a secret, as Wade explained.

2016: Kazem Finjan, the Iraqi Minister of Transport, held a press conference in the Dhi Qar district to announce the construction of a new airport. Finjan incredulously claimed that five thousand years ago, Sumerians had built an airport in the Dhi Qar Governorate to launch spaceships. He cited the work of Zecharia Sitchin (1920–2020) and others to support his assertions and stated:

> *When the Sumerians settled here, they knew full well that the atmosphere was suitable for flying to outer space. It was from here that the Sumerian spaceships took off towards the other planets.*
>
> *The Sumerians were the first to discover the 12th planet, which was acknowledged by NASA, and named Nibiru, and which completes its orbit around the sun every 3,600 years.*

2016: Real estate tycoon Brandon Fugal, who purchased Utah's infamous 512-acre Skinwalker Ranch from Robert Bigalow, told *Newsweek*:

> *It is the most scientifically studied paranormal hotspot on the planet, with the highest frequency of documented UFO sightings, bizarre cattle mutilations, electromagnetic anomalies, and unexplained phenomena.*

February 16, 2017: Clare Grafik, head of exhibitions at the 2017 London Photographers' Gallery, billed as "Conspiracy Week," told the BBC that conspiracy theories speak to people who feel that the world isn't providing them with the reality they want:

> *In a world that seems overwhelming and complex, it's attractive to find a narrative that somehow ties things down—even if that narrative is, to other people, completely outlandish. There's a natural human instinct to try to make sense of things, in whatever way you can.*

February 16, 2017: Gordon MacDonald, artist and curator of *Divisive Moments*, while researching ufology, noticed a trend:

> *Flying saucers tend to get spotted by white males in remote areas—the Swiss Alps, deserts in Nevada, rural Argentina, and Mexico—rather than by masses in urban areas. There's never been a claim that a spaceship was spotted by ten thousand people on Oxford Street, for instance—though perhaps there will be during our show.*

Divisive Moments used material from the extensive UFO Photo Archive and included abduction case studies such as *Contact: The Billy Meier Phenomenon* (1987) and *UFO Abduction at Botucatu*—the report of a repeated abduction of a Brazilian man, João Valério da Silva, and his eldest son—which featured photographs "taken" by their alien abductors and an alien language tape recording.

2017: J. Allen Hynek biographer Mark O'Connell published *The Close Encounters Man: How One Man Made the World Believe in UFOs* (Dey Street). O'Connell's book describes:

> *The astronomer who invented the concept of "Close Encounters" with alien life, inspired Steven Spielberg's blockbuster classic science fiction epic film and is the subject of History Channel's Project Blue Book, and made an entire nation want to believe in UFOs.*

With unprecedented access to Hynek's personal and professional files, O'Connell smashes conventional wisdom to reveal the intriguing man and scientist beneath the legend.

October 19, 2017: 'Oumuamua, a red-colored, cigar-shaped object was first detected by Robert Weryk, using Haleakala Observatory's Pan-STARRS telescope. Professor Avi Loeb, the chair of Harvard's astronomy department, theorized that it was of alien origin. 'Oumuamua is believed to have been the first object from another star system in the galaxy to pass through the solar system.

2017: Filmmaker Spyros Melaris, another self-identified participant in the Fox Television documentary *Alien Autopsy: Fact or Fiction*, confessed that he had shot the "autopsy" footage in his London apartment, using a model filled with animal organs. The TV documentary claimed to show footage of Roswell's "extraterrestrial" alien creature.

December 17, 2017: The *New York Times* published a UFO story on page one, written by Leslie Kean and retired *New York Times* reporter Ralph Blumenthal. Their spin shaped the article to show military interest in UFOs, not that billionaire Robert Bigalow had skillfully received funding for a personal military research program.

2017: The Pentagon acknowledged the secret program AATIP, tasked with investigating UAP sightings. The Pentagon released the F-18 gun camera footage of a possible extraterrestrial vehicle outperforming US Navy fighters off San Diego. This was the first time, after decades of denial, that the military admitted the existence of possible intelligent craft.

October 2017: The former Advanced Aerospace Threat Identification Program director Luis Elizondo left the AATIP, protesting that its work wasn't being taken seriously enough by the Defense Department. Although the government said that AATIP had officially shut down in 2012, Elizondo insisted the little-known "shadowy" enterprise was still operating.

2017: Retired naval commander David Fravor recalled an encounter with a UFO while conducting a training mission off the coast of California in 2004. He described the UFO as a wingless, oblong craft, about forty feet long and flying erratically at incredible speeds. The craft maneuvered in a way that defied accepted principles of aerodynamics. Fravor told *ABC News* it was not like anything he had ever seen during his career:

> *I can tell you, I think it was not from this world. I'm not crazy, haven't been drinking. It was—after eighteen years of flying, I've seen pretty much about everything that I can see in that realm, and this was nothing close.*

Fravor's UFO was tracked on radar by controllers on a nearby Navy ship, reporting that objects were dropping about eighty thousand feet from the sky, then headed "straight back up."

December 2017: The *New York Times* reported on the Pentagon's secret $22 million, five-year Advanced Aerospace Threat Identification Program (AATIP). The revelation that the US government was actively researching UFOs between

2007 and 2012 reignited world interest in UFOs and extraterrestrials.

2018: According to a survey, forty-one percent of Americans believe aliens have visited Earth in our ancient past, an indication of the popularity of the TV series *Ancient Aliens*—following in the wake of Erich von Däniken's 1968 book *Chariots of the Gods*.

July 8, 2018: *Pascagoula—The Closest Encounter: My Story* is published by abductee Calvin Parker, recalling one of the most classic close encounters on record. On October 11, 1973, Parker and Charles Hickson were abducted and medically examined by gray-skinned aliens. The full transcript of Calvin Parker's hypnotic regression session with the late Budd Hopkins, one of the world's foremost researchers of this phenomenon, is included.

August 23, 2018: In her comprehensive "A monstrous primer on the works of H. P. Lovecraft: Your guide to the fantasy author's nightmarish must-reads," Emma Stefansky perceived:

> *Lovecraft was a pioneer of the "speculative fiction" genre, and started the Cosmicism movement, which is marked by the belief that there are interstellar beings far outside the realm of human perception, and humans are an insignificant part of a very large, very terrifying universe. His narrators are unreliable, often addicted to substances, their minds altered and broken by the horrors they've witnessed.*

His works "traditionally feature humans catching glimpses of a bigger universe our minds were never built to comprehend," such as "Dagon", *At the Mountains of Madness*, and "The Colour Out of Space."

September 27, 2018: Arthur Berkeley published Philip Schneider: One of the bravest whistleblowers of the 20th century, with overwhelming evidence to confirm that the Oklahoma City and World Trade Centre bombings, and 9/11 were false flag attacks. Berkeley's twenty-five-page "booklet" reveals what Schneider knew about the government's secret agendas and extraterrestrials, and his suspicious death.

2018: *Newsweek* reported that MUFON officials and high-level donors to the organization propagated racist, antisemitic, and other extreme views.

January 3, 2019: Stan Michalak and Winnipeg UFO researcher Chris Rutkowski published When They Appeared: Falcon Lake 1967: The Inside Story of a Close Encounter, documenting the UFO sighting and chest and stomach burns experienced by Stefan Michalak. The Falcon Lake event is believed to be Canada's most famous UFO encounter.

January 3, 2019: China's robotic probe *Chang'e 4* made a soft landing on the moon's South Pole-Aitken Basin area, otherwise known as the "dark side" of Earth's only natural satellite. It was the first spacecraft in history to achieve a landing on this unexplored area, which is never visible from Earth.

March 10, 2019: Rev. Barry Downing, of Endwell, New York, published The Bible and Flying Saucers: Did a UFO Part the Red Sea? Downing said the parting of the Red Sea, as written in Exodus 14, could have happened as he suggested:

> *Though the ETs did carry out the Exodus, they were in some kind of spaceship called the pillar of fire by the Bible. The whole Exodus works out fine.*

Downing had previously published, in 2017, Biblical UFO Revelations: Did Extraterrestrial Powers Cause Ancient Miracles?

March 24, 2019: Former US Air Force Office of Special Investigations special agent Richard Doty addressed the UFO Mega Conference, dubbed "the Immersion Event," in Laughlin, Nevada. He acknowledged participating in the surveillance of UFO groups and disseminating false information. Doty claimed that in the 1980s he was tasked with hoaxing documents and feeding false information to UFO researchers, including Paul Bennewitz, noted for espousing his Duca War narrative.

2019: According to a Gallup survey, thirty-three percent of Americans believed that alien spacecraft have been sighted in the past. More than half of Americans also believe that the government knows more about the existence of alien life forms and is hiding something about UFOs.

April 2019: The US Navy announced it was drafting guidelines for reporting any sightings of UFOs and was "investigating each and every report." The initiative was intended to destigmatize such reports and make it easier for service members to come forward with less fear of ridicule. In a statement to *Politico*, the Navy stated:

> *There have been a number of reports of unauthorized and/or unidentified aircraft entering various military-controlled ranges and designated air space in recent years. For safety and security concerns, the Navy and the [US Air Force] takes these reports very seriously and investigates each and every report.*

> *As part of this effort, the Navy is updating and formalizing the process by which reports of any such suspected incursions can be made to the cognizant authorities. A new message to the fleet that will detail the steps for reporting is in draft.*

Although the Navy did not acknowledge the existence of alien life, they did conclude that these unexplained sightings should be investigated.

2019: University of North Carolina, Wilmington professor of religious studies Diana Pasulka published *American Cosmic: UFOs, Religion, Technology* (Oxford University Press), revealing that more than half of American adults and over sixty percent of young Americans believe in intelligent extraterrestrial life. Pasulka theorized that belief in UFOs and extraterrestrials has become a kind of religion, reflecting changing cultural attitudes and the shifting roles of religion and technology. She told Sean Illing, writing for *Vox*:

> *One way we can make sense of this by using a very old but functional definition of religion as simply the belief in nonhuman and supernatural intelligent beings that often descend from the sky. There are many definitions of religion, but this one is pretty standard.*

July 16, 2019: Rep. Mark Walker, the ranking member of the Intelligence and Counterterrorism Subcommittee, wrote a letter to Navy Secretary Richard Spencer requesting more information about the source of the UAP. Walker was concerned that the Pentagon wasn't sufficiently investigating the strange sightings regularly reported by Navy pilots:

> *Based on pilot accounts, sightings of UAPs often entail complex flight patterns and advanced maneuvering. The UAP technology appears to use revolutionary advances in quantum mechanics, nuclear science, electromagnetics, and thermodynamics.*

Walker expressed concern that the UAPs might result from significant advances in Chinese aeronautical engineering technology.

November 10, 2019: UFO researcher and former director of the British UFO Research Association Philip Mantle published *Roswell Alien Autopsy—The Truth Behind the Film That Shocked the World,* charging that the event was a staged hoax, using sheep brains and jelly stuffed into puppets.

2019: Maj. David Grusch, detailed to the National Reconnaissance Office, claimed that the head of a government task force on UAPs asked him to identify all highly classified programs relating to the task force's mission. In 2023, Grusch testified before Congress, revealing the Pentagon has been aware of "non-human" activity since the 1930s—with multi-decade programs involving UAP crash retrieval and reverse engineering.

2019: The Department of Defense declassified and released three videos taken by US Navy pilots showing flying objects that continue to remain a mystery.

2020s

April 2020: The *New York Times* reported over one thousand UAP sightings in 2020, however, that report's significance was confusing because it happened during the chaos and uncertainty of the Covid-19 pandemic. Still, there were other things of significance, according to Steve Gorman, writing for Reuters:

> *The parallel NASA and Pentagon* (*reporting of UAPs*) *efforts highlight a turning point for the US government after spending decades deflecting, debunking, and discrediting observations of unidentified flying objects, or UFOs, dating back to the 1940s.*

2020: Because of concerns about Covid-19, many New York residents, confined at home, reported seeing UFOs. Sightings across Upstate New York climbed from eighty-nine in 2019 to one hundred and sixty-two in 2020. The state spotted three hundred and ten UFOs in 2020, but compared to the rest of the country, was considered the state with the fewest UFO sightings, according to *Satellite Internet.*

July 3, 2020: MUFON executive director Jan Harzan, who at a 2013 symposium claimed to have been visited as a child by a "humming" alien, was arrested in Newport Beach, California, on charges of soliciting sex from a law enforcement detective posing online as a thirteen-year-old girl. As described by the Huntington Beach Police Department:

> *The suspect solicited the minor to meet for the purpose of engaging in sexual activity, and when the suspect agreed to meet the supposed minor, detectives were there to take him into custody.*

In response to the arrest, MUFON leadership reported that Harzan had been permanently removed as the organization's executive director and would no longer serve any role.

August 2020: To standardize and collect information about UAP sightings, the Pentagon set up the Unidentified Aerial Phenomena (UAPTF) Task Force as part of the US Office of Naval Intelligence:

> *The Department of Defense established the UAPTF to improve its understanding of, and gain insight into, the nature and origins of UAPs. The mission of the task force is to detect, analyze, and catalog UAPs that could potentially pose a threat to US national security.*

August 9, 2020: A UFO was observed near Wapwallopen, in Pennsylvania's Luzerne County. Witnesses reported that the object looked like a shooting star, then reversed direction, shooting up in the direction it came. Physical evidence of markings confirmed that the craft had landed, making it an example of Hynek's CE-2.

2020: The Navy formally released three UFO videos, first made public by the *Times* and former Blink-182 front man Tom DeLonge's To the Stars Academy—self-described as "a public benefit corporation that was established in 2017 as a revolutionary collaboration between academia, industry, and pop culture to advance society's understanding of scientific phenomena and its technological implications."

Videos released by the Pentagon show unknown objects demonstrating speed and maneuverability exceeding known aviation expertise. The Pentagon concluded these UAPs are either advanced earthly technologies, atmospherics, or something alien.

February 18, 2021: The rover *Perseverance* launched on July 30, 2020, landed on Mars to study a region called Jezero

Crater. The rover's main job was to seek signs of ancient life and collect samples of rock and regolith (broken rock and soil) for a possible return to Earth. According to NASA Science:

> *Because hardware cannot be repaired once the rover is on Mars, the team has to build a vehicle that can survive for years on a planet with punishing temperature shifts, constant radiation, and ever-present dust. To ensure readiness, they put Perseverance through a test program tougher than the trip to Mars and the environment it will encounter once there.*

March 15, 2021: Former award-winning *New York Times* reporter Ralph Blumenthal published *The Believer: Alien Encounters, Hard Science, and the Passion of John Mack* (High Road Books). Blumenthal coauthored the *Times* article in 2017 that broke the news of a secret Pentagon unit investigating UFOs.

April 1, 2021: *Captured! The Betty and Barney Hill UFO Experience (60th Anniversary Edition): The True Story of the World's First Documented Alien Abduction* was published by Stanton T. Friedman and Kathleen Marden, with the foreword written by Dr. Bruce Maccabee. As reviewed by Linda Moulton Howe, Emmy award-winning TV producer, reporter, and editor:

> The famous 1961 Betty and Barney Hill abduction by non-humans is taken apart, meticulously re-examined by Betty's niece Kathleen Marden and nuclear physicist Stanton T. Friedman, and reinforced by the pressure of facts.

June 2021: The first recorded use of the term "unidentified aerial phenomena," or UAP, was in an Office of the Director of

National Intelligence report titled *Preliminary Assessment: Unidentified Aerial Phenomena*. UAPs are all types of unidentifiable or unexplainable aerial sightings. The term UAP was later changed from "aerial" to "anomalous." According to the 2021 report, over five hundred UAP sightings have occurred since 2004—with almost one hundred and fifty occurring within the two years preceding the report.

June 10, 2021: Physicist and former *Nature* editor Mark Buchanan wrote an article in the *Washington Post* warning that attempting to establish contact with aliens could be "extremely dangerous" and possibly "end the life on earth":

> *Chances are, though, that we all should be grateful that we don't yet have any evidence of contact with alien civilizations. Attempting to communicate with extraterrestrials, if they do exist, could be extremely dangerous for us.*

Buchanan argued that since our solar system is relatively young, a more technologically advanced civilization could easily exploit our primitive vulnerabilities. He said that it might be "wiser to just wait."

June 15, 2021: In an interview with reporter Thomas Picciano of the *Binghamton Press & Sun-Bulletin*, Rev. Barry Downing, the pastor emeritus at Northminster Presbyterian Church in Endwell, New York, viewed the Bible through the lens of a ufologist:

> *Maybe the angels were ETs or aliens in our understanding all along, but they wouldn't use that language in biblical times. The biblical people were way pre-space age, so, to solve the problem, how do we translate or interpret the Bible?*

Downing's books include Biblical UFO Revelations: Did Extraterrestrial Powers Cause Ancient Miracles? (2017) and The Bible and Flying Saucers: Did a UFO Part the Red Sea? (2019).

2021: The National Aeronautics and Space Administration (NASA) is preparing a "squad" of twenty-four priests and theologians to assess how the world's major religions would react to the news that extraterrestrial life exists. The clergy will be tasked with questions about how the appearance of extraterrestrials would alter or affect earthly religions. NASA's report stated that life on other planets does not contradict any religious doctrine:

> *Modern priests accept hypotheses according to which planet Earth is not the only place in the universe where life could originate.*

The NASA-sponsored program is located at the Center for Technological Inquiry (CTI) at Princeton.

2021: A suspected UFO with flashing lights was filmed flying over Camp Wilson, a 998-square-mile US Marine installation at the southern tip of San Bernardino County in the Mojave Desert. Investigative journalist Jeremy Corbell, the only civilian invited to Congress's historic hearing in May 2022 on UAPs, obtained footage and pictures of the possible UFO and shared them with *Fox News Digital*. The UFO was described as a "large, silent and hovering triangular-shaped craft." The government claimed it was a training exercise.

July 2021: Former intelligence agent David Charles Grusch filed a legal complaint with the Department of Defense inspector general about the withholding of UAP-related information from Congress. He served as the reconnaissance office's representative to the Unidentified Aerial Phenomena Task Force from 2019–2021.

August 2021: The Pentagon established the Unidentified Aerial Phenomena Task Force to investigate observations of unknown flying aircraft.

2021: A Pentagon report found insufficient data to determine the nature of more than one hundred and forty credible sightings documented by Navy personnel.

March 9, 2022: Tim R. Swartz launched Zontar Press with *Timothy Green Beckley's Bizarre Bazaar: UFO Encounters—Ghosts and Hauntings—Unknown Creatures—Mysteries of the Hollow Earth and MORE! Stories Taken from the Files of Mr. UFO ... Timothy Green Beckley*, a compilation of articles about UFOs, ghosts, cryptids, and hauntings, being his first published book. The text included contributions from Beckley's longtime working partner Carol Ann Rodriguez, as well as from Swartz and Sean Casteel. Beckley, "Mr. UFO," who died in 2021, has been referred to as the "King of Fringe Publishers," and Casteel noted that:

> *He left behind a paranormal publishing empire that will forever be a testimony to one man's drive and determination to learn the truth about both our world and the hidden worlds that surround it.*

May 10, 2022: John Fuller published The Interrupted Journey: Two Lost Hours Aboard a UFO: The Abduction of Betty and Barney Hill, about the 1961 incident "that enraptured America and stands as the quintessential extraterrestrial encounter." The Interrupted Journey is the complete story of those missing hours and the Hills' nearly identical accounts, as revealed to doctors under psychotherapy and hypnosis. It stands as one of the most extraordinary abduction stories of our time.

July 22, 2022: *Nope*, the sci-fi-horror neo-Western written, directed, and produced by Jordan Peele, was released. The film grossed $172 million worldwide and was named one of the top ten films of 2022 by the American Film Institute. It starred Daniel Kaluuya and Keke Palmer as siblings attempting to document evidence of a UFO. *NPR* reviewer Aisha Harris said:

> *With this movie, Peele's contributing a new entry to the rich history of Black westerns (the Sidney Poitier-directed* Buck and the Preacher *is visually referenced, for one) and tapping into themes about a cultural obsession with taming nature and profiting off of pageantry. It's also significant to note how Peele playfully speaks to Black audiences and their frequent responses to horror movies through the clever title and OJ and Emerald's actions—like Regina Hall's ever-skeptical Brenda in the* Scary Movie *franchise, these characters are wary and smart about situations that are obviously ominous. "Nope" isn't just a phrase, it's a way of survival.*

2022: NASA formed a sixteen-member panel to investigate UAPs. The study, focused on sightings collected from civilian, government, and commercial sectors, included experts from scientific fields ranging from physics to astrobiology.

December 2022: The National Defense Authorization Act, spearheaded by Senators Kirsten Gillibrand and Marco Rubio and signed into law by President Biden, stated that any person with relevant unidentified aerial phenomena information can inform Congress without retaliation, regardless of any previous nondisclosure agreements.

December 16, 2022: Jennifer Granholm, the US Secretary of Energy, ordered that the 1954 decision by the Atomic Energy Commission to revoke Robert Oppenheimer's security clearance be vacated. Calling the AEC investigation a "flawed process that violated the Commission's own regulations," Secretary of Energy Jennifer Granholm said:

> *As time has passed, more evidence has come to light of the bias and unfairness of the process that Dr. Oppenheimer was subjected to while the evidence of his loyalty and love of country have only been further affirmed.*

2023: The Sky Canada Project (SCP) is being conducted by the Office of the Chief Science Advisor of Canada—the first study of its kind in over thirty years. The project seeks to understand how reports of UAPs are handled and look for ways to improve this.

January 14, 2023: Jaime Maussan, Mexico's most-famous ufologist, claimed a photo of a supposed UFO hovering over the FC Juárez soccer stadium showed "a ship of nonhuman origin."

A soccer fan's photo of an unknown dark object close to a bright setting sun behind Estadio Olympico Benito Juárez caused the sensation. A close-up of the small dark speck looks similar to a flying saucer. The computer-enhanced photo showed a smooth, dark almond-shaped object. Maussan said:

> *I share that the case was analyzed with AI equipment, and everything indicates that we are facing an unidentified anom-*

> *alous phenomenon "UAP." Given all of the above, I think it is a SHIP of nonhuman origin.*

January 28, 2023: US officials first detected a Chinese surveillance balloon and its payload when it entered US airspace near the Aleutian Islands. The balloon traversed Alaska, Canada and re-entered US airspace over Idaho. President Biden asked the military to present options and authorized them to take down the PRC device as soon as the mission could be accomplished without undue risk to US civilians under the balloon's path.

2023: NASA announced a partnership with the Defense Advanced Research Projects Agency, or DARPA, to develop a rocket that uses nuclear propulsion to carry astronaut crews to deep-space destinations like Mars. The system uses high heat from a fission reactor to turn liquid propellant into a gas, which is then funneled through a nozzle to power the spacecraft.

February 4, 2023: US President Joe Biden ordered the US Air Force to shoot down a Chinese-operated surveillance balloon over US territorial waters. The spy balloon, capable of geolocating electronic communications, was shot down by a US F-22 Raptor off the coast of South Carolina. The Chinese balloon had been detected in North American airspace, including Alaska, western Canada, and the contiguous United States, from January 28 to February 4, 2023.

February 13, 2023: White House press secretary Karine Jean-Pierre told the media that there was "no indication of aliens or extraterrestrial activity" involving what proved to be Chinese spy balloons and other benign commercial or research entities that were tracked over American territory.

February 16, 2023: President Biden, addressing the unknown objects floating over Canada and the United States, stated that:

> *These three objects were most likely balloons tied to private companies, recreation, or research institutions studying weather or conducting other scientific research.*

April 4, 2023: Former intelligence agent David Charles Grusch, thirty-six, provided the Intelligence Community Inspector General extensive classified information about deeply covert programs that have retrieved intact craft of nonhuman origin. In documents "cleared for open publication" by the Defense Office of Prepublication and Security Review at the Department of Defense, Grusch revealed that recoveries of UFOs have been made for decades by the government, its allies, and defense contractors. Grusch said:

> *Analysis has determined that the objects retrieved are of exotic origin (non-human intelligence of extraterrestrial or unknown origin) based on vehicle morphologies and material science testing and the possession of unique atomic arrangements and radiological signatures.*

He served as the reconnaissance office's representative to the Unidentified Aerial Phenomena Task Force from 2019–2021 and was the NGA's co-lead for UAP analysis. Grusch, a decorated war veteran, worked with both the National Geospatial-Intelligence Agency and the National Reconnaissance Office, where he worked on the UAP Task Force with top clearance levels.

April 28, 2023: Water may be more widespread and recent on Mars than previously thought, based on observations of

Martian dunes by China's *Zhurong* rover. The finding highlights potentially fertile areas in the warmer regions of Mars where conditions might be theoretically suitable for life to exist.

April 2023: Sean Kirkpatrick, head of the Pentagon's All-domain Anomaly Resolution Office, told senators that sightings of UAPs rose by more than one hundred and forty since the last report was released in January.

April 30, 2023: A Las Vegas Metro police officer's body camera video recorded an object that streaked low across the sky. About forty minutes later, a man called 911, saying he and his family saw a UFO fall from the sky and that there were two humanoids in his backyard. The caller said that the humanoids were eight feet tall and had big mouths and big shiny eyes that "were looking at us."

May 8, 2023: The United Kingdom's *Truthseeker* web site posted an article by Dmitry Rogozin, the former head of Russia's Roscosmos Space Agency. Rogozin expressed skepticism that the United States landed men on the Moon in 1969. He argued that he has yet to see sufficient proof. He said that he became skeptical after he saw how exhausted Soviet cosmonauts looked upon returning from their flights, compared to how seemingly unaffected the Apollo 11 crew appeared. Despite numerous conspiracy theories, the Apollo 11 mission was the first manned trip to the Moon, with Neil Armstrong and Buzz Aldrin being the first people to walk on the lunar surface.

May 22, 2023: *NBC News* reported that NASA plans to use nuclear rocket engines to get its astronauts to Mars. Scientists believe nuclear rocket engines could eliminate at least a third of that time, making long-duration spaceflights less risky for the humans on board.

May 2023: The Federal Aviation Administration was sued by wildlife and environmental groups over SpaceX's launch of its giant rocket from Texas. SpaceX's Starship soared twenty-four miles high before exploding over the Gulf of Mexico. The rocket's self-destruct system caused the nearly four-hundred-foot rocket to blow up as it spun out of control.

May 25, 2023: Virgin Galactic completed what was expected to be its final test flight before taking paying customers on brief trips to space. The craft landed at Spaceport America, situated on eighteen thousand acres adjacent to the US Army White Sands Missile Range in southern New Mexico. The company is preparing for commercial service, possibly as soon as late June 2023.

May 29, 2023: North Korea notified neighboring Japan that it plans to launch a satellite in the coming days. Experts believe it may be an attempt to put Pyongyang's first military reconnaissance satellite into orbit. Japan's coast guard said the notice it received indicated the launch window was from May 31 to June 11 and that the launch may affect waters in the Yellow Sea, East China Sea, and east of the Philippines' Luzon Island. Several days later Pyongyang admitted that the launch failed.

May 29, 2023: The United Arab Emirates unveiled plans to send a spaceship to explore the solar system's main asteroid belt. If successful, the spacecraft will soar at speeds reaching 20,500 miles per hour on a seven-year journey. It will culminate in the deployment of a landing craft onto a seventh, rare "red" asteroid that scientists say may "hold insight into the building blocks of life on Earth."

May 30, 2023: Scientists and tech industry leaders issued a warning about the perils artificial intelligence poses to humankind. Geoffrey Hinton, a computer scientist known as the godfather of artificial intelligence, was among the hundreds of leading figures who signed the statement, which cautioned:

> *Mitigating the risk of extinction from AI should be a global priority alongside other societal-scale risks such as pandemics and nuclear war.*

Concerns about artificial intelligence systems outsmarting humans and running amuck have intensified with the rise of a new generation of highly capable AI chatbots such as ChatGPT. Stanley Kubrick's 1968 film, *2001: A Space Odyssey*, offered an earlier warning, where the HAL 9000 computer began to assume control.

May 31, 2023: NASA held its first public meeting a year after launching a study into what they have designated as UAPs, or unidentified aerial phenomena. The space agency brought together an independent panel consisting of sixteen scientists and other experts, including retired astronaut Scott Kelly, the first American to spend nearly a year in space. The study, a first step in trying to explain mysterious sightings in the sky, contained no secret military data. Several committee members have been subjected to "online abuse" for serving on the team.

June 5, 2023: An article written by journalists Leslie Kean and Ralph Blumenthal in *The Debrief* identified whistleblower David Charles Grusch, who claimed that the United States has a secret UFO retrieval program and possession of multiple UFOs of nonhuman origin as well as records of dead pilots. The *New York Times, Politico,* and the *Washington Post* were unable to verify the story and turned it down.

2023: The Sky Canada Project will begin studying UAPs for the first time in almost thirty years. The study is being conducted by Canada's Office of the Chief Science Advisor and is tasked to understand how reports of UAPs are handled and look for ways to improve their methodology.

June 11, 2023: David Grush, thirty-six, was interviewed by Ross Coulthart, co-host of *Need to Know*, revealing that "we have non-human exotic technical vehicles that have either landed or crashed." Grush, from Pittsburgh, Pennsylvania, was a fourteen-year intelligence officer who worked for the National Geospatial-Intelligence Agency. The whistleblower admitted that he has never personally seen any NHI (non-human intelligence) beings but knows that they exist and has seen classified photos of intact spacecraft. Grush surmised that these beings may not be extraterrestrial but may come from a higher-dimensional physical space, co-located on Earth. Grush stated, "We definitely are not alone."

June 12, 2023: Ufologist Dr. Steven M. Greer, founder of the Disclosure Project, addressed the National Press Club, presenting evidence of illegal unacknowledged Pentagon UFO/UAP black-budget projects. He was joined by other government whistleblowers, who presented testimony.

June 2023: Ex-intelligence officer and whistleblower David Grusch, interviewed on *NewsNation,* revealed that in 1933 the Italian government under Benito Mussolini recovered a UAP, which it then "moved to a secure airbase in Italy for the rest of the fascist regime until 1944–1945." Grusch said Pope Pius XII "backchanneled that," and the Vatican "told the Americans what the Italians had and we ended up scooping it." Grusch said that there has been a massive international cover-up of alien life that's been going on for ninety years. He later testified before Congress on July 26, 2023.

2023: Professor Avi Loeb, the chair of Harvard's astronomy department from 2011 to 2020, claimed he uncovered remnants of an alien "spacecraft" at the bottom of the Pacific Ocean. Loeb combed the ocean's bottom for two weeks, searching for fragments from a 2014 meteor that crashed off the coast of Papua New Guinea. Professor Loeb believes that the meteor, dubbed IM1, originated from interstellar space. Loeb has been arguing for years that Earth may have been visited by interstellar technology.

June 28, 2023: For the first time, scientists were able to "hear" low-frequency gravitational waves—changes in the fabric of the universe that are created by huge objects moving around and colliding in space. Einstein predicted when really heavy objects move through space-time—the fabric of our universe—they create ripples that spread through that fabric. Scientists sometimes liken these ripples to the background music of the universe.

June 30, 2023: The James Webb Space Telescope released images of Saturn and three of its moons—Enceladus, Tethys, and Dione—and the planet's glowing icy rings. Using this advanced technology, scientists hope to uncover new ring structures and any new, hidden faint moons.

June 2023: The Senate's approved text for the Intelligence Authorization Act (IAA) for fiscal 2024 included deeper transparency regarding government encounters with UAPs and any associated attempts to inspect or reverse engineer recovered, unexplainable craft or materials. The proposal comes just after a former Pentagon official-turned-whistleblower alleged that the US has spacecraft of nonhuman origin. The legislation notes that it applies to "any activities relating to the following":

1. *Recruiting, employing, training, equipping, and operations of, and providing security for, government or contractor personnel with a primary, secondary, or contingency mission of capturing, recovering, and securing unidentified anomalous phenomena craft or pieces and components of such craft.*
2. *Analyzing such craft or pieces or components thereof, including for the purpose of determining properties, material composition, method of manufacture, origin, characteristics, usage and application, performance, operational modalities, or reverse engineering of such craft or component technology.*
3. *Managing and providing security for protecting activities and information relating to unidentified anomalous phenomena from disclosure or compromise.*
4. *Actions relating to reverse engineering or replicating unidentified anomalous phenomena technology or performance based on analysis of materials or sensor and observational information associated with unidentified anomalous phenomena.*
5. *The development of propulsion technology, or aerospace craft that uses propulsion technology, systems, or subsystems, that is based on or derived from or inspired by inspection, analysis, or reverse engineering of recovered unidentified anomalous phenomena craft or materials.*
6. *Any aerospace craft that uses propulsion technology other than chemical propellants, solar power, or electric ion thrust.*

June 2023: In a statement, a NASA spokesperson said:

> *One of NASA's key priorities is the search for life elsewhere in the universe, but so far, NASA has not found any credible evidence of extraterrestrial life and there is no evidence that UAPs are extraterrestrial.*

The statement also said that NASA explores the solar system and beyond to help answer fundamental questions, including whether we are alone in the universe.

July 1, 2023: The European Space Agency's Euclid observatory space telescope was launched by Space X from Cape Canaveral, Florida. Euclid will explore the mysterious realm, known as the dark universe, and should reach its one-million-mile destination in a month to begin its six-year survey. Named for the ancient Greek mathematician, Euclid will scour billions of galaxies and hope to glean insight into the dark energy and dark matter that make up most of the universe.

July 2023: Senate Majority Leader Chuck Schumer (D-N.Y.) introduced legislation that would require the Pentagon to release any information it has gathered around contact with "non-human intelligence," among other UAP. The proposed amendment would direct the National Archives and Records Administration to create a collection of records on UAPs and UFOs to be disclosed to the public immediately unless a review board provides reasons to keep them classified. Schumer said in a statement:

> *For decades, many Americans have been fascinated by objects mysterious and unexplained and it's long past time they get some answers. The American public has a right to learn about technologies of unknown origins, non-human intelligence, and unexplainable phenomena.*

July 26, 2023: Retired major David Grusch testified before Congress, charging that the Pentagon has been aware of "non-human" extraterrestrial activity since the 1930s—with multi-decade programs involving UAP crash retrieval and reverse engineering.

July 27, 2023: Sean Kirkpatrick, head of the Pentagon's All-domain Anomaly Resolution Office, fired back at retired major David Grusch, who accused the US of covering up a long-standing government program to recover extraterrestrials from unidentified craft. Kirkpatrick, in a memo, stated:

> *To be clear, AARO has yet to find any credible evidence to support the allegations of any reverse engineering program for non-human technology.*

Kirkpatrick further accused Grusch of insulting the officers of the Department of Defense and Intelligence Community.

September 12, 2023: UFO researcher Jaime addressed a UFO congressional hearing in Mexico and presented the remains of two ancient "non-human" alien corpses found fossilized in mines in Cusco, Peru, in 2017. The National Autonomous University of Mexico conducted radiocarbon dating tests on them, which Maussan claimed revealed them to be up to 1,800 years old; Maussan testified:

> *These specimen are not part of our terrestrial evolution... These aren't beings that were found after a UFO wreckage. They were found in diatom mines and were later fossilized. This is the first time (extraterrestrial life) is presented in such a form, and I think there is a clear demonstration that we are dealing with non-human specimens that are not related to any other species in our world.*

The mummified creatures, brought out in two glass display cases, had tiny bodies, three-fingered hands, and elongated heads that may offer the elusive proof we have been searching for.

The final word has yet to be heard, and yes, this story will be continued ...

Chapter 20
Conclusions

Like children looking through eyes filled with awe and dread, early man stared into the skies for protection and salvation. He believed that mighty gods, wiser and more technologically advanced, resided above, praying to these altruistic space brothers to save him from total destruction.

Flying Saucer Esoteric reveals a series of events, offering a novel perspective. It is akin to entering H. G. Wells's time machine and embarking on an amazing journey of acceptance and disbelief, of science and non-science, traveling from the beginning, through decades of time and space, to our present day.

My intention in writing this book was to expand the boundaries of ufology by embracing the scientific elements of space exploration, astrobiology, and human technological supremacy. I believe man created the pyramids and the Easter Island statues and was responsible for countless other archaeological, astronomical, and mathematical achievements. Man did it without help from Mars, Venus, or Clarion space brothers.

Adamski, Sitchin, and von Däniken were wrong. Einstein, Hynek, and Sagan were right.

Flying Saucer Esoteric is vastly different from my previous book, *Coal Region Hoodoo*. In that narrative, we explored all of the familiar territory—life after death, out-of-body experiences, Sheppton, Bigfoot, angels, and zombies. *Flying Saucer Esoteric* offers none of that but presents UFOs as science, pseudo-science, religion, mythology, and popular culture. And, of course, theories.

In her 1974 Redbook article "UFOs: Visitors from Outer Space," American cultural anthropologist Margaret Mead (1901–1978) argued that the UFO phenomena represented a tangible entity, not some abstract construct demanding our unwavering faith. Dismissing the question, "Do you believe in UFOs?" she wrote:

> *Belief has to do with matters of faith. It has nothing to do with the kind of knowledge that is based on scientific inquiry. We should not bracket UFOs with angels and archangels, devils, and demons. But this is just what we are doing when we ask whether people "believe" in UFOs—as if their existence were an article of faith. Do people believe in the sun or the moon or the changing seasons or the chairs they are sitting on?*

Mead argued that most people frame the UFO question around their personal belief system rather than looking to the scientific community for answers or theories.

Theories abound. That hasn't changed. At this point, UFOs or UAPs are either physical anomalies, psychic projections, or an interdimensional something else, yet to be defined. We don't know. I wish we did. And maybe we will!

* * *

If you loved this book, check out Maxim's other book Coal Region Hoodoo: Paranormal Tales from Inside the Pit.

Excerpt from Coal Region Hoodoo:

Night of the Living Dead

Shot in rural Evans City, Pennsylvania, Night of the Living Dead fleshed out its reputation as birthmother to the zombie film, pushing the boundaries of the horror genre from psychological suspense to buckets full of blood and gore. The beginning is one of cinema's classic opening scenes, with suspense building in every vintage frame. A car (a 1967 Pontiac LeMans) slowly moves up and down steep winding hills, atmospheric music in the background. It finally arrives at a cemetery in rural Evans City.

Evans City

Night of the Living Dead was filmed around the quaint town of Evans City, nestled in a valley surrounded by large hills and a beautiful landscape. It is located just north of Pittsburgh in Butler County. Evans City has approximately 1,800 residents, many sharing the same German heritage as the early settlers. The Evans City Cemetery and nearby community basked in notoriety after *Night of the Living Dead* was released. According to Mayor Dean Zinkhann, his city became a magnet that attracted numerous fans, including couples who renewed their wedding vows at the cemetery chapel. They came from all over the world, including Australia. Nevertheless, this film represents more than just an opportunity for a road trip and a wedding destination.

The Evans City Cemetery, just north of Pittsburgh in Butler County, was the rural location where *Night of the Living Dead* was filmed. In 1999, the film was deemed "culturally, historically, or aesthetically significant" by the Library of Congress and selected for preservation in the National Film Registry. (Photograph by Patricia A. Furek.)

The 1968 American horror film, produced one year before Woodstock's peace and love, was written, directed, and photographed by George A. Romero (1940–2017). In a 2010 interview with film critic Peter Keough, Romero described his zombie films as "snapshots of the time they were made" and influenced by the era's political climate. Moreover, Romero's independent film was cobbled from drips and drabs of other similar themes, hidden gems he successfully mined. For example, Romero and co-writer John Russo found inspiration in Richard Matheson's classic 1954 vampire novelette *I Am Legend*. Matheson's plot is about a virus created to battle cancer, which mutates into a plague turning people into carnivorous vampire-like creatures. Matheson's theme has been imitated in a host of other post-apocalyptic films, such as Vincent Price's *The Last Man on Earth* (1964) and Cormac McCarthy's *The Road* (2006).

Acknowledgments

There were many people who helped with this project. I would like to thank them all and apologize for any lapses in memory.

Thanks to Michael Anthony, Justin Bamforth, Dean Bertran, Timothy Green Beckley, James B. Boyd, Joey Champion, James Creachbaum, Christine Curley, David Freas, David Giordano, Stan Gordon, David Karchner, Shawn Kelly, Taryn Kerper, Barbara Kleckner, Ryan Oberst, Gwendelyn Purcell, Timothy Renner, Tim Swartz, Rich Rozelle, Barbara Smith, Gene Steinburg, Susan Swiatek, Mark Tomeo, John Weaver, and Cheryl Knight-Wilson. Special thanks to Charles "Rudi" Phillips for sharing his personal and extensive flying saucer collection with me.

References

BOOKS

Bamforth, J. *The Spectrum*. Normal Paranormal Publishing, 2018.

Bishop, G. *Project Beta: The Story of Paul Bennewitz, National Security, and the Creation of a Modern UFO Myth*. New York: Paraview Pocket Books, 2005.

Blum, R., and J. *Beyond Earth: Man's Contact with UFOs*. New York: Bantam Books, Inc., 1974.

Chambers, H. V. *The Facts on the Flying Saucer Controversy*. New York: Grosset & Dunlap, 1967.

Clarke, A. C. *The Promise of Space*. New York: Harper & Row, 1968.

Condon, E. U. *Scientific Study of Unidentified Flying Objects*. New York: Bantam Books, 1969.

Cutchin, J., & Renner, T. *Where the Footprints End: High Strangeness and the Bigfoot Phenomenon. Volume II: Evidence*. Red Lion, Pennsylvania: Dark Holler Arts, 2020.

References

Dudding, G. *The Kecksburg UFO Incident.* Spencer, WV: GSD Publications, 2013.

Edwards, F. *Flying Saucers – Here and Now!* New York: Bantam Books, Inc.,1967.

Edwards, F. *Flying Saucers – Serious Business.* New York: Bantam Books, Inc.,1966.

Fuller, J. G. *Incident at Exeter.* New York: Berkley Medallion Books, 1966.

Furek, M. W. *Coal Region Hoodoo: Paranormal Tales from Inside the Pit.* San Diego: Beyond the Fray Publishing, 2023.

Furek, M. W. *Sheppton: The Myth, Miracle and Music.* Charleston, SC: CreateSpace, 2015.

Gordon, S. *Silent Invasion. The Pennsylvania UFO-Bigfoot Casebook.* www.stangordon.com, 2010.

Hopkins, B**.** *Art, Life and UFOs***.** San Antonio: Anomalist Books, 2009.

Hynek, J. A., Imbrogno, P. J., and Pratt, B. *Night Siege: The Hudson Valley UFO Sightings.* New York: Ballantine Books, 1987.

Jacobsen, *A. Area 51: An Uncensored History of America's Top Secret Military Base.* Boston: Back Bay Books, 2012.

Jessup, M. *The Case for the UFO.* New York: Bantam Books, 1955.

Kanon, G. M. *The Great UFO Hoax: The Final Solution of the UFO Mystery.* Lakeville, MN: Galde Press, Inc., 1997.

Keel, J. The Mothman Prophecies. New York: Tom Doherty Associates, 1991.

Keyhoe, D. E. *Flying Saucers from Outer Space*. New York: Henry Holt and Company, 1953.

Lorenzen, C., and J. *Flying Saucer Occupants*. New York: Signet Books, 1967.

McWane, G., and Graham, D. *The New UFO Sightings*. New York: Warner Paperback Library, 1974.

Matthews, R. *Alien Encounters*. London: Arcturus Publishing Limited, 2021.

Menzel, D. H., and Boyd, L. G. *The World of Flying Saucers: A Scientific Examination of a Major Myth of the Space Age*. Garden City, New York: Doubleday & Company, Inc., 1963.

Murdin, P. *The Secret Lives of Planets*. New York: Pegasus Books, 2019.

Mysteries of Mind, Space & Time. The Unexplained. Vol 1. Westport, Connecticut: H. S. Stuttman, Inc., Publishers, 1992.

Mysteries of the Unknown: The UFO Phenomenon. Alexandria, VA: Time-Life Books, 1987.

Newton, M. Strange Pennsylvania Monsters. Atglen, PA: Schiffer Publishing Ltd. 2012.

Pilkington, M. *Mirage Men: An Adventure into Paranoia, Espionage, Psychological Warfare, and UFOs*. New York: Skyhorse Publishing, 2010.

Randle, K. D., and Schmitt, D. R. *The Truth About the UFO Crash at Roswell*. New York: Avon Books, 1994.

Randles, J., and Hough, P. The Complete Book of UFOs. New York: Sterling Publishing Co., Inc., 1996.

Renner, T. Bigfoot in Pennsylvania. Red Lion, Pennsylvania: Dark Holler Arts, 2017.

Sagan, C. *The Cosmic Connection: An Extraterrestrial Perspective.* Garden City, New York: Doubleday, 1973.

Sitchin, Z. *The 12th Planet.* New York: Avon Books, 1976.

Steiger, B. *Alien Meetings.* New York: Ace Books, 1978.

Steiger, B., and Whritenour, J. *Flying Saucers are Hostile.* New York: Award Books, 1967.

Story, R. *The Space Gods Revealed.* New York: Barnes & Noble Books, 1976.

Springfield, L. H. *Situation Red: The UFO Siege.* New York: Fawcett Crest, 1977.

Sullivan, W. *We Are Not Alone.* New York: Signet Books, 1964.

The Bigfoot Alien Connection Revealed. Centre Communications, Inc. 2020.

Trench, B. L. *The Flying Saucer Story.* New York: Ace Books, Inc., 1966.

Vallee, J. *Anatomy of a Phenomenon.* New York: Ace Books, Inc., 1965.

Vallee, J. *Passport to Magonia: From Folklore to Flying Saucers.* Chicago: Henry Regnery Co., 1969.

Walton, T. *The Walton Experience.* New York: Berkley Publishing Group, 1978.

Wilkins, H. T. *Flying Saucers Uncensored.* New York: Pyramid Books, 1955.

Zubrin, R. *Entering Space: Creating A Spacefaring Civilization.* New York: Jeremy P. Tarcher/Putnam, 1999.

Periodicals

Aggen, E. A. Jr. "The Absence of UFO Artifacts." *Flying Saucers*, No. 70 (September 1970): 20–21.

Aguilar, X. F. "Flying Saucers: The Money Making Myth." *Flying Saucers,* No. 68 (March 1970): 22.

Anderson, J. "Questions shroud the Roswell Incident." *Washington Merry-Go-Round,* (May 31, 1995).

Blum, R. "Are UFOs For Real?" *Readers' Digest* (June 1974): 89.

Burns, R. "Air Force and skeptics remain worlds apart on UFO aliens." *Philadelphia Inquirer,* (June 25, 1997).

Casteel, S. "Bizarre Bazaar: Tim Beckley's Marketplace of the Strange." *Paranormal Underground,* (May 2022): 10–15.

Clark, K. R. "Former 'M.A.S.H.' regular hosts '*U.F.O. Cover-up?*'" *Chicago Tribune,* (October 14, 1988).

Fox, M. "Budd Hopkins, Abstract Expressionist and U.F.O. Author, Dies at 80." *New York Times,* (April 24, 2011).

Furek, M. W. "Revisiting the Kecksburg UFO Incident." *Paranormal Underground,* (May 2022): 38–40.

"Good News, If True? On Air Force Dropping 'UFO Hunt.'" *Flying Saucers,* No. 70 (September 1970): 18.

Gordon, S. *Silent Invasion. The Pennsylvania UFO-Bigfoot Casebook.* www.stangordon.com, 2010.

"Government report has no answers about UFOs." Associated Press, Press Enterprise, (June 26, 2021). 4.

Guiley, R. E. Interview. "The Bigfoot Alien Connection." (January 27, 2019.)

Heiden, R. W. "Walter Cronkite and UFOs." *The Star Beacon*, (April 2023).

"Luis Elizondo reveals that our military has experienced alien abductions and implants." *The Gate to Strange Phenomena*, Vol. 38, (1), 1 & 2, (July 2022).

Mead, M. "UFO – Visitors from Outer Space?" *Redbook*, 57 (September 1974).

Monroe, R. "The Enduring Panic About Cow Mutilations." The New Yorker, (May 8, 2023). Retrieved from https://www.newyorker.com/news/letter-from-the-southwest/the-enduring-panic-about-cow-mutilations

"Monsters: Myth or Fact?" NBC Smithsonian Special (January 20, 1977). Narrated by Rod Serling.

Morello, C. "Unbelievable: Strange sights are common along Chestnut Ridge." The Philadelphia Inquirer, (February 12, 1989): B1 & 7B.

Schneck, M. "Is Bigfoot in Pennsylvania? Parts of the state have several reported Sasquatch sightings." *PatriotNews*, (June 18, 2019).

"Scientist: Many UFO sightings quake-related phenomena." Associated Press, (April 15, 1992).

Sheppard, R. Z. "Books: Worlds in Collusion." Time, (August 2, 1976).

Stoneley, J. "The Sentinel Stars: Some Top Scientists Begin to Believe That Man Not Alone In Restless, Changing Universe." *Grit*, (February 16, 1975): 15, 16, 30.

"UFO experts: Silent invasion has begun." Associated Press (March 21, 1992).

Internet sources

"25 Greatest Science Books of All Time." *Discover* (December 8, 2006). Retrieved from https://www.discovermagazine.com/the-sciences/25-greatest-science-books-of-all-time

Andrew, S. "The US Navy just confirmed these UFO videos are the real deal." CNN (September 18, 2018). Retrieved from https://www.cnn.com/2019/09/18/politics/navy-confirms-ufo-videos-trnd/index.html

Andrews, E. "World War II's Bizarre 'Battle of Los Angeles.'" History.com (May 6, 2020). Retrieved from https://www.history.com/news/world-war-iis-bizarre-battle-of-los-angeles

February 26, 1942: "Sailing in the Timor Sea, the Royal Netherlands Navy cruiser *Tromp* witnessed a large aluminum-shaped UFO, flying towards them at an estimated speed of 3,500 mph. The officer on duty was unable to identify it as any known aircraft."

"Area 51." *Britannica* (April 21, 2023). Retrieved from https://www.britannica.com/place/Area-51

Barlow, N. "Mars: An Introduction to its Interior, Surface, and Atmosphere." Cambridge University Press. Retrieved from https://assets.cambridge.org/97805218/52265/excerpt/9780521852265_excerpt.pdf

Bender, B. "Republican lawmaker presses Navy on UFO sightings." *Politico* (July 30, 2019). Retrieved from https://www.politico.com/story/2019/07/30/navy-mark-walker-ufo-1441105

Bennett, M. "Recent UFO Sightings In Pennsylvania: Here's What They Saw." Patch.com (July 9, 2020). Retrieved from https://patch.com/pennsylvania/across-pa/ufo-awareness-day-sightings-pennsylvania-what-they-saw

Bernard, L. "Bigfoot sightings in the Pennsylvania wilds." Pennsylvania Wilds (May 24, 2019). Retrieved from https://pawilds.com/bigfoot-sightings-pennsylvania-wilds/

"Billy Meier: The Controversial Contactee." *Gaia* (February 27, 2020). Retrieved from https://www.gaia.com/article/billy-meier-the-controversial-contactee

Booth, B. J. "The Kecksburg UFO Crash." UFO Evidence.org (2011). Retrieved from http://ufoevidence.org/documents/doc1294.htm

Borunda, D. "Unidentified object flying over Mexican soccer stadium was of 'nonhuman origin,' famous ufologist claims." *USA Today* (January 20, 2023). Retrieved from https://www.yahoo.com/now/unidentified-object-flying-over-mexican-202539691.html

Bowman, V. "Aliens exist but we may simply not see them, says first British astronaut into space." *The Telegraph* (January 6, 2020). Retrieved from https://www.yahoo.com/news/aliens-exist-living-among-us-173131625.html

Brooks, M. "*The Blob* (1958) – Review." Mana Pop (January 24, 2020). Retrieved from https://manapop.com/film/the-blob-1958-review/

Burke, D. "Story of Shag Harbour UFO examined by folk-lorist." *CBS News* (October 2, 2016). Retrieved from https://www.cbc.ca/news/canada/nova-scotia/shag-harbour-ufo-folk lorist-story-1.3788102

"Carl Jung's Fascinating 1957 Letter on UFOs." Open Culture (May 31, 2013). Retrieved from https://www.openculture.com/2013/05/
carl_jungs_1957_letter_on_the_fascinating_mod ern_myth_of_ufos.html

Carter, J. "Florida Scoutmaster's Close Encounter With UFO." Anomalien.com (August 20, 2020). Retrieved from https://anomalien.com/florida-scoutmasters-close-encounter-with-ufo/

Carter, J. "Brush Creek UFO Incident: Two Miners Saw UFOs and Aliens." Anomalien.com (December 7, 2020). Retrieved from https://anomalien.com/brush-creek-ufo-inci dent-two-miners-saw-ufos-and-aliens/

Chappell, B. "The Pentagon got hundreds of new reports of UFOs in 2022, a government report says." *NPR* (January 13, 2023). Retrieved from https://www.npr.org/2023/01/13/1149019140/ufo-report

Chow, D., Costello, T., & Seidman, J. "NASA has sights set on Mars with help from a nuclear rocket engine." *NBC News* (May 22, 2023). Retrieved from https://frontier.yahoo.com/news/nasa-sights-set-mars-help-175925344.html

Cook, E. "Congressman Says Alien UFO Tech Is Being 'Reverse Engineered' in Secret." *Newsweek* (March 7, 2023). Retrieved from https://www.newsweek.com/congressman-tim-burchett-ufo-technology-reverse-engineered-1786068

Daugherty, G. "George Adamski Got Famous Sharing His UFO Photos and Alien 'Encounters'. He claimed to have conversed with Venusians using hand gestures and mental telepathy." History.com (January 9, 2020). Retrieved from https://www.history.com/news/george-adamski-ufo-alien-photos

Daugherty, G. "When Top Gun Pilots Tangled With A Baffling Tic-Tac-Shaped UFO." History.com (June 5, 2019). Retrieved from https://www.history.com/news/uss-nimitz-2004-tic-tac-ufo-encounter

Dickinson, D. "Spot failed Soviet Venus prove in Earth orbit." *Universe Today* (March 20, 2019). Retrieved from https://phys.org/news/2019-03-soviet-venus-probe-kosmos-earth.html

Dinkel, M. "Acorn from Space: The Kecksberg Incident." Pennsylvania Center for the Book, 2010. Retrieved from https://pabook.libraries.psu.edu/literary-cultural-heritage-map-pa/feature-articles/acorn-space-kecksburg-incident

Dwelly, J. "The Flannan Isle Mystery: The Three Lighthouse Keepers Who Vanished." SkyHistory (June 14, 2023). Retrieved from https://www.history.co.uk/articles/the-flannan-isle-mystery-the-three-lighthouse-keepers-who-vanished

Elderkin, B. "6 Lesser-Known Cults That Will Give You More Nightmares Than *American Horror Story*." *Gizmodo.com* (September 11, 2017). Retrieved from https://gizmodo.com/6-lesser-known-cults-that-will-give-you-more-nightmares-1800917042

Feehly, C. "Will We Know Alien Life When We See It?" *RealClearScience* (January 5, 2023). Retrieved from https://www.realclearscience.com/2023/01/06/will_we_know_alien_life_when_we_see_it_874144.html

"Florida Scoutmaster." UFOHelp.com (May 22, 2023). Retrieved from http://www.ufohelp.com/Classic%20Sightings/Florida%20Scoutmaster.htm

"Forensic Expert Says Bigfoot Is Real." *National Geographic* (October 23, 2003). Retrieved from https://www.nationalgeographic.com/culture/article/forensic-expert-says-bigfoot-is-real

Galloway, C. *The Andromeda Strain.* CriterionForum.org (June 28, 2019). Retrieved from https://criterionforum.org/Review/the-andromeda-strain-arrow-video-blu-ray

Garamone, J. "F-22 Safely Shoots Down Chinese Spy Balloon Off South Carolina Coast." US Department of Defense (February 4, 2023). Retrieved from https://www.defense.gov/News/News-Stories/Article/Article/3288543/f-22-safely-shoots-down-chinese-spy-balloon-off-south-carolina-coast/

Garber, M. "The Man Who Introduced the World to Flying Saucers." *The Atlantic* (June 15, 2014). Retrieved from https://www.theatlantic.com/technology/archive/2014/06/the-man-who-introduced-the-world-to-flying-saucers/372732/

Gordon, S. "Kecksburg, PA, UFO Incident: Some Interesting Details 56 Years Later." Phantoms and Monsters (December 10, 2021). Retrieved from https://www.phantomsandmonsters.com/2021/12/kecksburg-pa-ufo-incident-some.html

Gorman, S. "NASA's UFO panel convenes to study unclassified sightings." Reuters (October 24, 2022). Retrieved from https://frontier.yahoo.com/news/nasas-ufo-panel-convenes-study-003226536.html

Harris, A. "Jordan Peele subverts expectations (again) with 'Nope.'" *NPR* (July 21, 2022). Retrieved from https://www.

npr.org/2022/07/21/1112634101/jordan-peele-subverts-expectations-again-with-nope

Heiser, D. "Chariots of the Frauds: The Real Erich von Daniken." *Paleobabble* (April 6, 2013). Retrieved from https://drmsh.com/chariots-frauds-real-erich-von-daniken/

Hernandez, S. "UFO sightings in Upstate NY nearly doubled in 2020. Where did aliens visit most?" *NYup.com* (March 8, 2021). Retrieved from https://www.newyorkupstate.com/news/2021/03/ufo-sightings-in-upstate-ny-nearly-doubled-in-2020-where-did-aliens-visit-most.html

Higgs, J. "HG Wells's prescient visions of the future remain unsurpassed." *The Guardian* (August 13, 2016). Retrieved from https://www.theguardian.com/books/2016/aug/13/hg-wells-visions-of-the-future-remain-unsurpassed

Huneeus, A. "Rare document on the Trindade UFO case." OpenMinds (August 26, 2010). Retrieved from https://www.openminds.tv/trindade-ufo-case-205/5060

Huneeus, A. "Remembering Jim Moseley (1931–2012), the Voltaire of American Ufology." OpenMinds (November 23, 2012). Retrieved from http://www.openminds.tv/remembering-jim-moseley-1931-2012-the-voltaire-of-american-ufology

"Intruders Foundation." Ufopedia (May 1, 2023). Retrieved from https://www.ufopedia.it/Intruders_Foundation.html

Jaksic, V. M. "How Orson Welles' 1930s *War of the Worlds* radio adaptation went viral."

CBC (September 15, 2020). Retrieved from https://www.cbc.ca/television/how-orson-welles-1930s-war-of-the-worlds-radio-adaptation-went-viral-1.5719569

Janos, A. "What Really Happened at Roswell?" History.com (May 8, 2023). Retrieved from https://www.history.com/news/roswell-ufo-aliens-what-happened

James, S. J. "HG Wells: A visionary who should be remembered for his social predictions, not just his scientific ones." *Independent* (September 22, 2016). Retrieved from https://www.independent.co.uk/arts-entertainment/hg-wells-a-visionary-who-should-be-remembered-for-his-social-predictions-not-just-his-scientific-ones-a7320486.html

John Carter of Mars Series. Edgar Rice Burroughs Universe. (May 23, 2023.) Retrieved from https://www.edgarriceburroughs.com/series-profiles/john-carter-of-mars-series/

Joshi, S. T. "Howard Phillips Lovecraft: The Life of a Gentleman of Providence." (April 29, 2023.) Retrieved from https://www.hplovecraft.com/life/biograph.aspx

Kane, M. "Is Bigfoot an extraterrestrial visitor? Some researchers think so." *Masslive* (October 19, 2015). Retrieved from https://www.masslive.com/news/worcester/2015/10/is_bigfoot_an_extraterrestrial.html

Karl Pflock. *Extraterrestrial Contact.* (May 11, 2023.) Retrieved from http://ufoevidence.org/Researchers/Detail105.htm

Kay, S. "How Takoma Gave the World the Flying Saucer." *Grit City Magazine* (October 2019). Retrieved from https://gritcitymag.com/2019/10/how-tacoma-gave-the-world-the-flying-saucer/

Ke, B. "This Chinese man claims he 'slept with an alien' and is now waiting for a hybrid child." *NextShark* (June 1, 2023). Retrieved from https://nextshark.com/meng-zhaguo-incident-chinese-man-slept-with-alien

Kean, L. "The Conclusion of the NASA Lawsuit: Concerning the Kecksburg PA UFO Case of 1965." The UFO Chronicles (October 10, 2019). Retrieved from http://www.theufochronicles.com/2009/11/conclusion-of-nasa-lawsuit-concerning_10.html

Kean, S. "The Undying Appeal of Nikola Tesla's 'Death Ray.'" Science History Institute (October 6, 2020). Retrieved from https://sciencehistory.org/stories/magazine/the-undying-appeal-of-nikola-teslas-death-ray/

"Kecksburg Crash UFO: Undoubted Federal Object." The Quester Files (September 24, 2021). Retrieved from http://www.thequesterfiles.com/html/kecksburg_crash_ufo--_undoubte.html

"Kenneth Arnold Sighting." UFO Databank. Retrieved from http://www.ufodatabank.com/arnold.htm

Kennan, A. "The Pascagoula Abduction." *Country Roads* (September 21, 2021). Retrieved from https://countryroadsmagazine.com/art-and-culture/people-places/the-pascagoula-abduction/

"Kidnapped by UFOs. Interview with Budd Hopkins — Author, Abductee." (May 1, 2023.) Retrieved from https://www.pbs.org/wgbh/nova/aliens/buddhopkins.html

Killen, J. "Past Tense Oregon: UFO photos taken near McMinnville in 1950 still raise questions." *Oregon Live* (May 12, 2015). Retrieved from https://www.oregonlive.com/history/2015/05/past_tense_oregon_ufo_photos_t.html

Kirk, S. "55 years later: How the Silver Bridge collapse changed West Virginia." *12WBOY* (December 15, 2022). Retrieved from https://www.wboy.com/news/west-virginia/

55-years-later-how-the-silver-bridge-collapse-changed-west-virgin

Lacitis, E. "An Eastern WA man records 180,000 UFO sightings, even if others debunk them." *The Seattle Times* (October 14, 2022). Retrieved from https://www.seattletimes.com/pacific-nw-magazine/as-one-eastern-wa-man-records-ufo-sightings-others-debunk-them/

Liptak, A. "The Unidentified Adventures of Raymond A. Palmer." *Kirkus* (July 28, 2016). Retrieved from https://www.kirkusreviews.com/news-and-features/articles/unidentified-adventures-raymond-palmer/

Little, B. "Bigfoot was Investigated by the FBI. Here's What They Found." *History.com* (January 22, 2020). Retrieved from https://www.history.com/news/bigfoot-fbi-file-investigation-discovery

Little, B. "How the CIA Tried to Quell UFO Panic During the Cold War." History.com (January 6, 2020). Retrieved from https://www.history.com/news/ufo-sightings-cia-robertson-condon

Lohnes, K. "The Fermi Paradox: Where Are All the Aliens?" *Britannica* (June 19, 2023). Retrieved from https://www.britannica.com/story/the-fermi-paradox-where-are-all-the-aliens

"Long John Nebel, 66." *The New York Times* (April 11, 1978). Retrieved from https://www.nytimes.com/1978/04/11/archives/long-john-nebel-66-was-host-for-allnight-talk-show-on-radio-almost.html

Lowe, M. "The Mysterious Contact Memories of Herbert Schirmer." UFO Insight (January 17, 2018). Retrieved from https://www.ufoinsight.com/aliens/encounters/contact-memories-herbert-schirmer

"Lucretius." *Stanford Encyclopedia of Philosophy* (October 17, 2018). Retrieved from https://plato.stanford.edu/entries/lucretius/

Lussier, G. "*Contact* Is More than A Movie About Science vs. Religion." *Gizmodo.com* (July 11, 2017). Retrieved from https://gizmodo.com/contact-is-more-than-a-movie-about-science-vs-religion-1796775188

MacIsaac, T. "4 Pilots Who Say They've Seen UFOs." *Epoch Times* (November 18, 2013). Retrieved from https://www.ufocasebook.com/2013/4-pilots-see-ufos.html

Mancini, M. "10 Out-of-This-World Facts About Plan 9 From Outer Space." *Mental Floss* (April 19, 2016). Retrieved from https://www.mentalfloss.com/article/78785/10-out-world-facts-about-plan-9-outer-space

"Mantell Case – 1948." *MUFON* (April 28, 2023.) Retrieved from https://mufon.com/2021/05/14/mantell-case-1948/

Margaritoff, M. "Astounding Bigfoot Facts That Delve Into The Legend Of The Notorious Ape-Man." *AllThatsInteresting* (April 27, 2021). Retrieved from https://allthatsinteresting.com/bigfoot-facts

Margaritoff, M. "Inside the Montauk Project, The US Military's Alleged Mind Control Program." *AllThatsInteresting* (May 7, 2022). Retrieved from https://allthatsinteresting.com/montauk-project

Marquis, E. "U.S. Recovered 'Intact And Partially Intact Vehicles' Of Non-Human Origin: Whistleblower" Yahoo.com (June

5, 2023). Retrieved from https://autos.yahoo.com/u-recovered-intact-partially-intact-190000314.html

Mason, R. L. "Book Review: *The Day After Roswell.*" *UFO Digest* (December 26, 2010). Retrieved from https://www.ufodigest.com/article/book-review-the-day-after-roswell/

Meares, H. "The Unsolved Mystery of the Lubbock Lights UFO Sightings." History.com (January 10, 2020). Retrieved from https://www.history.com/news/lubbock-lights-ufo-sightings

Merlan, A. "Americans Now Correctly Believe UFOs Could Be Alien Craft." *Vice News* (August 20, 2021). Retrieved from https://www.vice.com/en/article/bvzbw3/more-americans-now-correctly-believe-ufos-could-be-alien-craft-from-outer-space

Mullen, L. "Dedication of the Carl Sagan Center." NASA (November 26, 2001). Retrieved from https://solarsystem.nasa.gov/people/660/carl-sagan-1934-1996/.

"NASA's Perseverance Rover Goes Through Trials by Fire, Ice, Light and Sound." NASA Science (May 18, 2020). Retrieved from https://mars.nasa.gov/news/8671/nasas-perseverance-rover-goes-through-trials-by-fire-ice-light-and-sound/

O'Connell, M. J. "Allen Hynek" (biography). Center for UFO Studies (April 17, 2023). Retrieved from http://www.cufos.org/Hynekbio.html

Osborne, H. "Skinwalker Ranch: The UFO Hotspot in Utah That Has Men Obsessed." Newsweek (April 28, 2022). Retrieved from https://www.newsweek.com/ufo-skinwalker-ranch-utah-pentagon-paranormal-1701730.

Pennsylvania Bigfoot Society. *PBS* (September 1, 2022). Retrieved from https://www.pabigfoot.com

Pfarrer, S. "What did the children see? Whately filmmaker's documentary examines a famous UFO incident outside an African school." *Daily Hampshire Gazette* (October 6, 2022). Retrieved from https://www.gazettenet.com/Whately-film maker-investigates-mysterious-UFO-story-from-Africa-in-Ariel-Phenomenon-48213733

Pfeiffer, L. *The Day the Earth Stood Still. Britannica* (April 12, 2023). Retrieved from https://www.britannica.com/topic/The-Day-the-Earth-Stood-Still-film-1951

Picciano, T. "What Endwell pastor and author makes of UFO sightings: They may be angels and in the Bible." *PressConnects* (June 15, 2021). Retrieved from https://www.pressconnects.com/story/news/connections/faith/2021/06/15/ufos-and-bible-pastor-and-author-downing-says-they-may-angels/7684053002/

"Pioneer 10." Solar System Exploration (July 19, 2021). Retrieved from https://solarsystem.nasa.gov/missions/pioneer-10/in-depth/

Pruitt, S. "China Makes Historic Landing on 'Dark Side' of the Moon." History.com (January 3, 2019). Retrieved from https://www.history.com/news/china-plans-historic-landing-on-dark-side-of-the-moon

Redfern, N. "More on the Mysterious Bigfoot. The UFO Connection." Mysterious Universe (September 17, 2020). Retrieved from https://mysteriousuniverse.org/2020/09/more-on-the-mysterious-bigfoot-the-ufo-connection/

Redfern, N. "Kenneth Arnold, The Man Who Started the UFO Phenomenon: In Arnold's Very Own Words." Mysterious Universe (May 6, 2023). Retrieved from https://mysteriousuniverse.org/2023/05/Kenneth-Arnold-The-Man-Who-Started-the-UFO-Phenomenon-In-Arnold-s-Very-Own-Words-/

Rink, J. "The Strange Death of Majestic 12 Member James Forrestal – What Did He Know?" Super Soldier Talk (January 7, 2019). Retrieved from https://supersoldiertalk.com/the-strange-death-of-majestic-12-member-james-forrestal-what-did-he-know/

Rojas, A. "Update on Area 51 whistleblower Bob Lazar." Open Minds (June 27, 2013). Retrieved from https://www.openminds.tv/update-on-area-51-whistleblower-bob-lazar-1064/22527

Root, C. "The Man Who Hitched a Ride To Venus (Allegedly)." *Denver Public Library* (October 19, 2022). Retrieved from https://history.denverlibrary.org/news/man-who-hitched-ride-venus-allegedly

Ruehl, F. "Is Bigfoot Possibly an Alien Entity?" HuffPost (August 7, 2012). Retrieved from https://www.huffpost.com/entry/is-bigfoot-possibly-an-alien_b_1578844

Sablich, J. "The UFO Sightings That Launched 'Men in Black' Mythology." *History.com* (January 15, 2020). Retrieved from https://www.history.com/news/men-in-black-real-origins.

"Scientists take position." *Ufologie* (November 27, 1978). Retrieved from https://ufologie.patrickgross.org/htm/hynekun.htm

Shannon, J. "'We can't ignore this': UFO sightings spark concern from more than just conspiracy theorists." *USA Today* (June 1, 2021). Retrieved from https://www.yahoo.com/news/t-ignore-ufo-sightings-spark-100116674.html

Shapiro, R. "The 5 Most Credible Modern UFO Sightings." History.com (June 5, 2019). Retrieved from https://www.history.com/news/ufo-sightings-credible-modern

Sheaffer, R. "James W. Moseley (1931–2012)." Bad UFOs (November 27, 2012). Retrieved from https://badufos.blogspot.com/2012/11/james-w-moseley-1931-2012.html

Snow, K. "Kecksburg Crash 1965." The National Paranormal Society (2016). Retrieved from http://national-paranormal-society.org/kecksburg-crash-1965/

Sooke, A. "The strange photographs used to 'prove' conspiracy theories." BBC (February 16, 2017). Retrieved from https://www.bbc.com/culture/article/20170216-five-photographs-used-to-prove-conspiracy-theories

Speigel, L. "ETs Built Earth's First Airport, Iraqi Transport Minister Says." *HuffPost* (October 13, 2016). Retrieved from https://www.huffpost.com/entry/first-airport-on-earth-iraq_n_57fbb625e4b068ecb5e05fed?section=us_weird-news

Stefansky, E. "A monstrous primer on the works of H.P. Lovecraft. Your guide to the fantasy author's nightmarish must-reads." *Polygon* (August 23, 2018). Retrieved from https://www.polygon.com/2018/8/23/17762378/hp-lovecraft-books-cthulhu-necronomicon-stories

Stranger in a Strange Land: The Original Uncut. Kirkusreviews (January 1, 1990). Retrieved from https://www.kirkusreviews.

com/book-reviews/robert-a-heinlein/stranger-in-a-strange-land/

Swartz, A. B. "The Infamous 'War of the Worlds' Radio Broadcast Was a Magnificent Fluke." *Smithsonian* (May 6, 2015). Retrieved from https://www.smithsonianmag.com/history/infamous-war-worlds-radio-broadcast-was-magnificent-fluke-180955180/

Shelton, J. "The Kecksburg Incident: Mysterious UFO Crash of The '60s." *GroovyHistory.com* (December 10, 2020). Retrieved from https://groovyhistory.com/kecksburg-incident-ufo-crash

Tearle, O. "A Summary and Analysis of H. G. Wells' *The War of the Worlds*." Interesting Literature (June 2021). Retrieved from https://interestingliterature.com/2021/06/wells-the-war-of-the-worlds-summary-analysis/

Thames, N. "Carl & Margery Higdon | The Carl Higdon Alien Abduction Story." Inception Radio Network (May 7, 2021). Retrieved from https://timefordisclosure.com/carl-margery-higdon-the-carl-higdon-alien-abduction-story/.

"The George Adamski Case: Presenting the facts about George Adamski's life and mission." (April 30, 2023.) Retrieved from https://www.the-adamski-case.nl/his-life/

The Mothman Prophesies. Bookotron.com (May 24, 2023). Retrieved from http://bookotron.com/agony/reviews/keel-the_mothman_prophecies.htm

"This scoutmaster had a run-in with a UFO. The kids saw it too." *NexusNewsFeed.com* (January 15, 2021). Retrieved from https://nexusnewsfeed.com/article/unexplained/this-scoutmaster-had-a-run-in-with-a-ufo-the-kids-saw-it-too-1/

"To the Stars Academy of Arts and Science Acknowledges the Pentagon's Official Release of UAP Video Footage." TTSA (September 1, 2022). Retrieved from https://tothestars.media/blogs/press-and-news/to-the-stars-academy-of-arts-science-acknowledges-the-pentagons-official-release-of-uap-video-footage

The UFO Incident. IMDB (May 16, 2023). Retrieved from https://www.imdb.com/title/tt0073834/

"Tunguska explosion in 1908 caused by asteroid grazing Earth."*Astronomy* (October 9, 2020). Retrieved from https://www.astronomy.com/science/tunguska-explosion-in-1908-caused-by-asteroid-grazing-earth/

"UFOs and Bigfoot; Evidence of an Inter-Dimensional Connection." *Gaia* (March 27, 2020). Retrieved from https://www.gaia.com/article/ufos-bigfoot-evidence-interdimensional-connection

Verma, V. "Missouri UFO Crash: Reverend Saw Three Dead Aliens & Their Spaceship." *Journal News*. (July 15, 2023). Retrieved from https://journalnews.com.ph/missouri-ufo-crash-reverend-saw-three-dead-aliens-their-spaceship/

Vincent, B. "Senate's intelligence authorization bill questions 'reverse engineering' of government-recovered UAPs." *DefenseScoop* (June 27, 2023). Retrieved from https://defensescoop.com/2023/06/27/senates-intelligence-authorization-bill-questions-reverse-engineering-of-government-recovered-uaps/

Weisberger, M. "1947 'alien autopsy' film frame is up for auction as an NFT." *LiveScience* (May 28, 2021). Retrieved from https://www.livescience.com/alien-autopsy-footage-nft-auction.html

Whalen, A. "UFO Organization Leader Arrested for Allegedly Soliciting Sex From a Detective Posing as Child." *Newsweek* (July 15, 2020). Retrieved from https://www.newsweek.com/ufo-sightings-mufon-arrest-organization-jan-harzan-arrested-1517779

"What is Area 51 and what goes on there?" BBC News (September 19. 2019). Retrieved from https://www.bbc.com/news/world-us-canada-49568127

Wright, W. J. "The Terrifying True Story of The Cash-Landrum UFO Incident." *Grunge.com* (December 21, 2020) Retrieved from https://www.grunge.com/299546/the-terrifying-true-story-of-the-cash-landrum-ufo-incident/

Wright, W. J. "The Truth About The Alien Invasion In The Hudson Valley." *Grunge.com* (January 23, 2023). Retrieved from https://www.grunge.com/487429/the-truth-about-the-alien-invasion-in-the-hudson-valley/

About the Author

Maxim W. Furek is recognized as an academic and avid student of the paranormal. His eclectic background includes aspects of psychology, addictions, and rock journalism. He has a master's degree in Communications from Bloomsburg University and a bachelor's degree in Psychology from Aquinas College.

He has written numerous rock biographies, as well as paranormal-themed books, such as *Coal Region Hoodoo: Paranormal Tales from Inside the Pit.*

He has been interviewed on podcasts, including *Exploring the Bizarre,* with the legendary Timothy Green Beckley, and on Art Bell's *Midnight in the Desert.* His book *Sheppton: The Myth, Miracle, and Music* was featured on Australia's *Mysterious Universe.*

He contributes to *Fate* magazine, Normal Paranormal, and *Paranormal Underground.*

His previous book, *Coal Region Hoodoo,* has been described as "A fascinating look into Pennsylvania's paranormal wormhole through a never-seen-before sociological and popular culture lens."

www.maximfurek.com

Also by Maxim W. Furek

Coal Region HooDoo: Paranormal Tales from Inside the Pit

www.ingramcontent.com/pod-product-compliance
Lightning Source LLC
Chambersburg PA
CBHW032342280326
41935CB00008B/418
* 9 7 8 1 9 5 4 5 2 8 7 7 2 *